CISTERCIAN STUDIES SERIES:
NUMBER EIGHTY-EIGHT

Theodoret of Cyrrhus

A HISTORY OF THE MONKS OF SYRIA

A History of the Monks of Syria

by Theodoret of Cyrrhus

Translated with an Introduction and Notes by R. M. Price

CISTERCIAN PUBLICATIONS

A translation of the *Religious History* of Theodoret of Cyrrhus based on the critical edition of P. Canivet and A. Leroy-Molinghen in the series Sources Chrétiennes (Paris: Éditions du Cerf, 1977–79).

A Cistercian Publications title published by Liturgical Press

Cistercian Publications
Editorial Offices
Abbey of Gethsemani
3642 Monks Road
Trappist, Kentucky 40051
www.cistercianpublications.org

The work of Cistercian Publications is made possible in part by support from Western Michigan University

© 1985 Cistercian Publications, Inc., © 2008 by Order of Saint Benedict, Collegeville, Minnesota. All rights reserved. No part of this book may be reproduced in any form, by print, microfilm, microfiche, mechanical recording, photocopying, translation, or by any other means, known or yet unknown, for any purpose except brief quotations in reviews, without the previous written permission of Liturgical Press, Saint John's Abbey, PO Box 7500, Collegeville, Minnesota 56321-7500.

Library of Congress Cataloging-in-Publication Data

Theodoret, Bishop of Cyrrhus.
    A history of the monks of Syria.
    (Cistercian studies series; no. 88)
    Translation of Philotheos historia, based on the critical edition entitled Histoire des moines de Syrie, edited by P. Canivet and A. Leroy-Molinghen and published in the series Sources chrétiennes by Editions du Cerf, Paris, 1977–79.
    Bibliography: p. 208.
    Includes indexes.
    1. Monasticism and religious orders—Syria—History. 2. Monks—Syria—Biography. 3 Nuns—Syria—Biography. 4. Syria—Church history. 5. Syria—Biography. I. Title. II. Series.

Preface

NO APOLOGY is needed for the first English translation of the *Religious History* by Theodoret of Cyrrhus, our major source for the monasticism of northern Syria in the fourth and fifth centuries. The text translated is that of the recent *Sources Chrétiennes* edition (Paris, 1977-9) by P. Canivet and A. Leroy-Molinghen. My two departures from it (in XXV.1 and XXVI.18) are both trivial. I do, however, defend the authenticity of two of the several passages which these editors condemn as interpolations (see the commentary on I.10 and XXVI.13).

The lack of translations into modern languages – Canivet's is the first – has restricted acquaintance with the text, but scholars have not neglected it. The studies of the seventeenth-century French scholars Garnier and Tillemont are still fundamental, and have been supplemented during the last hundred years by many scholarly monographs. These include the Russian biography of Theodoret by Glubokovsky, the German contributions by Lietzmann and Schiwietz, and the recent English work by Peter Brown. However, it is the work of French writers that continues to dominate the field. The fine studies of Festugière, and the fieldwork of French archaeologists during the period of the French mandate in Syria, form the foundation for Canivet's *Le monachisme syrien selon Théodoret de Cyr* (1977), the most comprehensive study both of the composition of the *Religious History* and of the data it presents. This extensive literature, together with English writing on Late Antique Syria by A.H.M. Jones, Liebeschuetz and others, provides that massive sum of acquired knowledge from which my own commentary modestly derives.

I would like to make a few acknowledgements: first to my parents, who taught me to love learning and provided me with a traditional classical education; also to Peter Brown, who introduced me to the *Religious History* fifteen years ago; then to the well-stocked libraries of London, especially those of Heythrop College and of my own community, the Brompton Oratory; and finally to my publishers, who commissioned this translation at a time when most academic publishing houses are displaying more discretion than valor.

The Oratory, London   R.M. Price

TABLE OF CONTENTS

INTRODUCTION ix
A HISTORY OF THE MONKS OF SYRIA
(*THE RELIGIOUS HISTORY*)
Prologue 3
I. James (of Nisibis) 12
II. Julian (Saba) 23
III. Marcianus 37
IV. Eusebius (of Teleda) 49
V. Publius 58
VI. Symeon the Elder 63
VII. Palladius 69
VIII. Aphrahat 72
IX. Peter (the Galatian) 81
X. Theodosius 89
XI. Romanus 94
XII. Zeno 96
XIII. Macedonius 100
XIV. Maësymas 110
XV. Acepsimas 114
XVI. Maron 117
XVII. Abraham 120
XVIII. Eusebius (of Asikha) 126
XIX. Salamanes 129
XX. Maris 131
XXI. James (of Cyrrhestica) 133
XXII–III. Thalassius, Limnaeus, John 150
XXIV–V. Zebinas, Polychronius, Asclepius 154
XXVI. Symeon (Stylites) 160
XXVII. Baradatus 177
XXVIII. Thalelaeus 180
XXIX. Marana and Cyra 183

| XXX. | Domnina | 186 |
| Epilogue: | On Divine Love | 190 |

LIST OF WORKS CITED ... 208

INDEX OF NAMES ... 214

INDEX OF SUBJECTS ... 220

Introduction

THEODORET OF CYRRHUS (AD 393–466) is a writer with a variety of claims on the attention of students of christian antiquity.¹ As a controversial writer, he was the main champion of Antiochene Christology against the attacks of Cyril of Alexandria and his adherents, and lived to see his stand vindicated at the Council of Chalcedon. As an apologist, he wrote what has been judged the finest vindication of the superiority of Christianity over paganism – *The Cure of Hellenic Maladies*. As an exegete, he expounded the Church's traditional typological interpretation of Scripture, in conscious correction of both the allegorism of Origen and the literalism of Theodore of Mopsuestia. As an historian, he penned an *Ecclesiastical History*, a continuation of Eusebius down to 428, notable for its fluency and vigor. A further historical work is the text translated here, the *Religious History* or *Ascetic Life* (see Prologue 10 for these titles), an account of around thirty notable ascetics of northern Syria from the time of Constantine to Theodoret's own day.

This amounts to an *œuvre* unequaled in range by any of his contemporaries. It is true that he lacked originality and is never really profound, but he had a clear perception of what in any topic was really at issue; his reasoning is sharp and incisive, his exposition lucid and uncluttered. Add to this the verve and elegance of his style, and Theodoret emerges as the most attractive writer of his generation; meanwhile, his role on the stage of the history of the Church was second only to those of Cyril of Alexandria and Leo of Rome. Yet he has never attracted quite the attention he deserves. At the Ecumenical Council of 553 the vindication of Cyril and condemnation of Theodore, his supposed teacher, were accompanied by the anathematization of his specific writings against Cyril and in defense of Theodore and Nestorius; it was only his standing at Chalcedon that protected him from personal condemnation. From then on his name was viewed with circumspection, and his writings were denied canonical status. The modern age that has rehabilitated Theodore and Nestorius naturally looks on Theodoret with a kindlier eye; but the crude, if useful, schematization that sees the Council of Ephesus as a duel between Cyril and Nestorius, and Chalcedon as the victory of Leo over Eutyches, has kept Theodoret at the rear of the stage, despite his unique position as a leading contestant in the whole twenty-five years of the debate and his weighty theological contribution, which is second only to Cyril's.

A quite separate, but not dissimilar bias has contributed to the neglect of his *Religious History* in particular. It is our principal source for early Syrian monasticism, a movement as preeminent in its anchorites as was Egypt in coenobitic monasticism. Later developments have favored coenobitism over anchoritism, in the East as well as the West; consequently, Egyptian monasticism receives pride of treatment, and the Syrian variety can appear even slightly deviant, as a rococo exaggeration of the genuine article. As a result, Theodoret's eulogy of the monks of Syria, while never forgotten as a prime historical source, has not enjoyed the same respect and canonical status as the classic accounts, by Cassian and Palladius, of their Egyptian peers.

Recent scholarship, however, has achieved some correction of this imbalance: both Theodoret and the monks of Syria are now accorded more sympathetic attention than for centuries past. This is a result partly of the rehabilitation of the Antiochene school of theology: even Nestorius is nowadays more often defended than condemned. It is also the result of new emphases in the study of Late Antique asceticism: the role of holy men in society has become a main topic of research, and here Theodoret's work is arguably the most important single source.[2]

I

ONE OF THE MOST DELIGHTFUL features of the *Religious History*, as well as a main element in its historical reliability, is Theodoret's inclusion of personal reminiscences of his own contacts with Syrian monks over the whole course of his life. To understand these, we need to have some knowledge of his own biography, for which, indeed, the scattered data of the *Religious History* are a prime source.

Theodoret was born, probably in 393, of a well-to-do, though not aristocratic, Antiochene family. It was from his mother that he inherited his interest in monks. Seven years before his birth, she went to the hermit Peter, on the outskirts of Antioch, in quest of healing for an eye complaint; the hermit not only cured her, but also converted her to what we call the 'devout life', marked outwardly by a rejection of rich dress, jewelry, and cosmetics (IX.5-8). She continued to visit him, and he worked a whole series of cures for her and her household (IX.9, 10, 14, 15); she also became the client of other holy men, such as Symeon the Elder (VI.14). Theodoret's father also felt a need for the help of monks: when after thirteen years of marriage his wife had still not conceived, he went the round of holy men until the hermit Macedonius promised to obtain him a son from God. Belatedly, after four years, the promise was fulfilled by the birth of Theodoret. Macedonius insisted that the child, as God's gift, had to be dedicated to God's service: this insistence, together with the piety of the mother, who had no wish to bear a child for a worldly career, determined Theodoret's vocation right from his birth (XIII.16-18).

As a boy, Theodoret saw much of holy men in the vicinity of Antioch; monks, whether anchorites or coenobites, did not reside within the city itself. His mother sent him once a week to receive Peter's blessing (IX.4); he accompanied his mother on a visit to the celebrated Aphrahat and was blessed by him (VIII.15); he often saw Macedonius, who constantly reminded him of his dedication to God's service (XIII.18). This dedication was confirmed by Theodoret's receiving, as a boy, the office of lector (XII.4). Meanwhile, his education would have followed the normal course: the study of Greek grammar and the already established syllabus of the Greek classics, from Homer to Demosthenes. The Atticizing style and vocabulary of the *Religious History* is itself proof that this formation was not neglected. But if Greek remained Theodoret's sole written language, he grew up speaking Syriac as well, and therefore could converse freely with the monks of Syria, most of whom knew no Greek. Did these monks press Theodoret towards a religious vocation? Peter, who blessed him weekly, remarked sagely that he could not become a monk since his parents were too attached to him (IX.4). Clearly, they understood his consecration to God to involve an ecclesiastical career at Antioch, but not a vocation to the monastic life with the separation from them that this would entail. Yet, Theodoret's contact with monks developed into a serious interest in asceticism. He tells us that he visited the hermit Zeno to question him on 'philosophy', i.e. the monastic life (XII.4), and that, together with comrades who shared his attraction to the ascetic life, he spent a week at the celebrated monastery founded by Ammianus and Eusebius at Teleda, up on the limestone plateau to the east of Antioch (IV.10). It was probably at this period too that he made repeated visits to a second monastery at Teleda, which Symeon, soon the famous Stylite, had just left (XXVI.4) These were doubtless but a few of many visits to hermits and monasteries, as the young Theodoret pondered on his vocation.

Within a few years, at an unspecified date, the death of both his parents enabled Theodoret to fulfil his pious wishes (*ep.* 113): he disposed of all his property, and entered a monastery (*epp.* 80, 81). The community he settled on was one of those at Nicerte (or Nicertae) near Apamea; its foundation in the preceding century is mentioned at III.4. There he stayed, gaining a reputation as a writer, till in 423 he was made bishop of Cyrrhus, a city north-east of his native Antioch; and at Cyrrhus he remained (apart from a brief period of exile from 449 to 451) till his death in 466. During this long period he maintained his identity as a monastic bishop, firmly refusing to acquire any wealth or property (*ep.* 113) and happy to return for a spell in 449 to what he could call 'my monastery' (*ep.* 119).

As bishop, Theodoret had plentiful opportunity to maintain contact with monasteries and hermits. While, in the *Religions History*, his experiences as a child and youth supplement the oral tradition about deceased monks, his contacts as a bishop were his source in the *Religious History* for monks still alive (or who, like Eusebius of Asikha or Maris, had died quite recently). Of the living hermits to whom major notices are allotted in chapters XXI to XXX Theodoret is able to record personal contact with all save one (Baradatus, XXVII). It is because of the priority that he accords in this section to his personal testimony that most of the monks treated are of his own diocese of Cyrrhus: but he also devotes notices, and records visits, to ascetics further afield: Symeon Stylites in the territory of Antioch (XXVI.14ff.); Thalelaeus in that of Gabala, sixty miles south of Antioch (XXVIII.4); Marana and Cyra in that of Beroea (XXIX.5). As a bishop, Theodoret enjoyed privileged access to recluses: Eusebius of Asikha would, finally, converse with Theodoret alone (XVIII.2); Maris (XX.3), Limnaeus (XXII.3), James of Nimouza (XXV.2) and Marana and Cyra (XXIX.5) allowed him to unblock their doors and gain access. It is to his credit that he used his episcopal authority to induce some ascetics to moderate their austerities when old age or sickness required it. He induced Polychronius to accept two companions (XXIV.4) and leave the open air for a cell (§9), though he failed to persuade him to renounce carrying a huge root of oak (§6). Truly delightful is the account he gives of how he induced the sick James to agree to be screened from the sun, lie down and take off his chains (XXI.5–8): his diplomatic skills are as evident here as in his more famous and prolonged involvement in the high ecclesiastical politics of the time.

II

WITHIN THIS CHRONOLOGY of Theodoret's ecclesiastical career and contacts with holy men we must attempt to determine the precise date of the composition of the *Religious History*. The only incontestable data are the *terminus post quem* of 437 provided by the death of Acacius of Beroea (II.9) and the *terminus ante quem* of 448 provided by Theodoret's listing this work among his other writings in a letter of that year (*ep.* 82). But a more precise dating is a practical necessity, in view of Theodoret's frequent dating of events by specifying the number of years between them and the time of writing. Here recent scholars have been divided between a preference for 440 and one for 444; the debate is a replay of that between Garnier, whose arguments for 444 were published posthumously in 1684, and Tillemont, whose advocacy of 440, as an approximate date, was published, also posthumously, in 1711.[3]

The debate revolves round a mere two passages: XXI.27 on the reaction of the hermit James to an Isaurian incursion; and XXVI.9 on the number of years during which Symeon Stylites had maintained a total lenten fast. The argument for 444 from the former passage runs as follows. James became a hermit at the time of an Isaurian incursion that other sources date to 405; according to XXII.7 James 'has already completed the thirty-eighth year' of his asceticism; it follows that Theodoret is writing in 444. It is strange that this argument has been so often repeated. As Tillemont pointed out, what we learn from Theodoret is that James was already an ascetic at the time of the incursion. There is no reason to suppose he *became* an ascetic then.[4] Meanwhile, at XXVI.9 we read, with reference to Symeon's first great lenten fast, that 'from then till today twenty-eight years have passed'. Garnier dated this first great fast to 416, and so produced 444 for the date of writing. Tillemont, however, and the great majority of later scholars prefer 412, a date which firmly implies 440 for the date of writing.[5] Here, a new argument has been advanced by Leroy-Molinghen, the co-editor of the *Sources Chrétiennes* edition. Some manuscripts contain a revised edition of this account of Symeon, produced at some unspecifiable date after the deaths of both Symeon and Theodoret. In this edition the words just quoted are altered to 'from then till his death forty-three years have passed'. It follows, she argues, that Theodoret's original edition was penned fifteen years before Symeon's death (459), i.e. in 444.[6] This argument is neat, but unconvincing. The reviser is most unlikely to have possessed any direct evidence for the date of the *Religious History*. His 'forty-three' figure must rather derive from his own incorrect calculation of the chronology of Symeon; he has calculated it precisely as Garnier did, and need have had no additional evidence at his disposal. In all, it remains preferable to deduce from XXVI.9 that 440 is the date of composition – at least for the account of Symeon. Apart from the epilogue *On Divine Love*, manifestly added later,[7] the *Religious History* is a uniform, coherent text, and we have no reason to suppose that it took years to write. Consequently, the only practical working hypothesis is that this same year, 440, is the date of the *Religious History* as a whole.

III

As a work of literature, the *Religious History* possesses certain virtues as obviously as it lacks others. The vocabulary admits only a few words unknown to Plato and Demosthenes; unclassical official or ecclesiastical terms, such as 'count', 'bishop', 'monastery' are strictly avoided.[8] Of course, by modern standards this is not a great virtue, and it must be admitted that Theodoret's use of the classical vocabulary, though accurate, lacks delicacy and nuance, as if he were writing in a foreign language. But this is just to observe that he is a typical late antique author. More individual is the great merit of the work: its vigor and sprightliness in narration. If we compare the *Religious History* to the slightly earlier *History of the Monks in Egypt*, similar in content though less sophisticated in style, we are struck by Theodoret's more artful dramatic skill, while in a comparison with Athanasius's more famous *Life of Antony* Theodoret emerges as a lesser spiritual writer but an incomparably superior storyteller. From the story of James of Nisibis cursing laundry-girls (I.4) to that of Domnina soaking the hand of a visiting bishop with her perpetual tears (XXX.2), the *Religious History* contains a wealth of unforgettable tales and vignettes, consistently vivid, often (for a modern reader) haunting in their strangeness. The defect of the work is that it is magnificent as a series of stories, but feeble as a series of portraits. Theodoret's holy men are insufficiently differentiated, to the point where most of the stories, accidental details aside, would equally fit most of his holy men. It is the same ideal of saintliness that is reiterated again and again; and monotony is accentuated by the tone of panegyric, with its rigorous refusal to attribute to any of the holy men defects or limitations.[9] Indeed, the reader has to stand back to notice that there is, after all, a logical sequence—partly chronological, partly geographical—in the order of the individual biographies that make up the work. The following analysis will make this clear.

A. Monks already deceased:
I. James, of Mesopotamia, † 337/8
II. Julian Saba, of Mesopotamia, † 367
III. Marcianus, of the region of Chalcis, † 380s
IV. Eusebius, of the region of Antioch, fl. 350s
V. Publius, of Euphratesia, fl. 350s
VI. Symeon the Elder, of the region of Antioch, fl. 370s
VII. Palladius, of the region of Antioch, fl. 370s
VIII. Aphrahat, of Antioch, † c.410
IX. Peter, of Mt Silpius near Antioch, † c.403
X. Theodosius, of Cilicia, d. at Antioch, † c.405
XI. Romanus, of Mt Silpius near Antioch, † c.400
XII. Zeno, of Mt Silpius near Antioch, † 410s
XIII. Macedonius, of Mt Silpius near Antioch, † c.420
XIV. Maesymas, of the region of Cyrrhus, fl. late 4th century
XV. Acepsimas, of the region of Cyrrhus, fl. late 4th century
XVI. Maron, of the region of Cyrrhus, † 410s
XVII. Abraham, from the region of Cyrrhus, † 420s
XVIII. Eusebius, of the region of Cyrrhus, † 430s
XIX. Salamanes, by the Euphrates
XX. Maris, of the region of Cyrrhus, † c.430

B. Monks still alive
XXI. James, of the region of Cyrrhus
XXII-III. Limnaeus and others, of the region of Cyrrhus
XXIV-V. Polychronius and others, of the region of Cyrrhus
XXVI. Symeon Stylites, of the region of Antioch
XXVII. Baradatus, of the region of Antioch
XXVIII. Thalelaeus, of the region of Gabala
Women:
XXIX. Marana and Cyra, of Beroea
XXX. Domnina, of the region of Cyrrhus

Introduction

The sequence is one of individual holy men, most of them hermits; however, a number of them were founders of religious communities. Theodoret mentions the following coenobitic foundations.

A. Mesopotamia:
II.3-5 Foundation in Osrhoene, c.320

B. Near Antioch:
II.9 Foundation at Gindarus, c.330
IV.2 Foundation at Teleda, c.350
IV.13, XXVI.4 Later foundations at or near Teleda
X.3 Foundation in extreme S.-E. Cilicia, c.360
VI.13 Foundation on Mt Amanus, 380s
XXVI.8 Foundation east of Antioch, early 400s

C. Euphratesia:
V.3-5 Foundation at Zeugma c.350
XVIII.1 Mention of monastery near Cyrrhus in c.365
XXII.2 Mention of monastery near Cyrrhus in c.390

D. Regions of Chalcis and Apamea:
III.4-5 Foundations in c.360s
XXIX.2 Foundation of nunnery at Beroea, 420s or 430s

IV

BEFORE WE HAZARD any conclusions on the development of monasticism in northern Syria, we must ask ourselves how comprehensive is the treatment of holy men and coenobitic foundations in the *Religious History*. In his *Ecclesiastical History* IV.28 (25) Theodoret gives a list of the most outstanding hermits of the later fourth century. Of the twenty-three names, only two (Paul of Apamea and Zeugmatius of the region of Cyrrhus) receive no mention in the *Religious History*. In contrast, the list of Syrian monks in the contemporary *Ecclesiastical History* of Sozomen (VI.33-34) shows how uncomprehensive Theodoret's treatment is. Among the monks of Mesopotamia Sozomen includes the shadowy Aones, absent from Theodoret: 'it is said that this Aones originated the strict philosophy apart from all men among Syrians, just as Antony did among the Egyptians'. Of the monks of northern Syria in the fourth century he names seven, of whom only one (Marosas) is mentioned in the *Religious History* (IV.12). Meanwhile, Theodoret's treatment of coenobitic foundations is also obviously patchy; it is striking that in treating his own diocese of Cyrrhus he mentions religious communities only incidentally and concentrates on developments in the eremitical life. His treatment of the monasteries of the Antiochene region is fuller, but here too there are striking omissions even of early foundations: Mt Silpius, just outside the city, was a great ascetic center, and Theodoret treats several hermits who lived there (IX, XI–XIII), but he makes no mention of the coenobitic communities familiar to us from the Antiochene sermons (AD 386–97) of John Chrysostom.[10]

These omissions are due to a large extent, obviously, to a deliberate decision by Theodoret: 'To recount everything is impossible not only for me but for all writers; even if it were possible, I consider it superfluous and an ambition without gain' (XXX.7). But the omissions are also due to his patchy knowledge of the past history of Syrian monasticism. Consider for example his treatment of a favorite area within his own immediate purview – the development of open-air asceticism in the region of Cyrrhus. He knew that the first influential exponent of this pattern of life was a hermit, called Maron, who died before his arrival at Cyrrhus: 'it was he who planted for God the garden that now flourishes in the region of Cyrrhus' (XVI.3). Yet Theodoret's chapter on this major figure is exceedingly thin and slight. Clearly, Maron's disciples had been more concerned to imitate him than to transmit a detailed tradition of his life and labors.

The point may appear obvious, but it is easy to lose sight of it when we consider the relation of the development of monasticism in Syria to that in Egypt. Of Theodoret's holy men only James of Nisibis and Julian Saba predate Nicaea (A.D. 325), and they are both Mesopotamian rather than Syrian. For the following period (325–360) Theodoret reports only a handful of holy men and coenobitic foundations; it is thereafter that his material becomes plentiful. Contrast the situation in Egypt, where by the time of Nicaea St Antony had been an ascetic for over fifty years and Pachomius had already made his first foundations. It is easy to suppose, in consequence, that Syrian monasticism was the later development, dependent on the stimulus of Egyptian models. But if St Antony had never been made famous by Athanasius's biography, and if Theodoret had been writing fifty years earlier, at a time when memories of the early fourth century were less dim, this impression of Egyptian priority might not have arisen.

This does not, of course, prove the equal antiquity of Syrian monasticism. What positive evidence is there? The archaeological evidence is indecisive. As Isaac of Antioch († c.460) tells us,[11] the monasteries of the fourth century were small and plain, but expanded in the fifth century beyond recognition; and it was the glories of the fifth and sixth centuries rather than the humbler origins that left the traces still visible today.[12] There is, however, evidence for the early expansion of Syrian monasticism in the christianization of the countryside. Sozomen in his account of monasticism in northern Syria (VI.34) relates that the monks had at first to encounter the hostility of a population which, outside the city of Antioch itself, was still largely pagan, but that they gradually converted the countryside to Christianity. This is a plausible account of the process of conversion, since relations between Greek-speaking Antioch and the Syriac-speaking countryside were not sufficiently close or friendly[13] to make evangelization by the city itself likely to have been attempted or likely to have been successful. Now the date of the christianization of the countryside in the territory of Antioch is revealed by the numerous inscriptions found on the limestone plateau to the east of the city. Here, the two earliest Christian inscriptions date to 336/7; in the following decade the proportion of Christian as opposed to pagan inscriptions steadily increases; the latest pagan inscription found in the area is dated to 367/8.[14] The implication of this evidence, taken with the testimony of Sozomen, is that Christian asceticism was strong and widespread in this region as early as 340, although all that Theodoret records for this district at around this date is the foundation of the great monastery at Teleda (IV.2).

That the development even of coenobitic monasticism in Syria was not dependent on Egyptian influence is supported by the location and plan of the north Syrian monasteries—even if, as we have noted, the visible remains date to the fifth and sixth centuries. Doubtless the evidence is not unambiguous: it has been observed that the early monastic buildings and inscriptions, being more common in southern than in northern Syria, might be taken to suggest that coenobitism gradually spread northwards, from Egypt upwards into northern Syria.[15] But that would be to ignore the very different character of north Syrian coenobitism, as manifested in the visible remains. It has been pointed out by both Lassus and Tchalenko, the leading French experts on this subject,[16] that, while the monasteries of southern Syria, like those of Egypt, display in the close-knit plan of communal buildings within a walled enclosure a confined lifestyle, cut off from the world and almost oppressively communal, the monasteries of northern Syria normally followed an open plan, with the various buildings spaced out and no enclosing wall. Significant too is their location on frequented routes; contact with the outside world seems to have been cultivated rather than shunned. This contrasting character makes a picture of monastic expansion from Egypt through southern Syria to the region treated by Theodoret implausible and misleading. Was there instead a local tradition of asceticism from which Syrian monasticism developed, independent of Egyptian models?

V

ASCETICISM IN SYRIAN CHRISTIANITY[17] may be traced back to the presumed Syrian origin of the *Gospel according to Matthew*,[18] with its emphasis on the theme of discipleship, on a following of Christ involving celibacy (19.11–12), poverty (19.21) and homelessness (19.29) in the service of announcing the kingdom, in a proclamation to be accompanied by miraculous signs of exorcism and healing (10.7ff). That this ideal was widely practised by early Christian missionaries is implied by the *Apocryphal Acts of the Apostles*: shamelessly unhistorical, these are still revealing of the ideas and lifestyle of the communities that produced them, ascetic groups in Syria and Asia Minor in the second and third centuries. Take the description of St Thomas in §20 of the *Acts of Judas Thomas*:

> He goes about the towns and villages, and if he has anything he gives it all to the poor, and he teaches a new God, and heals the sick and drives out demons and does many other miracles. . . . He continually fasts and prays, and eats only bread with salt, and his drink is water, and

he wears one garment alike in fair and in wintry weather, and he accepts nothing from anyone and what he has he gives to others.

This is so close to the *Gospel of Matthew* and to the work and lifestyle of later holy men that it proves an essential continuity in Syrian asceticism going right back to the example of Christ.

A striking development occurred, however, in the importance attached to celibacy, which is present but unemphasized in the life and teaching of Christ. The *Apocryphal Acts* wax lyrical on the purifying power of chastity, and speak frequently as if only the celibate are proper Christians; in consequence, these are often dismissed as heretical writings that illustrate deviant rather than mainstream Christianity. Yet the disparagement of marriage that arises naturally in fervent exhortation to celibacy must not be misread as a dogmatic assertion that marriage is actually sinful—no more than in a later ascetic writer like St Jerome; in fact, the constant attack on adultery in these *Acts* implies acceptance of lawful marriage.[19] Their central theme remains that full access to God can be enjoyed only by those who follow Christ in strict chastity and poverty. It is only by modern standards that this sounds deviant: even the mainstream Apologist Athenagoras of Athens (*c*.170) could write, 'You would find many among us, both men and women, growing old unmarried in the hope of being united more closely with God' (*Plea* 33).

In the churches of Syria and Mesopotamia this idea found expression in the creation of a special order, intermediate between the laity and the ordained clergy, of the 'sons and daughters of the Covenant', best known to us from the *Sixth Demonstration* of Aphrahat the Persian (written in 337). These sons and daughters of the Covenant were men and women who at their baptism made a commitment to lifelong celibacy; they were not monks and nuns, since they were free to possess property and practised only mild austerity. They served the Church and its cult in a humble capacity, and were a witness to the tradition that attributed unique value to sexual continence, even separated from the other evangelical notes of poverty and homelessness.[20]

The respect and attention that ascetics receive in all this early literature had a practical side in the pastoral role they were called upon to perform. The special access to God that they gained through celibacy and ascetic practices had its outward expression in charismatic gifts which they could exercise for the benefit of the whole Church, especially the gifts of healing and exorcism. Even in the work of evangelization eloquent preaching was not the prime instrument: St Paul could say, 'My word and my proclamation were not in persuasive words of wisdom but in the demonstration of spiritual power' (1 Co 2:4). The work of healing was proof that God was with the missionary, and that he willed the salvation of the individual. So in the *Apocryphal Acts* missionary work and miracle go hand in hand, and the power to work miracles is the possession of those who by following Christ literally are special instruments of his power. This same charismatic role was exercised by celibates at a humbler level too: the early third-century *Epistles on Virginity* in the Pseudo-Clementine corpus, another Syrian text, describe the role of celibates within small Christian communities, who, without being equipped as preachers and teachers, take on a special burden of prayer and fasting, visit the poor and distressed, and are able to apply the remedy of exorcism (I.12).

In addition to this practical side, the special significance of the celibate life received expression, even in the Pseudo-Clementine *Epistles*, in a variety of literary themes. Celibates are described as following in the footsteps of the great virgins of the Bible – Elijah, Elisha, Mary, John the Baptist, the Beloved Disciple, St Paul (I.6). If they live worthy of their vocation, they are uniquely conformed to Christ (I.7), just as they have the Holy Spirit dwelling within them (I.8). And in their detachment from the world and their single-minded service of God, they are said to 'lead a heavenly and divine life, like the holy angels', while in heaven they will attain the honor of dwelling not with those of the elect who were married but with the angels themselves (I.4).

Now it is surely this tradition, native to Syria, from which stem the ascetics of Theodoret. In them we find the same asceticism – celibacy, fasting, vigils – , the same charismatic powers of healing and exorcism, and the same themes of asceticism as an imitation of the great biblical saints and a sharing in the life of the angels.[21] Of course, the later period had its innovations – permanent coenobitic communities, for example, or the open-air asceticism of a Maron or Symeon Stylites – , but the ideal and practice of 'monasticism', i.e. the 'single' life of the *monachos* (Greek) or *ihidaya* (Syriac), goes back in Syrian Christianity through the celibates of the second and third centuries to the Matthaean presentation of the ideal of discipleship.[22] Our fragmentary sources for the second and third centuries may fail to give us names and biographies of individual ascetics; but we know enough to be able to assert that the standard text-book treatment of monasticism, that starts with Antony of Egypt in the late third century and proceeds to Syrian monasticism as if it were a subsequent and dependent development, is seriously misleading. The main features of Syrian asceticism, and the repertoire of appropriate biblical themes, go back to the obscure origins of Syrian Christianity. Therefore they deserve to be called primitive, rather than be viewed as a late, perhaps dubious, development, extraneous to the essence of Christianity.

VI

HOWEVER MUCH WE STRESS the continuity between primitive Christian asceticism and the more familiar monasticism of the late antique period, there remains the question why there was a notable expansion in the fourth and fifth centuries both in the number of ascetics and in the attention and respect they received from other members of the Church. Answers to this question naturally link this expansion to contemporary changes in Church and society.

One explanation, that appears already in ancient sources,[23] links the monastic expansion to the end of the Roman persecution of the Christians, and therefore of the possibility of martyrdom. It is certainly true that the holy men of the late antique period inherited much of the glory that had previously been attached to the confessors, those who suffered for the faith. The holy man inherited the fight against Satan for the benefit of the Church, and unique powers of intercession, not to mention the alms of the pious. But to see the monks of the late antique period as martyrs *manqués*, driven into asceticism by the passing away of a more glorious form of witness to Christ, is too evidently dependent on viewing asceticism as a late development. In fact, the theme that the contemplative life is itself a form of witness to Christ, and as such superior to an unperfected man's merely dying for Christ, goes back to Clement of Alexandria at the turn of the second century (*Stromata* IV. ch. 4 and 9). And the persecutions were too occasional and sporadic for dying for Christ to be a satisfactory spiritual ambition: Origen had an intense longing for martyrdom from boyhood, but he did not view this as a substitute for the severe ascetic regimen that he maintained throughout his adult life.[24]

Some historians have laid stress on a reason for monastic retirement drawn from the opposite pole of human motivation, namely, the pressures of economic hardship. The social and economic decline of the Later Roman Empire has been seen as the main cause why men and women abandoned the unequal struggle to maintain themselves in secular life and turned instead to a life of monastic poverty, partly to make a virtue of necessity, and partly to come under the protection of powerful monastic communities.[25] It is obvious that this factor provides no explanation why ascetics should have been revered rather than despised as drop-outs, but it does help to account for the huge size of coenobitic communities in some regions. The exceptional size of many of the Egyptian monasteries may presumably be linked to the retrenchment of agriculture and squeezing out of the small, independent farmer that was a feature of at least parts of the Nile valley in the fourth century.[26] The region of Theodoret's holy men, that of northern Syria, however, experienced in the fourth and fifth centuries precisely the opposite economic development: huge rural areas, hitherto under-exploited, enjoyed an unprecedented agricultural expansion, accompanied by the breakdown of many large estates into a huge number of modest farms.[27] Even in an area already heavily exploited and still dominated by great estates, such as the plain of Antioch, the laments of Libanius over the recalcitrance of some tenants illustrate that even in the late antique world the great landowner could not always ride roughshod over his peasantry.[28] It seems scarcely necessary to add that, in any case, many monks, especially the leading ones, were not oppressed peasants at all, but came from the prosperous classes of society.[29]

A further explanation links the 'flight to the desert' not to economic pressures but to spiritual tension within the Christian Church, a result of the heady changes of the fourth century. This explanation runs as follows. The conversion of the emperors to Christianity (inconceivable to Tertullian and Origen only a century earlier) stimulated the rapid christianization of the whole of society. To be a Christian was now a material as well as a spiritual advantage. As a result, the Church was flooded with converts of very mixed motives and an imperfect understanding of the requirements of the Christian life. Meanwhile, the bishops who should have stemmed the tide turned instead to seek their own advantage, as they wallowed in the wealth that now poured into ecclesiastical coffers and engaged in bitter rivalry for imperial favor. Earnest Christians found themselves increasingly out of place in a degenerate Church: the desire to escape from this sorry scene and parade a way of life diametrically opposed to worldly Christianity was the great stimulus to monastic expansion. This is a familiar thesis,[30] but it can scarcely survive an impartial reading of the sources. First, in a markedly uncentralized society the conversion of the emperors percolated down only slowly; even in the court circles where an influence was immediately felt, it was not till the fifth century that a brilliant government career and open paganism became incompatible. More important for conversion at the grass-root level was the local initiative of bishops and monks: the change in governmental attitude enabled more open evangelization than had been possible in the third century, but there was little in the way of material incentives to win converts.[31] Secondly, the problem of low standards in the Church was not a new one; tepidity and worldliness among Christians are as much a theme in writings of the turn of the first century (e.g. the Letters to the Churches in the *Book of Revelation* and the *Shepherd* of Hermas) as in any late antique text. The development of public penance, with its acknowledgment within the very sacramental system that even baptized Christians desired rather than possessed holiness, was complete by the beginning of the third century. The rules and penalties of the Church did not undergo further relaxation in the fourth century; indeed, the greatest of recent historians of the Later Roman Empire, A.H.M. Jones, can accuse the Church of excessive inflexibility and a failure to adapt its norms to the needs of society.[32] The notion of monasticism as a protest movement fails finally before the evidence of the actual attitude of monks towards both the bishops and the laity. With some exceptions (notably the Messalian heretics), monks were reluctant to claim spiritual superiority.

One constant theme of Theodoret's *Religious History*, as of Athanasius's *Life of Antony*, is the willingness of monks to assure laymen that life in the world could be acceptable to God; another favorite theme of these two works is the humility and obedience that monks displayed towards their bishops. In all, monasticism cannot be viewed as a movement of protest against spiritual degeneracy in the mainstream Church.

Nevertheless, we are touching here on what must be the true explanation for monastic expansion and the increased reverence ascetics received. As long as the Church was a small body, with a sense of separateness from society reinforced by occasional persecution, it could maintain that unbounded self-esteem that is typically associated with sectaries. The primitive Christians had a strong sense of themselves as a holy people, existing in the flesh but not in accordance with the flesh, living on earth but exhibiting a heavenly citizenship (*Ad Diognetum* 5). The fact that the vast majority of Christians aimed at nothing higher than the basic moral decencies did not dent Christian self-esteem, since this could be buttressed by contemplating the vices of the pagans (as in Cyprian's *To Donatus*). But as the Church expanded to incorporate whole social groups, being a Christian ceased to seem so special a claim on God's favor, and the comforting spectacle of pagan vices became a rarer one. Inevitably, the ordinary Christian of the fourth century did not enjoy the self-confidence of his predecessor of two or three centuries earlier; to be certain of God's favor seemed now to require something beyond the observance of the ordinary layman. Asceticism had long been practised as a way to special graces: now for the first time it was widely pursued as the only way to be certain of salvation.[33] In addition, the ascetic's traditional role of intercession on behalf of his fellow Christians came to receive a new emphasis. Direct access to God (*parrhesia*) was traditionally attributed, as in the New Testament, to all the baptized, and this remained a theme of baptismal catechesis; but in practice the ordinary Christian layman no longer had the confidence that his own prayers were acceptable to God.[34] Instead, he felt a need for mediators—holy men and women who through the strictest self-denial had won that access to God which he himself could not claim without presumption. Ascetics who attained a special reputation could now expect to have a flood of clients in quest of the assurance afforded by their prayers and blessing. It is this spiritual anxiety of Christian laymen in the late antique period, this sense of their own spiritual inadequacy, that provides the essential explanation of the growth both in the number of Christians who chose the ascetic path to salvation and in the attention and respect these ascetics received from those who remained in the world.

In sum, the expansion of asceticism in the fourth and fifth centuries finds its explanation in the conversion of the Roman world, a process that transformed Christianity from a small sect into the religion of a whole society. As we have seen, this does not mean that monks were in revolt against the development. Rather, they shared in the humility and rigorism that increasingly characterized the Church as it came to seem obvious that the direct access to God that could assure someone of personal salvation and enable him to pray effectively for others required not just Christian baptism, which was now too common to seem a source of special grace, but a total rejection of earthly goods and a life of ceaseless prayer.

VII

THE RELIGIOUS HISTORY enables us to pursue further this topic of the holy man as mediator. One key feature of this role is immediately apparent to the reader of the work: the services of the holy man were not sought merely by the scrupulous or the exceptionally pious, obsessed with doubts as to their own salvation. The favor of God was recognized as necessary for success in this world as well as in the next. When Theodoret's mother sent her boy each week to receive a blessing from the hermit Peter (IX.4), it was as much his bodily as his spiritual health that she was concerned to safeguard. A holy man could even be asked to relieve a horse of a bladder complaint (VIII.11). Nothing is more indicative of the true spirit of the holy man's celibacy than his readiness to bless childless women and cure them of sterility (XI.4, XIII.16, XXVI.21); the monk who prayed for successful procreation was no enemy of sex or family life. His own extraordinary lifestyle did express a belief that life in the world was life at a certain distance from God, but in his pastoral ministrations he was concerned to bridge this gap and to assure lay people through his prayers that God's favor was available to them, that they could win God's protection in this world and the next without themselves becoming ascetics.

It is in this context of the holy man's mediatorial role that we must place the miracle stories that are so numerous in the *Religious History* and similar sources. If blessing clients was the holy man's standard pastoral activity, the occasional miracle could be seen as a necessary, as well as a spectacular, adjunct, and this in two ways. First, the miracles of the holy man were evidence that he did possess the power to secure his clients divine protection, and so proved the efficacy of his blessing. Secondly, it was reasonable to suppose that, if the need arose, the holy man's blessing could secure miraculous, as well as providential, protection; in this way constant blessing implied occasional miracle. The historian who sets aside the miracles attributed to holy men as either legends or exceptional freaks is missing the extent to which they illuminate the whole role of the holy man, a service of prayer and blessing where his working of miracles was but the occasional highlighting of something constant: the power of the holy man to assure his clients of God's favor.

The most original and influential recent article on holy men — Peter Brown's 'The Rise and Function of the Holy Man in Late Antiquity' (1971) — is concerned to bring out a further aspect of their mediatorial role, that of the holy man as the adjudicator between men, or social groups, in conflict, as often the patron of the poor against their oppressors. Certain stories in the *Religious History* immediately come to mind — that of Abraham securing a loan to enable a village to pay its taxes and promptly being adopted as its 'patron' (XVII.3), or that of Macedonius interceding for the guilty Antiochenes before the imperial officials sent to determine their punishment (XIII.7). Brown links the rise of the holy man to the rapid social and economic developments of the time, since these threw up tensions and conflicts that needed authoritative mediation to resolve. The monk was well placed to fill the role of judge and mediator, standing, as he did, outside and above the nexus of society. His extreme, sometimes histrionic, asceticism fitted in well. It constituted 'a long drawn-out, solemn ritual of dissociation, of becoming the total stranger (p. 131), and thereby he became the plausible spokesman for a divine law that was not the concoction of some particular interest group and was therefore acceptable to all. This thesis, of the Syrian holy man as 'the good patron writ large', knocks many hoary myths off their shaky pedestals:

the picture of late antique society as stagnant and constricted, the attribution of eremitical withdrawal to flight away from social responsibilities, the denigration of the reverence paid to holy men as abject superstition.[35]

VIII

THE ROLE THAT LEADING MONKS came to play as mediators between men, and supremely between man and God, illuminates both their own standing and the needs of the society they served. But we are still some way from understanding the reverence paid to holy men as a religious phenomenon. For certainly we cannot reduce reverence for holy men to a recognition of their usefulness: man's desire to admire is as basic as his need for assistance, and the flocks of pilgrims who beset a James of Cyrrhestica or Symeon Stylites were concerned in the first place simply to behold a living example of true perfection. What was it in the holy man that made him appear an awesome figure rather than an unsocial freak? The monk led a life at the opposite extreme from the culture of the cities. Unwashed, unkempt, often homeless, usually poorly educated, making a positive virtue out of physical deprivation, he shocked and appalled a cultivated pagan like Libanius of Antioch; and even the Christian townsman had a prejudice to overcome before he could see in this uncouth figure the spiritual paragon of the age.[36] Yet the Christian laity, led by their clergy, came to view the monk as the perfect Christian. What accounts for this veneration?

Let us turn again to the *Religious History*. We need first to determine the aim of the work. In a concluding section Theodoret declares that he has described a variety of ascetics 'so that each person, as he receives the impress of his favorite life, may have as a rule and regulator of his own life the one presented in our account' (XXX.7). The theme is tired and conventional. In fact, Theodoret presents in the *Religious History* numerous examples of essentially the same ascetic pattern. And it does not appear that he was genuinely concerned to guide would-be ascetics: he has little to say of the topics of prime interest to them—the details of formation, the problems and temptations to be encountered, the inner life of prayer. His monks are consistently fully formed and faultless; they are essentially viewed from the outside, as by a spectator of their achievements. The work is clearly intended for the awestruck observer who wishes to venerate the monks rather than imitate them, let alone join them. In consequence, Theodoret's presentation of his holy men should provide an accurate answer to the question we have posed: what was it in the ascetic pattern of life that so impressed the ordinary Christian, so stirred his veneration?

The first part of our answer lies in one of the broadest themes in the ideology of monasticism. A reading of the *Religious History*, as of comparable texts, makes it clear that the ideal the monk was seen to realize was not some specifically human perfection, defined by the limitations inherent in man's nature, but a transcending of these limitations through the power of divine grace, and entry into a higher spiritual life unconfined by man's normal physical and psychological needs. This higher life was envisaged as an imitation on earth of the heavenly life of the angels. The theme of the monastic life as the 'angelic life' is often touched upon, explicitly or implicitly, in the *Religious History*. It is in another work, however, that Theodoret develops it at length, *The Cure of Hellenic Maladies*:

> Intercourse with females is superfluous for the angels: as immortal they have no need of increase, and as bodiless they are incapable of sexual activity. Another reason for calling them holy is that there is nothing of the earth about them: instead, separated from all earthly passions, they labor as a heavenly choir, singing hymns to their maker. They also serve by ministering to the divine will, in accordance with its commands, sent out as they are by the God of all creation to further the salvation of men . . . . It is in imitation of their mode of life that so many men have embraced the service of God, shunning even licit intercourse as a distraction from the things of God, and forsaking their homes and families: this they do in order to be anxious only about the affairs of the Lord and to escape all bonds that might prevent the mind from soaring into heaven and gazing in desire at the invisible and ineffable beauty of God. They fill the cities and the

villages, the hilltops and the ravines. Some of them by living in community fashion in their souls the images of wisdom; others living in twos or threes, or in solitary isolation, protect their eyes from the lure of visible beauty, and win for their souls the freedom to bask in the contemplation of things spiritual. If men yoked to the body and troubled by passions many and various embrace an exalted style of life which has nothing to do with the body and belongs to heavenly beings, what words would then suffice to depict the life of incorporeal natures, a life free from every passion and anxiety? (III.91-2).

The notion of the 'angelic life' summed up for Theodoret and his contemporaries all the main features of the ascetic life: the rejection of marriage, suppression of bodily urges, freedom from irrational impulses, perpetual prayer, succoring of one's fellow-men.[37]

We have still to ask which elements of this lifestyle excited particular attention. Which one of these features receives the greatest emphasis in the *Religious History*, as appealing especially to its readers? The answer is not entirely obvious. Theodoret is often dependent on emphases and omissions in his sources of information, and is not manifestly calculating or crudely tendentious. He can concentrate in one chapter on aspects of the holy man that are quite subordinate in others. And the reader must beware of importing his own emphases as he reads, and of being over-influenced by the early chapters of the work, the ones where Theodoret is most dependent on the shape of the tradition as it had reached him. He will do best to concentrate on the lives of the ascetics best known to Theodoret personally, those of his own day and his own diocese – the ascetics of Cyrrhestica treated principally in chapters XXI to XXV. Which topics predominate here? The pastoral role of holy men receives no special emphasis: indeed James is defended for driving away visitors without a blessing (XXI.33-34). Miracles, the highlights of their pastoral role, are mentioned only briefly and in passing (XXI.14, XXII.3, XXIV.7). Nor was Theodoret concerned, by and large, with the details of the interior life: the section on James's experience of diabolical visitations (XXI.23-28) is unique in the whole work; and while these hermits' devotion to prayer is naturally mentioned (e.g. XXIV.3), Theodoret does not enter into the details of their prayer-life. Instead, the main emphasis is on their physical endurance: one favorite form this took among these ascetics was living all the time in the open air, exposed to burning heat in the summer and to frost and snow in the winter (e.g. XXI.3) and the tedium and inconvenience of a total lack of privacy (XXI.5, 32); other elements were constant standing (e.g. XXIV.4) and the wearing of heavy chains (e.g. XXI.8). Since these details might create the impression that these hermits were 'abnormal self-tormentors, not more healthy in mind than in body'—to use the words of the liberal historian J.B. Bury—[38] Theodoret was concerned to add that they exhibited consistent 'simplicity, mildness, modesty, gentleness of speech, sweetness in company' (XXIV.5), while remaining firmly indifferent to human admiration (XXI.11).

This concentration on the mortification of the body is disconcerting to the modern reader, who attaches an infinitely greater value to the life of the mind. But it arises from a simple and obvious factor: it was precisely the external aspects of asceticism that were visible and manifest to the lay observer. The monastic lifestyle excited veneration principally because it proved that human limitations could be overcome, and man participate in the life of angels. The great champions of the monastic movement were those who attained such victory over the flesh that they lived for decades almost without sleep and with a minimum of food; it was the sight of this that demonstrated that they had transcended the human condition, and could be presumed to enjoy a perfect life of prayer, a constant access to God.

IX

IN THIS EMPHASIS ON THE EXTERNALS of asceticism, there would appear to be a further factor at work. Theodoret displays at times a concern to explain how some particularly histrionic feat of bodily mortification served some ulterior purpose. The most striking case occurs in his account of Symeon Stylites, easily the most famous of Theodoret's holy men, both in their own day and in ours. Symeon's great achievement was to maintain for almost forty years the posture of standing on the top of a pillar. He attracted huge crowds of pilgrims from as far afield as Gaul and Persia. Now at an earlier stage in his ascetic progress he had tied himself to a rock by a long chain, until persuaded that he could equally stay near the rock without using a chain (XXVI.10). Why then did he not keep to perpetual standing on the ground: was not the ascent onto a pillar another piece of pointless exhibitionism? Theodoret offers two answers (XXVI.12). The first is that Symeon ascended the pillar for the practical reason that he was tired of being fingered by the visitors who beset him continually. This explanation is a feeble one, since it was precisely Symeon's ascent of the pillar that attracted the crowds of pilgrims, who prior to that cannot have been sufficiently numerous to be a real nuisance. Secondly, Theodoret suggests that Symeon's action could be compared to the extraordinary actions of some of the Old Testament prophets, such as Isaiah walking naked or Jeremiah putting on a wooden collar. Such actions served, he explains, to draw the inquisitive, amazed at such conduct, so that they could then be given instruction in the things of God. But merely eccentric behavior would simply have excited ridicule. The strange actions of the prophets were, of course, much more than this: they were symbolic gestures that added to prophetic words the decisive reinforcement of prophetic actions having a power of their own; but Theodoret does not attempt a deeper explanation of Symeon's behavior along corresponding lines. Theodoret's desire for the rational explanation that was not genuinely forthcoming surfaces elsewhere. He describes, for instance, how Thalelaeus chose to live in a suspended cylinder: when he himself asked the hermit what the reason was, he received the somewhat thin reply that he hoped through discomfort in this life to escape the torments of hell. Theodoret comments delightedly, 'I was overwhelmed with admiration for his shrewdness, because he not only contended beyond the course laid down and devised further contests of his own will, but also knew the reason for them and could teach it to others' (XXVIII.4).

One is left with the disconcerting impression that Theodoret's own Hellenic spirit of rationalism and moderation was something of a hindrance in dealing with the more extraordinary features of Syrian Christianity. Normally he was content to record the strange acts and gestures of his holy men, but when he betrays a need to assure himself that these had some ulterior spiritual purpose, we sense that

Theodoret's own outlook was not quite that of the holy men themselves. For in contrast to his Hellenic assumptions (which we today largely share), their lives point to a very different climate of thought. The histrionic element in Syrian asceticism reveals a mentality in which outward actions have their own value, quite apart from their influence on the soul; it was a spirituality where interior cultivation was not the one, all-absorbing concern. Suspension in a cage or enchainment to a rock did not so much *effect* as *express* the suppression of physical needs, the victory of the spirit; Symeon ascended a pillar not to achieve a predictable effect on his soul or those of others, but simply in order to manifest thereby the ascent of the whole person to God. Bodily gesture of this kind were seen not merely to have psychological effects but to possess intrinsic meaning and value in their visible reality. In this way the Syrian ascetics, while mortifying the flesh, esteemed the body.

What, then, the holy men of northern Syria offered to the beholder, or the reader of Theodoret's account, was a spiritual life that was actually visible, and a direct object of veneration, quite apart from conjecture on the state of the soul. The student of Christian spirituality may wish to penetrate to the 'inner life', as if that were more real; the secular historian may seek an explanation of the rise of the holy man in the tensions and needs of the society around him. But Theodoret's narratives draw our attention in the first place to outward behavior of strong symbolic resonance, and to the desire of the pious layman, in all ages perhaps, to venerate the visible manifestations of divine grace. It is this that gives the *Religious History* its power and abiding value.

NOTES

1. The best introduction to Theodoret's life and writings is F. Young, *From Nicaea to Chalcedon*, 33-38, 50-56 (on the *Rel. Hist.*), 265-289. See too J. Quasten, *Patrology*, III: 536-554. There has been no longer general survey of Theodoret since N. Glubokovsky, *Blazhennyi Theodorit* (1890).
2. P. Brown, 'The Rise and Function of the Holy Man in Late Antiquity' (1971), which cites the *Rel. Hist.* repeatedly, has had a great and immediate impact in the English-speaking world.
3. The arguments of J. Garnier for 444 (*Auctarium Theodoreti*; PG 84: 238-240) are accepted by Glubokovsky, *Blazhennyi Theodorit* (1890) II: 415-6, Schiwietz, *Das morgenländische Mönchtum*, III (1938) 32, n.4, and Canivet, *Le monachisme syrien* (1977), 32-3. 440 was preferred, as at least an approximate date, by Le Nain de Tillemont (*Mémoires*, XV: 327, 357, 877), and is strongly supported by work in this century on the chronology of Symeon Stylites (as noted by Festugière, *Antioche*, 348, n.2).
4. The date of 405 is that in Marcellinus, *Chronicon*, describing a stage in the Isaurian war that Zosimus, IV.25 dates, with convincing detail, to 404. The raid in question in *Rel. Hist.* XXI.27 is probably that dated by Palladius (PG 47: 55A) to the autumn of 404 – though a date in 403 or 405 can be supported from other sources (see Tillemont, *Histoire des Empereus*, V: 473-5). The date of 404, taken with the correct interpretation of XXI.27, implies a *terminus ante quem* of 442/3 for the composition of the *Rel. Hist.* and actually excludes 444.
5. Garnier deduced 416 from a combination of the following: (1) Symeon died in 460 (actually in 459); (2) Evagrius (in fact, virtually all sources) gives fifty-six years as the duration of Symeon's labors; and (3) to get the date of his first great fast, which coincided with his arrival at Telanissus, we must deduct from the fifty-six years the 2 + 10 years he labored, according to *Rel. Hist.* XXVI.4-5, before coming to Telanissus. However, the ancient computation of Symeon's labors that offers the total of fifty-six reckons the period before Telanissus as only nine years (Delehaye, *Les Saints Stylites*, xv-xvii), thus implying 412 for the arrival at Telanissus. Canivet (*Le monachisme syrien*, 177-8) accepts this date, but places the fast three years later. As he notes, Theodoret's account (XXVI.7) does not exclude this, but it is contrary to the detailed account in the *Syriac Life* 24-26.
6. A. Leroy-Molinghen in *Byzantion* 34 (1964), 381-2.
7. See *Epilogue: On divine love*, note 1, below; here too Garnier's dating (followed by Canivet) is mistaken.
8. *Episkopos* occurs only at I.10 (unless this chapter is largely an interpolation) and *monasterion* only at III.14.
9. The sole exception, IV.10, mentions the anger of a monk only in order to praise his superior's equanimity.
10. For John Chrysostom on the monasteries around Antioch see the texts given in Festugière, *Antioche*, 329-346.
11. A. Vööbus, *History of Asceticism in the Syrian Orient*, II: 145.
12. G. Tchalenko, *Villages antiques de la Syrie du Nord*, I: 20.
13. W. Liebeschuetz, *Antioch*, 61-2.
14. Tchalenko, *Villages antiques*, I: 145 n.; Liebeschuetz, *Antioch*, 237.
15. H. Butler, *Early Churches in Syria*, 83.
16. Lassus, *Sanctuaires Chrétiens de Syrie*, 272-3; Tchalenko, *Villages antiques*, I:19.
17. See S. Brock, 'Early Syrian Asceticism', *Numen* 20: 1-19, and R. Murray, 'The Features of the Earliest Christian Asceticism', in P. Brooks, ed., *Christian Spirituality*,

65-77. A Vööbus, *History of Asceticism in the Syrian Orient*, Vol. 1, is full but less reliable: some of his sources (e.g. the *Chronicle of Arbela*) are dubious, and his thesis of a decisive Manichaean influence is unconvincing.
   18. B. Streeter's suggestion that Mt was written at Antioch (*The Four Gospels*, 500ff.) is a conjecture that has won wide support.
   19. E.g. *Acts of Judas Thomas* 79, 'There shall come false apostles and prophets of lawlessness, who, not satisfied with one wife, ruin many women'.
   20. For Aphrahat and 'the Covenant', see Vööbus, *History of Asceticism*, I: 173-208, and R. Murray in *New Testament Studies* 21 (1975) 59-80.
   21. See our subject index under 'Ascetic practices', 'Asceticism, themes of', and 'Miracles'.
   22. Schiwietz (*Das morgenländische Mönchtum*, III: 46-8, 407-8) argues that monasticism was indeed an importation into Syria, but from Mesopotamia rather than Egypt. For instance, Gindarus, the earliest known monastery in the region of Antioch, was founded from Mesopotamia (*Rel. Hist.* II.9) , and Aones, described by Sozomen (VI.33) as the first Syrian hermit, lived near Carrhae in Mesopotamia. But since the primitive asceticism from which all this grew was just as strong in Syria as in Mesopotamia, it seems better to take the two regions together as a single unit. For the essential point – the lack of Syrian dependence on Egypt – Schiwietz, III: 413-8 adds the numerous differences in the details of prayer and fasting, and in ascetic practises: the open-air life, perpetual standing and wearing of chains, though common in Syria, were extremely rare in Egypt.
   23. *Pachomii Vita Prima* 1 – a fourth century text.
   24. Eusebius, *Eccl. Hist.* VI.2-3.
   25. Oppression of the peasantry is still stressed in this context by W. Frend, *The Rise of Christianity* (1984), 574f. Contrast P. Brown, *The Making of Late Antiquity*, 83-6, which identifies the key pressure not as the subjugation of the poor but as social tensions between members of the intermediate class, that of the 'comfortable farmer'.
   26. For a diminution of the cultivated area in the Fayyum in the early fourth century see P. Jouguet, *Papyrus de Théadelphie*, 23-5.
   27. This is the main theme of Tchalenko, *Villages antiques* – on the limestone region to the east of Antioch. But other areas in northern Syria enjoyed the same expansion: Liebeschuetz, *Antioch*, 72.
   28. Libanius, *Or.* 47, *De patrociniis*, in Loeb *Selected Works*, II: 500ff.
   29. The following of Theodoret's monks are known to have come from a prosperous background: Asterius (II.7), Marcianus (III.2), Publius (V.1) Aphrahat (VIII.1), Theodosius (X.1), Zeno (XII.1-2), Symeon Stylites (see XXVI, note 3), Marana and Cyra (XXIX.2), Domnina (XXX.3).
   30. E.g., Gibbon, *The Decline and Fall of the Roman Empire*, ed. J. B. Bury, IV: 57-8.
   31. *Rel. Hist.* XVII.3-4 provides one of the exceptional examples to the contrary. For a few further instances, with some exaggerated generalization, see R. MacMullen, *Christianizing the Roman Empire*, 52-58.
   32. A.H.M. Jones, *The Later Roman Empire*, 979-985.
   33. See *Rel. Hist.* XXI.33 and XXVIII.4.
   34. See *Rel. Hist.* XXIV.8. For the *parrhesia* of the baptized see G. Bartelink, Παρρησια, 12f., with citation from John Chrysostom, Theodore of Mopsuestia and Theodoret.
   35. In the process, there is some exaggeration both of the similarity of monastic to other forms of patronage, and of the peculiar tensions of the Late Antique period: the problems that the holy man as good patron had to solve – of psychosomatic disease, childlessness, rural distress due to injustice or bad harvests – are common to every age.
   36. John Chrysostom, *8 Catéchèses Baptismales*, VIII.2-6; *Sources Chrétiennes* 50: John feels it necessary to tell his Antiochene congregation not to despise some monks who are visiting from the countryside.

37. For holy men being addressed as 'your angel', see Dawes and Baynes, *Three Byzantine Saints*, 78. However, monks did not suppose that life on earth could truly anticipate life in heaven. They looked forward to the life to come as a reversal and antithesis of the ascetic's present experience (e.g. Ephraem, *Hymni et Sermones*, ed. T. Lamy, IV: 164).
38. *History of the Later Roman Empire*, I: 384.

A History of the Monks of Syria

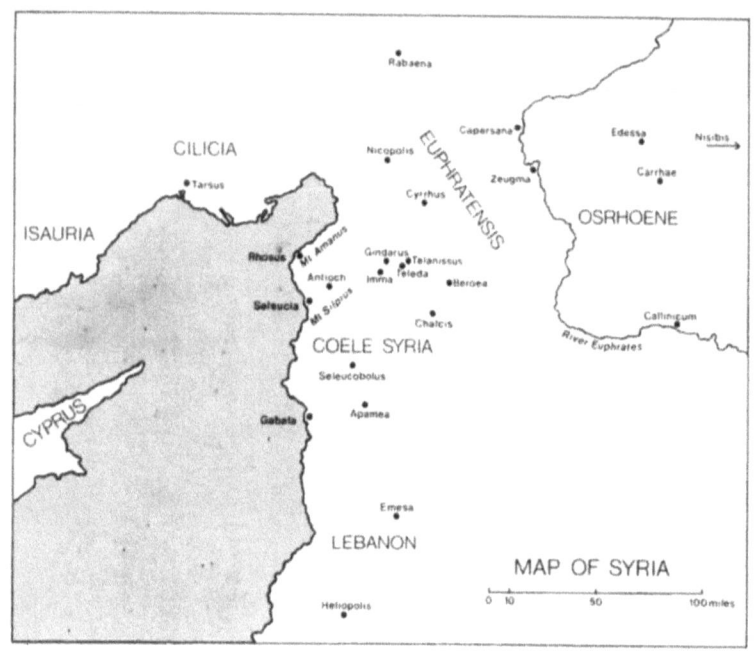

Prologue

HOW FINE IT IS[1] to behold the contests of excellent men, the athletes of virtue,[2] and to draw benefit with the eyes; when witnessed, the objects of our praise appear enviable and become desirable, and impel the beholder to attain them. No middling profit, however, derives from the mere narration of such achievements, communicated by those who know of them to the hearing of those who do not. Some say that sight is more trustworthy than hearing: however, we also believe hearing when it judges what is said from the truthfulness of the speakers. Just as the tongue and palate have been entrusted with decision over sweet and sour and other qualities of this kind and deliver their verdict accordingly, so too hearing has been empowered to discriminate between utterances, and knows how to distinguish those that bring some profit from harmful ones.

2. If the memory of profitable narratives remained inviolate and the injury of oblivion did not, like some spreading mist, render it extinct, it would of course be superfluous and redundant to record such actions, since the benefit from them would most easily make its way to posterity. But since time injures bodies by inflicting old age and death,

and injures achievements by causing oblivion and blunting memory, surely no one could reasonably be indignant with us for trying to write down the way of life of the men who have loved God; just as those who have been entrusted with treating bodies prepare medicines in order to fight the disease and aid the patients, so the welcome labor of such composition becomes like some preventive medicine, a device against oblivion and an aid to memory. When poets and historians record acts of bravery in war, when tragedians make conspicuous in tragedy misfortunes that had rightly been hidden away and leave their memory written up, when certain others expend their words on comedy and laughter, how would it not be absurd if we let be consigned to oblivion men who in a mortal and passible body have displayed impassibility[3] and emulated the bodiless beings? What penalty would we not justly pay for letting be dimmed the memory of these contests worthy of admiration? If they, in emulation of the consummate philosophy[4] of the holy men of old, did not engrave their memory in bronze letters, but receiving the impress of all their virtue have made themselves, as it were, living images and statues of them, what pardon could we reasonably receive if we do not honor their celebrated life in writing?
3. Especially when the athletes and pancratiasts who compete in the Olympic games are honored with images, and even the victorious charioteers appearing in the horse-races receive this same honor. And not only these but also men who are womanish and effeminate, so that it is ambiguous whether they are men or women, are painted on panels by those who love to gaze on them, in emulous zeal to extend their memory as long as possible, although this memory causes not profit but injury to their souls: nevertheless, they who love either these or those, even to their own detriment, honor them in portraiture; since death despoils the nature that is mortal, by mixing colors and placing their appearance on panels they contrive that their memory will last much longer than their life. But we are recording a life that teaches philosophy and has emulated the way of life in heaven; we do not portray their bodily features nor do we display for those in ignorance representations of them, but we sketch the forms of invisible souls and display unseen wars and secret struggles.
4. For such too is the armor which Paul, the general and champion of their host, has put upon them: 'Take up,' he says, 'the panoply of

God, so that you may be able to withstand in the evil day and having done all to stand,'[a] and again, 'Stand therefore having girded your loins with truth and having put on the breastplate of righteousness and having shod your feet with the preparation of the Gospel of peace, above all taking the shield of faith with which you will be able to quench all the flaming darts of the evil one, and receive the helmet of salvation and the sword of the Spirit that is the speech of God';[b] it was after putting this panoply upon them that he led them into combat. For such too is the nature of the enemy: bodiless, invisible, encroaching unperceived, plotting secretly, setting ambush and attacking suddenly. This same general taught this when he said, 'Not ours is the wrestling against flesh and blood, but against the principalities, against the powers, against the world-rulers of the darkness of this age, against the the spiritual beings of evil in the heavenly places.'[c] Nevertheless, though having such adversaries, the company of these saints or rather each one of them, surrounded by enemies of such number and such a nature (for they do not assail them together but attack now one, now another), have won so radiant a crown of victory as to rout their adversaries, pursue them forcibly and erect a trophy with nothing standing in the way.

5. It is not their nature that afforded them victory—for it is mortal and full of innumerable passions—but their resolve,[5] attracting divine grace. As fervent lovers of the beauty of God, choosing to do and suffer all things gladly on behalf of the Beloved, they bore nobly the revolt of the passions and were steadfast in shaking off the showers of the devil's darts. Repressing the body and subduing it, to use the apostolic phrase,[d] they soothed the inflammation of the irascible part and compelled the madness of the desires to be at rest.[6] So by fasting and sleeping on the ground they lulled the passions and put a stop to their restiveness; they compelled the body to make a treaty with the soul and put an end to their innate war.

6. So, after arbitrating peace between them, they expelled the whole array of their adversaries; for they are not able to make war when they lack the thoughts that betray the interior and are deprived of the cooperation of the human limbs, since the devil uses our own

[a]Eph 6:13. [b]Eph 6:14-17. [c]Eph 6:12. [d]Cf. 1 Co 9:27.

limbs as weapons against us; for if the eyes are not enticed nor the hearing bewitched nor touch titillated nor the mind receptive of evil intentions, the zeal of those plotting harm is in vain. For just as a city built on a height, walled round with a strong circuit and surrounded on all sides by a deep moat, would not be taken by an enemy unless one of those within played traitor and slipped open some postern, so too it is impossible for the demons making war from outside to overcome a soul surrounded by divine grace, unless the compliance of some thought open some postern in our senses and receive the enemy within it.[7] The men we are extolling had been taught this plainly by divine Scripture. Hearing God saying through the prophet that 'death has come up through the windows',[e] they barred up the senses with God's laws as if with bolts and bars and entrusted their keys to the mind. The tongue did not open the lips except at the command of the mind, nor was the pupil allowed to peep out from the eyelids without permission; the hearing, though unable to wall up the entrance with eyelids or lips, rejected words that were senseless and admitted only those that the mind took pleasure in; so they taught the sense of smell not to hanker after fragrant odors, since by nature they produce flaccidity and limpness. So too they expelled the satiety of the belly and taught it to accept what satisfied, not pleasure, but need, and indeed just so much as could prevent death from hunger. So too they deposed the sweet tyranny of sleep, and freeing the eyelids from slavery to it taught them to be masters not slaves, and to accept its services not when it assailed but when they themselves invited it to assist nature briefly. So therefore, taking thought for the guard of walls and gates and bestowing harmony on the thoughts within, they laughed at the antagonists assailing from without, who because of the protection of divine grace were unable to force a way in, since they found no traitor who chose to admit the foe. Although the enemies have an invisible nature, they could not master a visible body subject to the necessities of nature; for its charioteer and musician and helmsman by holding the reins well induced the horses to run in proper order, by striking the strings of the senses in rhythm made them produce sound that was perfectly harmonious, and by moving the rudder skilfully put an end to the blows of the billows and the blast of the winds.

[e] Jer 9:21.

7. Therefore these who have followed the path of life through innumerable labors and broken the body in with sweat and toil, who have not experienced the passion of laughter but spent all their life in mourning and tears, who have deemed fasting Sybaritic nourishment, laborious vigil a most pleasant sleep, the hard resistance of the ground a soft couch, a life of prayer and psalmody a pleasure measureless and insatiable, these who have attained every form of virtue – who would not rightly admire them? Rather, who could extol them as they merit? I, too, am well aware that no words can attain to their virtue. Nevertheless, the attempt must be made: it would not be right if men who became perfect lovers of true philosophy should for this very reason fail to receive even modest praise.

8. We shall not write a single eulogy for all together, for different graces were given them from God: the blessed Paul taught this when he said, 'To one through the Spirit is given a word of wisdom, to another a word of knowledge according to the same Spirit, to another gifts of healing in the same Spirit, to another workings of powers, to another prophecy, to another varieties of tongues, to another the interpretation of tongues;'[f] and to indicate the source of all these he added, 'All these are worked by one and the same Spirit, apportioning individually to each one as he wills'.[g] Since, therefore, they have received different gifts, we shall rightly compose the narrative of each one individually. We shall not work through the whole course of their actions, since a whole life would not be enough for such writing. Instead, we shall narrate a selection from the life and actions of each and display through this selection the character of the whole life, and then proceed to another.

9. We shall not try to transmit to history the way of life of all the saints who have been prominent everywhere, for neither do we know those who have been prominent everywhere nor is it possible for them all to be written down by one man. So I shall record the life of those alone who have appeared like stars in the east and reached the ends of the world with their rays. The account will proceed in narrative form, not following the rules of panegyric but forming a plain tale of some few facts.

[f] 1 Co 12:8-10.   [g] 1 Co 12:11.

10. I ask those who will read this *Religious History* or *Ascetic Life* – let one call the composition as one chooses – not to disbelieve what is said if they hear something beyond their own power, nor to measure the virtue of these men by themselves, but to recognize clearly that God is wont to measure the gifts of the all-holy Spirit by the resolve of the pious and gives greater gifts to those with more perfect resolve. Let me say this to those who have not been initiated into divine truths with real accuracy, for the initiates of the sanctuary of the Spirit know the munificence of the Spirit and what miracles he works in men through the agency of men, drawing the faithless to a knowledge of God by the mighty working of prodigies. Quite obviously, he who will disbelieve what we are about to tell does not believe either in the truth of what took place through Moses, Joshua, Elijah and Elisha, and considers a myth the working of miracles that took place through the sacred Apostles. But if truth bears witness on behalf of those men, let him believe these stories also to be free of falsehood, for the grace that worked in those men is the same that through these men performed what it has performed.[8] Grace is ever-flowing: it elects the worthy and through them as through springs pours forth the streams of beneficence.

11. Of some of what I shall tell I was myself the eye-witness; whatever I have not seen I have heard of from those who have seen these men, those who as lovers of virtue were counted worthy to see them and be taught by them. Trustworthy as writers of the Gospel teaching are not only Matthew and John, the great and first Evangelists, the eye-witnesses of the Master's miracles, but also Luke and Mark, whom 'the first eye-witnesses and ministers of the Word'[h] instructed accurately in not only what the Lord suffered and did but also what he taught continually. Despite the fact that he had not been an eye-witness, the blessed Luke at the beginning of his work says that his narration concerns facts about which there is full assurance. And we, hearing that he was not an eye-witness of these very narratives but received this teaching from others, pay equal attention to him and Mark as to Matthew and John, for each of the two is trustworthy in his narration because he was taught by those who had seen. For this

[h] Lk 1:2.

very reason we too shall tell of some things as eye-witnesses and of others trusting the narration of eye-witnesses, men who have emulated their life. I have expended rather many words on this point in my wish to carry conviction that I shall be narrating the truth; so starting from there, I shall begin my narrative.

NOTES

1. The Prologue is an elegant tissue of commonplaces. Its conventional character can be gauged from a comparison with the Preface and Prologue of the *Lausiac History* of Palladius (written *c.*420): the two texts are quite independent, but share many of the same themes.

2. The use of language from athletics, and at §4-6 from warfare, to describe asceticism recurs frequently in the *Religious History*, as in other early monastic literature (cp. Athanasius, *Life of Antony* 7-10, Jerome, *ep.* 14). There is a debt both to St Paul (Phil 3:13-14, Eph 6:11-17) and to the accounts of Christian martyrdom: e.g. Eusebius, *Eccl. Hist.* VI.4.3, where a martyr is called an 'athlete of piety', and V.1-2 (the contemporary account of the martyrs at Lyons in 177).

3. By 'impassibility' (*apatheia*) is meant freedom from the irrational emotions of concupiscence, fear, and anger, normally inseparable from life on earth (cp. Theodoret, *On Psalm 50*; PG 80: 1245A); it is linked in the *Religious History* to surpassing human limitations and attaining to the 'angelic life', on which see my *Introduction*, section VIII.

4. The application of the word 'philosophy' to Christian asceticism, however unintellectual, occurs in several fourth century Fathers, e.g. Eusebius and John Chrysostom (see Lampe, *P.G.L.*, 1483). There was preparation for this in the Platonic understanding of philosophy as a path to tame the passions (Porphyry, *To Marcella* 31) and purify the mind so as to enable the intuition of higher truths (Porphyry, *Life of Pythagoras* 46). See Theodoret, *Cure of Hellenic Maladies* XII.19-37, where he argues that Plato's philosophical ideal of detachment from worldly affairs and assimilation to God has been more successfully realized by the monks than by the pagan philosophers.

5. Cp. Theodoret, *On Psalm 50.7* (PG 80: 1244-5): as a result of the fall, man's nature has become mortal and therefore subject to the assault of the passions; 'nature has an inclination of sin, being beset by the passions, but nevertheless resolve is victorious, when it makes use of the cooperation of labors'. Such language is not Augustinian, but neither is it 'Pelagian': the love for God that enables such victory is itself a gift of the Holy Spirit, stemming from the passion of Christ (Theodoret, *On Romans*; PG 82: 96D).

6. Here, and in the following paragraph, Theodoret uses the scheme and much of the language of Plato's psychology (*The Republic* 436-444, *Phaedrus* 246), which, in its main outlines, he expounds and approves in *Cure of Hellenic Maladies* V.29-31. Briefly, the two emotional parts of the soul, the irascible faculty and the desires, have to be directed and checked by the third part, the intellect or reason. It is important to note that in this scheme the emotions are valued positively: *Cure of Hellenic Maladies* V.76-79, 'The rational part of the soul directs the passions, which themselves are necessary and useful for our nature. For desire is most advantageous, and so is the irascible faculty, its opponent. It is because of the former that we yearn for things divine . . . , while the irascible faculty has been given to cooperate with reason, in order to prevent the excess of desire. . . . So desire and the irascible faculty, blended with each other and disciplined by each other, effect the perfect blend of virtue. It is reason that has control over actions, so as to restrain the former faculty and stimulate the latter, or alternatively to suppress the latter and urge on the former.' Cp. *Sayings of the Desert Fathers*, Theodore §4, 'Again he said this, "A Christian discussing the body with a Manichee expressed himself in these words: 'Give the body discipline, and you will see that the body is for Him who made it.'"'

7. Cp. Cassian, *Conferences* VIII.19, 'The blessed Antony proved and established that demons cannot possibly find an entrance into the mind or body of anyone, nor

have they the power of overwhelming the soul of anyone, unless they have first deprived it of all holy thoughts, and made it empty and free from spiritual meditation.'

8. Cp. *History of the Monks in Egypt*, Prol. 13, 'Even in these times the Saviour performs through them what he performed through the prophets and apostles. For the same Lord now and always works all things in all men.'

1
JAMES
(of Nisibis)

MOSES, the divine legislator, who laid bare the bottom of the sea, flooded with water the moistureless desert and worked all the other miracles, wrote down the way of life of the holy men of old, not using the wisdom he had adopted from the Egyptians but receiving the splendor of grace from on high. For from what other source could he have learnt of the virtue of Abel, the devotion of Enoch, the righteousness of Noah, the priestly piety of Melchizedek, the call, faith and endurance of Abraham, his attentive hospitality, the celebrated sacrifice of his son and the list of his other achievements, and, to speak in summary, the contests, victories and utterances of those glorious men, if he had not received the rays of the rational and divine Spirit? I too need this assistance at present, as I try to write down the life of the glorious saints of our own time and the recent past, and seek to set out a rule, as it were, for those who wish to emulate them. I must therefore invoke their prayers, and so begin my narration.

2. Nisibis is a city on the frontier of the Roman and Persian empires which formerly paid tribute to the Romans and was subject to

James [of Nisibis]

their sovereignty. Originating from this city, the great James[1] embraced the eremitical and quiet life, and gaining the tops of the highest hills lived upon them. In spring, summer, and autumn he used the thickets, with the sky for roof; in the winter season a cave received him and provided scanty shelter. He had food not sown and produced with labor but that which grows up by itself: it was by gathering the natural fruits of wild trees and edible plants and vegetables that he provided his body with the bare necessities for life, rejecting the use of fire.[2] Also superfluous for him was using wool: the roughest goat's hair filled its place, for from this were made both his tunic and his simple cloak.

3. While he thereby wore down his body, he provided his soul unceasingly with spiritual nourishment. Purifying the eye of his thought, he prepared a clear mirror for the Holy Spirit; and 'with unveiled face, beholding as in a mirror the glory of the Lord, in the words of the divine Apostle, he was 'changed into his image from glory to glory, as from the Lord the Spirit'.[a] And so his familiar access to God increased every day, and his requests for what he needed to ask from God were granted immediately. So too he possessed prophetic foreknowledge of the future and received by the grace of the all-holy Spirit power to work miracles.[3] I shall recount a few of these, to reveal to those unacquainted with them the luster like that of the Apostles that shone in him.

4. At that time the madness of men over idols was in full vigor, lifeless statues usurped divine honors, and the majority of men paid no heed to the worship of God. Contempt was the lot of those who refused to share in their sottishness and, because of firm stability, had an accurate discernment of reality, who laughed at the feebleness of the idols and worshiped the Creator of the universe. In this period James went to Persia, to observe the piety planted there and convey to it the help it needed. As he was passing by a spring, some girls who were standing at washing-troughs and cleaning clothes under their feet, far from feeling awe at his novel appearance, cast aside all modesty and stared at the man of God with brazen looks and eyes dead to shame. They did not cover their heads, nor even let down

[a] 2 Co 3:18.

their clothes, which they had tucked up. Indignant at this, the man of God decided to display God's power opportunely, in order to free them from impiety by means of a miracle. So he cursed the spring, at which the stream immediately vanished away; and then he cursed the girls, and chastised their impudent youth with premature grey hair. His words had immediate effect: their black hair was changed, and they looked like young trees decked in spring with the leaves of autumn. As the water of the spring ran away, and looking at each other's heads they saw that drastic alteration, they perceived their punishment, and ran into the town to tell what had happened. At this the townsfolk rushed out to meet the great James, and begged him to calm his anger and remit the punishment. Without a moment's delay he made supplication to the Master and bade the water gush forth once more; immediately it appeared again out of its underground sources, recovering its course at the command of the righteous one. After receiving this favor, they begged him to restore to their daughters' hair its former color. It is said that he consented to this as well and asked for the girls who had received that correction, but when they did not appear he let the punishment stand, as a lesson in self-control, a reason for good behavior, and a perpetual and clear reminder of the power of God.[4]

5. Such was the miracle of this new Moses, which did not result from the blow of a rod but received its efficacy from the sign of the cross. I myself am filled with admiration for his gentleness, in addition to his working a miracle. He did not, like the great Elisha, hand over those shameless girls to carnivorous bears,[b] but applying a harmless correction that involved only a slight disfigurement he gave them a lesson in both piety and good behavior. I do not say this to accuse the prophet of harshness—may I be spared such folly—but to show how, while possessing the same power, he performed what accorded with the gentleness of Christ and the new covenant.

6. On some other occasion he saw a Persian judge give an unjust verdict. At this he laid a curse on a huge stone that lay nearby, and commanded it to shatter and explode, and thereby confute the man's unjust verdict. Immediately the stone broke up into a thousand pieces.

[b]Cf. 2 Kgs 2:24.

The bystanders were panic-stricken, and the judge, now filled with terror, revoked his earlier verdict and decreed instead a just one. Here too James emulated his own Master, who, to show that he submitted to his passion freely and could easily have chastised the miscreants if he had wished to, did not inflict punishment on them but demonstrated his power by causing with a word the lifeless fig-tree to wither up.[c] James too imitated this love for men when he did not chastise the unjust judge but by striking a stone taught him justice.

7. Because he was conspicuous for these actions and beloved by all and his name circulated in everyone's mouth, he was compelled to accept the office of bishop, receiving the charge of his native city. Although he exchanged that life on the hills and chose against his will to dwell in a city, he did not alter either his food or his clothing, but although there was a shift of place his way of life underwent no change.[5] His labors took on increase and became far more numerous than they had been before: to fasting, sleeping on the ground and wearing sackcloth was now added the whole range of care for the needy—I mean looking after widows and tending orphans, reproving the perpetrators of injustice and justly assisting their victims. What need is there, for those who know it, to list all that besets those who have received this charge? James entered on these labors with exceptional eagerness, because he was exceptional in his love and reverence for the Lord of the sheep.

8. The more he acquired the wealth of virtue, the more he enjoyed the grace of the all-holy Spirit. Once, when he was on his way to some village or town—I am unable to indicate the place exactly—some poor people came up to him, displaying one of their comrades as dead and begging to be given what was needed for his burial. He yielded to their request and made supplication to God as for a dead man, asking God to forgive the sins of his life and count him worthy of the choir of the righteous. While he was saying this, the soul of the man, who had up to this point been feigning death, actually departed, and grave-clothes were supplied for the body. When the inspired man had gone on a short way, the concocters of this play-acting told the man laid out to get up. When they saw that he did not hear, that

[c]Cf. Mt 21:19.

the charade had become a reality and the assumed expression had changed into a natural one, they overtook the great James; imploring loudly, prostrating themselves at his feet and saying that poverty was responsible for their audacious acting, they begged him to absolve their sin and restore the life taken away to the man laid out. Imitating the Master's love for men, he accepted their petition, and displayed his working of miracles by using prayer to restore to the man laid out the life that prayer had taken away.

9. This seems to me to resemble the miracle worked by the great Peter, who consigned to death Ananias and Sapphira who had concealed and deceived,[d] for James likewise deprived of life one who had concealed the truth and practised deceit. But while the former recognized the concealment — for the grace of the Spirit revealed it — and so imposed the penalty, the latter, in his ignorance of what lay behind the acting, applied prayer as the remedy and thereby cut short the dissembler's course of life. Also, while the divine Apostle did not release the dead from their misfortune — for terror was needed in the first stage of proclaiming salvation —, James, who was full of the grace of an Apostle, both applied chastisement as the occasion demanded and then swiftly revoked it, since he knew this was what would benefit the wrongdoers. But now we must go on to other matters, and these too we must relate in summary.

10. When Arius, who was the father and originator of blasphemy against the Only-begotten and the All-holy Spirit and had stirred his tongue against its Creator, filled Egypt with tumult and confusion, and the great emperor Constantine, the Zerubbabel of our flock — like him he led back out of exile the faithful in captivity and raised aloft the shrines of God that had been hurled to the ground — when, to resume, he summoned at this time all the leaders of the churches to Nicaea, the great James arrived with the rest, to fight for the true doctrines like some hero and champion of the whole host, since Nisibis was then under the sovereignty of Rome. At the great council many spoke extremely well, but many spoke otherwise, for there were some few who were of the opposing persuasion. They did not have the courage to lay bare their own impiety, but covered it over with

[d]Cf. Ac 5:1-10.

some snares that were not recognized by all but were quite obvious to those accurately initiated into the truth. The profession of faith that is now proclaimed as authoritative throughout the world was read aloud; one and all subscribed, and professed this faith and persuasion with hand and pen. The majority were glad to do this, but seven advocates of Arius's blasphemy, while assenting by word and signature, kept to the opinion contrary to their word. This accorded with the prophecy that says, 'This people honors me with their lips but in their heart they are far from me',[e] and also with the voice of Jeremiah exclaiming explicitly, 'You are near to their mouth and far from their reins';[f] in agreement with this and on the same subject the blessed David said, 'They bless with their mouth but in their heart they curse',[g] and again, 'Their words were smoother than butter and they are javelins'.[h] These men urged the great Alexander, bishop of Alexandria, to have pity on Arius, who had been excommunicated by all that host. When he, recognizing their falseness and suspecting the wickedness of Arius, would therefore not accept this request, some others from among the inveterate simpletons enumerated many pretexts for humanity, saying that this delights also the God of the universe. While the great Alexander called this unjustified humanity towards one man a form of inhumanity harmful to the majority and said it would be a cause of injury to all the flocks, the divine James urged them all to mortify themselves with fasting and simultaneously for seven days to beseech God to grant what would benefit the churches. Since they all welcomed the proposal of the inspired man, whom they knew to shine with apostolic charisms, fasting was combined with prayer, while the Helmsman of the churches decreed what would benefit them. When the appointed day arrived on which the majority anticipated the reconciliation of the miscreant, and the time had come for the divine liturgy and everyone expected to see the enemy of God receive pardon, at this very moment there occurred a truly divine and extraordinary miracle. While in a disgusting and noisome place that wretch was evacuating the refuse from his gluttony, he evacuated its receptacle as well; so with his inwards dissolved and ejected along with his excrement, the miserable creature instantly breathed his

[e]Is 29:13.   [f]Jer 12:2.   [g]Ps 62:4.   [h]Ps 55:21.

last and underwent this most shameful death, called to answer for his noisome blasphemy in a noisome place and slain by the tongue of the great James. Holy Scripture admires the priest Phinehas, and rightly, for slaying Zimri who had become a cause of destruction to the people. This is why the blessed David said in a psalm, 'Phinehas stood up and interposed and the plague was stayed, and it has been reckoned to him as righteousness from generation to generation for ever.'[i] Nevertheless, while Phinehas used a weapon of war to perform that just and celebrated slaying, the tongue sufficed for James in place of sword and spear when he destroyed the impious man to prevent him beholding the glory of God. This alone was adequate to confute the folly of the heirs of Arius's impiety; for this great man, as he was the herald and advocate of the doctrines we maintain, so utterly abhorred their impiety that he pierced its originator right through, using his tongue for a weapon. When this sacred council dissolved and each man returned home, James too went back, rejoicing like a victorious champion in the trophies of piety.[6]

11. After time had passed, that great and marvellous emperor departed life with the crowns of piety, and his sons inherited the sovereignty. Then the king of the Persians—Sapor was his name—, despising the sons as not equal in power to the father, marched against Nisibis with a huge troup of horse and a huge army on foot; he also brought the greatest possible number of elephants.[7] Dividing up his army as for a siege, he invested the city all the way round, set up engines, built bastions and dug in palisades, fencing in the gaps between them by branches placed cross-wise. He ordered the soldiers to heap up mounds and raise towers against towers; on these he then mounted his archers, ordering them to discharge their arrows against those stationed on the wall, while he ordered others to undermine the wall from beneath. When all this proved ineffectual, frustrated by the prayer of the inspired man, he finally set a great number of hands to stop the course of the river that flows past; and stopping most of the river by damming so as to mass it together, he released it all at once against the wall, using this as some mighty engine. The wall could not take the shock of the water: shaken by the impact, the

[i] Ps 106:30–31.

James [of Nisibis]

whole of it along this stretch fell down. They let out a great cry, as if the town would now be easy to capture, for they knew nothing of the great bulwark of the inhabitants. Seeing the city made inaccessible by the water, however, they postponed the assault. So now that their labor had abated, they withdrew to a distance to rest themselves and tend their horses. The inhabitants of the city had recourse to still more urgent prayer, with the great James as their intercessor. All those of age hastily rebuilt the wall, paying no attention to beauty or due arrangement but putting everything together haphazardly, stones, bricks, and whatever anyone could carry. In one night the works went forward and reached a height sufficient to prevent the charge of horses and the access of men without ladders. Then they all begged the man of God to appear on the wall and rain down curses on the enemy; he agreed and went up, and seeing the innumerable host besought God to send on them a cloud of gnats and mosquitoes. He spoke and God sent, persuaded as by Moses.[j] The men were wounded by the divine bolts; and the horses and elephants, bursting their bonds, ran hither and thither in confusion, unable to bear these stings.

12. When the impious king saw that all his machinations had failed to bear fruit, that the assault by means of the river had been fruitless (since the wall that had fallen down had been built up again) and that his whole army was in distress from its labors, suffering from the open air and harassed by the plague sent by God, — and when too he saw the man of God walking on the wall and supposed it to be the emperor himself supervising the work, as he was seen dressed in purple robe and diadem, — he was indignant against those who had deceived him and persuaded him to march, saying the emperor was not present. After passing sentence of death against them, he disbanded his army and returned to his own palace as quickly as he could.

13. Such are the miracles that God wrought in the case of this Hezekiah[k] also, not inferior to those earlier ones but greater, it seems to me, for what miracles could surpass a city's not being taken despite its wall falling down? I myself, in addition to this, am also filled with admiration at the way James, when applying a curse, did not ask for the introduction of thunderbolts and lightning, as the great Elijah did

---

[j] Cf. Ex 8:16.   [k] Cf. 2 Kgs 19.

when each of the commanders of fifties came to him with his fifty.¹ He heeded the Lord, saying explicitly to James and John when they tried to work this same miracle, 'You do not know of what spirit you are'.ᵐ Therefore he did not ask for the earth to gape under them nor did he call for the army to be consumed with fire, but rather that it be wounded by those tiny creatures and, recognizing the power of God, at some later date learn piety.

14. So great was the familiar access to God that this man of God possessed, so great too was the grace he enjoyed from above. Persevering in these and growing each day in the things of God, he laid down this life with the greatest renown and set out on his migration from here. After time had passed and this town was handed over by the then-emperor to the kingdom of Persia,ᵍ all the inhabitants of the city departed, but took with them the body of their champion, aggrieved and bewailing their exile, but chanting the power of their victorious hero; for if he had survived they would not have come under barbarians. Having proceeded through these particulars concerning the man of God, I shall move on to another narration, begging to receive a share of his blessing.

---

¹Cf. 2 Kgs 1:10–12.   ᵐLk 9:55 (var.).

NOTES

1. James was first a hermit in the mountains near Nisibis (in Mesopotamia) and later bishop of the city. We know from other sources that he died in 337/8. Ephraem's *Carmen Nisibenum* XIV (written in c.359) mentions James's fasting and simple preaching, and describes him as the bishop who 'gave birth' to the Church of Nisibis. He was the first metropolitan bishop of the city, and legends soon developed round him. Theodoret's account records the state of the James legend one hundred years later and is not reliable history. In particular, the miracles related attach doubtfully to James: that of §4 appears also in the *Life* of Ephraem, that of §8 is elsewhere attributed to Gregory Thaumaturgus and to Epiphanius, those of §10–13 are chronologically impossible (see below). Theodoret's account, and the more authentic evidence, is discussed by P. Peeters in *Analecta Bollandiana* 38 (1920) 285–373. Peeters comments on this first chapter: 'It is with this incoherent web of commonplaces, misplaced anecdotes and legendary fictions that opens a book filled with personal reminiscences and actual observation, one of the most attractive in all ancient Greek hagiography' (p. 312).

2. Cp. the account of the ascetics of Nisibis in Sozomen, *Eccl. Hist.* VI.33: 'They are called "Grazers", since they neither have houses nor eat bread or cooked food nor drink wine, but living on the mountains they praise God in prayers and hymns, in accordance with the law of the Church; when it is time for nourishment, they wander over the mountain, like animals driven to pasture, each with a sickle, and feed on plants.' On these ascetics see Vööbus, *History of Asceticism in the Syrian Orient*, I: 150ff. and II: 22ff.

3. The theme of the purified soul as the mirror of God was conventional by Theodoret's time and so cannot be pressed as indicative of his understanding of the spiritual ascent. More noteworthy is the idea that it is the self-purification enabled by withdrawal into solitude that wins for the holy man the gifts required for helping his fellow-men through prayer and the working of miracles: eremiticism and the life of charity are not opposed. 'Familiar access' translates *parrhésia*, which is sometimes used in the *Rel Hist.* of boldness of speech in addressing one's fellow-men (e.g. XIII.5,8) but more frequently of a degree of favor with God that enables a holy man to make effective intercession and work miracles, both in this life and the next (so here and at I.14, III.9, VII.3, VIII.15, IX.7, X.7, XVIII.4).

4. On Syrian holy men as 'notable cursers', see P. Brown, 'The Rise and Function of the Holy Man,' 122. The James legend clearly relished miracles of punishment: it is notable how Theodoret is determined to interpret them as evidence of God's mercy (§5, 6, 9, 13).

5. For monks becoming bishops without renouncing asceticism see also II.9, V.8, X.9, XVII.5; cp. Sulpicius Severus, *Life of Martin* X.1–2. Stories abound of ascetics, or would-be ascetics, yielding to ordination only under compulsion, partly through humility and partly because pastoral responsibilities excluded a purely contemplative life: examples include St Augustine, Daniel the Stylite, and Macedonius of Antioch (*Rel. Hist.* XIII.4). Pastoral responsibilities could, however, be seen as a simple extension of the holy man's care for his clients and visitors, and the ordained holy man could in his new sphere make effective use of the charismatic gifts he had gained through his asceticism. On Martin of Tours, see P. Rousseau, *Ascetics, Authority and the Church*, 152–165.

6. This account of James' involvement in the death of Arius is fictitious: James's presence at the Council of Nicaea is confirmed by other evidence, but Arius actually

died at Constantinople in 336, eleven years later. The correct account is given in Theodoret, *Eccl. Hist.* I.14(13). Canivet and most editors of the *Rel. Hist.* deduce that the treatment of Arius's death in this section must be a later interpolation, but the stylistic evidence favors its authenticity, and the whole section becomes pointless if no special achievement is attributed to James at Nicaea. Theodoret was certainly indifferent to chronological accuracy: e.g., the siege of Nisibis that involved James is dated in the *Rel. Hist.* to 337/8 but in the *Eccl. Hist.* (II.30) to c.360.

7. Sapor II of Persia took advantage of Constantine's death in 337 to make an incursion into Roman Mesopotamia, and laid siege to Nisibis for two months. Contrary to the legend related here, and repeated in Theodoret, *Eccl. Hist.* II.30 (26), James died during the siege, and Ephraem attributes protection of the city to James dead rather than James alive (*Carmina Nisibena* XIII.19); the details of the siege given here are an embroidered version of the later siege in 350.

8. In 363 the emperor Jovian surrendered Nisibis to the Persians.

II
JULIAN
(Saba)

JULIAN,[1] whom the people of the country in honour surnamed 'Saba' (the word means 'Old Man' in Greek), set up his ascetic cell in the land once called Parthia but now Osrhoene. It extends westwards to the very bank of the river (its name is the Euphrates), while towards the rising sun its frontier is that of the Roman empire. It is succeeded by Assyria, the western border of the kingdom of Persia, which later people have called Adiabene. In this province are many great and populous cities, and a great extent both of inhabited countryside and of uninhabited desert.

2. Repairing to the extremity of this desert, this man of God found a cave not made by hands, nor well and beautifully dug out, but able to provide some scanty shelter for those wanting refuge. He was glad to settle in the place, thinking it of more value than palaces shining with gold and silver. In it he resided, taking food once a week. As food he had bread made of barley and indeed of bran, as relish he had salt, as a most pleasant drink fresh water from springs,[2] and this not proportioned to satiety, but limited to what was needed for the food swallowed down beforehand. As his luxury, indulgence,

and elaborate banquet he had the hymnody of David and perpetual intercourse with God. As his enjoyment of this was insatiable, he refused to experience repletion; instead he was always taking his fill and always crying out, 'How sweet to my throat are thy oracles, beyond honey and honeycomb to my mouth'.[a] Again he had heard the blessed David saying, 'The judgments of the Lord are true and justified altogether, more to be desired than gold and much stone of price, and sweeter than honey and honeycomb'.[b] He had heard him saying again, 'Take delight in the Lord and may he grant you the petitions of your heart',[c] and further, 'May the heart of those that seek the Lord rejoice',[d] and 'Gladden my heart to fear thy name',[e] and 'Taste and see that the Lord is good,'[f] and 'My soul has thirsted for God, the strong, the living',[g] and 'My soul has cleaved after thee'.[h] He transferred into himself the love of the one who had uttered these sayings. For this was why the great David too sang them, to teach that he could make many his partners as fellow-lovers of God; and he was not cheated of his hope but wounded with divine love both this inspired man and innumerable others. For Julian received such a firebrand of longing that he was intoxicated with desire, and while seeing nothing of earthly things dreamt only of the Beloved at night and thought only of him by day.

3. Many who learnt of this, his consummate philosophy, some living in the neighborhood, others far away (for his fame sped everywhere on wings), hastened along to beg to be received into his wrestling-school and to live the rest of their lives under him as under some gymnastic master and trainer; for not only do birds catch other birds through calling to themselves by song those of the same species and entangling them in snares laid around, but men also entrap their fellow-men, sometimes for their harm, sometimes for their salvation. And so ten men were soon gathered together, then twice and three times that number, and later they made up the number of a hundred.

4. Even when they became so many, that cave received them, for they learnt from the Old Man to belittle care for the body; they too, like their trainer, ate barley-bread seasoned with salt. Later, gathering

[a] Ps 119:103. [b] Ps 19:9–10. [c] Ps 37:4. [d] Ps 105:3. [e] Ps 86:11. [f] Ps 34:8.
[g] Ps 42:2. [h] Ps 63:8.

wild vegetables, filling pots with them and mixing in a sufficient quantity of salty water provided those in need of special care with conserves. However, the damp of the place was harmful to these vegetables, for it naturally caused them to mould and decay. So when this misfortune occurred in the case of the conserves—for the cave admitted damp from all sides—, his disciples begged the Old Man to let them build a little hut adequate for the containers of the conserves. At first he would not grant their request, but some time later he complied, for he had been taught by the great Paul not to seek his own will but to accommodate himself to the lowly.[i] He gave them the dimensions for the cell, small and limited, and went off far away from the cave to make his customary prayers to God, for he used to take a walk in the desert often of fifty stades,[3] sometimes of twice this amount, and separating himself from all human company and turning into himself enjoy solitary intercourse with God and gaze as if in a mirror upon that divine and inexpressible beauty. Taking advantage of this free time, those counted worthy of his care built the hut according to dimensions that, while fitting the need, exceeded those laid down. Returning after ten days like some Moses from ineffable contemplation on the mountain, he saw that the building had become bigger than he wanted it. 'I fear, my friends,' he said, 'that by enlarging our abodes on earth we may diminish those in heaven; yet the former are temporary and of use to us briefly, while the latter are eternal and cannot come to an end.' But while he said this to instruct his choir in the more perfect way, he consented none the less, heeding the voice of the Apostle, 'I seek not my own advantage but that of the many, that they may be saved.'[j]

5. He instructed them to offer, when inside, common hymnody to God, and after dawn to go out in the desert in twos: one was to offer due worship to the Master kneeling, while the other sang fifteen Davidic psalms standing; they were then to change the task round, one standing up to sing while the other stooped to the ground to worship.[4] This they continued to do from early morning till late afternoon. Taking a short rest before sunset, they all gathered in the cave from all sides, some from here, some from there, and offered in unison the evening hymnody to the Master.[5]

[i] Cf. 1 Co 10:24, Rom 12:16.   [j] 1 Co 10:33.

6. The Old Man also used to take one of the more outstanding to share in his liturgy. He was often accompanied by a man who was by race a Persian and in physique tall and remarkable, and who possessed a soul more wonderful than his physique; James was his name.[6] After the death of the Old Man he was conspicuous in every virtue; he was distinguished and celebrated in not only the philosophical retreats of that region but also those of Syria, in which indeed he died, having lived, it is said, a hundred and four years. This man, sharing his walk to the desert, was following the Old Man at a distance, for the teacher would not let him come close, for fear that this would cause conversation between them and that this conversation would rob the mind of its reflection upon God. As he was following behind, he saw lying in the path a huge serpent. On seeing it, he did not dare advance; but after wishing several times to retire out of fear, he recovered again strength of mind. He then knelt down, picked up a pebble and hurled it. But he saw that the serpent remained in the same posture and could not move at all. Realizing that it was dead, he took the death of the beast to be the work of the Old Man. After finishing the walk and completing the liturgy of hymnody, when the time of rest had come, the Old Man sat down and told him to rest his body a little. At first he sat in silence, but when the Old Man began some conversation James begged him with a smile to reveal to him something of which he was ignorant. When the Old Man bade him speak, he said: 'I saw a huge serpent stretched out on the path. At first I was afraid of it, supposing it to be alive. But when I saw it was dead, I made my way rejoicing. Tell me, father (he concluded): who killed it? For you were leading the way and no one else went along.' The Old Man replied, 'Do not be inquisitive about things like this that can bring no profit to those who meddle with them.' But the wonderful James insisted none the less, eager to learn the truth. The Old Man tried for a good time to hide it, but could not bear to torment his disciple for still longer: 'I will tell you what you are eager to learn,' he said, 'but I charge you to let no one else share your knowledge of what I am about to say while I am alive, for it is right to hide things like this, that often arouse arrogance and vanity. But when I depart from here and get free of such passions, I do not prohibit you from speaking and relating the power of divine grace. So know well (continued the great

Julian) that as I was walking along the path that beast came against me and opened its mouth, eager to devour me. But I, invoking the name of the Lord and making the sign of the cross with my finger, cast off all fear, and immediately saw the beast fall to the ground; and hymning our common Saviour I continued my journey.'⁷ Concluding his narrative thus, he got up and took the path to the cave.

7. On another occasion, an adolescent born of a noble family and delicately nurtured begged the Old Man with more zeal than strength to share his journey to the desert, not the normal journey that everyone made each day but a very long absence that occupied often seven days and often even ten. This celebrated youth was Asterius. The inspired Old Man forbade the young man, mentioning the lack of water in the desert, but the young man persisted in begging to enjoy this favor. Overcome by his entreaty the Old Man yielded. The other followed readily at first, but when the first, second and third days passed, he was scorched by the sun's rays—for it was summer, and at the height of summer their heat, of course, is quite intense—and continuously consumed by thirst. At first he was ashamed to tell of his suffering, remembering what the teacher had said beforehand; but when overcome and oppressed by a swoon, he begged the Old Man to have pity on him. The Old Man reminded him of his remarks beforehand and told him to go back. But when the young man said he did not know the path leading to the cave and even if he did would not be able to walk since his strength was exhausted by thirst, the holy man took pity on the youth's suffering and accorded pardon to his bodily weakness. Kneeling down he besought the Master, wet the ground with fervent tears, and sought a way to save the young man. He who does the will of those who fear him and listens to their entreaty made the streams of tears, as they touched the dust, into a spring of waters; and when the young man was thereby replenished with fresh water, he immediately ordered him to depart.

8. The spring has lasted even till now, witnessing to the prayer (like that of Moses) of the inspired Old Man: just as Moses once of old by striking with his rod that infertile rock caused a flood of fertile river-water, in order to satisfy the thirst of those many thousands,[k] so

---

[k] Cf. Ex 17:6.

this man of God by watering with his tears that most arid sand drew forth streams of spring-water, to cure the thirst not of many myriads but of a single adolescent.

9. Illuminated in his soul by divine grace, he foresaw quite clearly the perfection that the young man would possess. And he, a long time later, called by divine grace to be the trainer of many others in the same virtue, fixed his ascetic wrestling-school in the district round Gindarus, a very large village placed in subjection to Antioch.[8] Apart from drawing to himself many other athletes of philosophy, he also drew the great Acacius[9] – I mean the famous, the celebrated one, pre-eminent in the monastic life, who emitted bright beams of virtue and was counted worthy of the episcopal office and assigned to be the shepherd of Beroea. Entrusted for fifty-eight years with tending this flock, he did not abandon the form of ascetic life, but mixed ascetic and civic virtue. Taking the strictness of the one and the accommodation of the other, he conjoined into one two things that stand apart.

10. Of this virtue the hunter and trainer was that Asterius, who remained so fervent a lover of the great Old Man that he made the journey to him often twice a year, often even three times. On his way there he was wont to bring dried figs to the brethren, placing the load on three or four beasts of burden. Gathering two measures, as sufficient for the Old Man for the whole year, he placed this load on his own shoulders, both calling and making himself his teacher's beast of burden, and carrying this load he walked along, completing not ten or twenty stades but a trek of seven days. On one occasion, the Old Man, seeing him carry the load of figs on his shoulders, said in displeasure that he would not make these his food, since it was not right that the other should undergo such toil and he luxuriate in his exertion. When Asterius swore that he would not relieve his shoulders of the load unless the Old Man agreed to eat the food he had brought, the aged man said, 'I shall do what you bid; only put down the sack at once'.

11. In this he was imitating the first of the Apostles, who, when the Lord wished to wash his feet, at first refused, insisting firmly that this should never happen. But when he heard that he would be cut off from fellowship with the Master if he did not consent to this, he begged

for his hands as well as his feet to be washed and also his head.¹ So too the great John, when ordered to baptize the Saviour, at first acknowledged his own servitude and indicated the Master; but later he performed what was ordered, not acting in presumption but obeying the Master.ᵐ So too this divine man was distressed that while another labored he himself should enjoy the fruit, but when he saw the fervent eagerness of his servant, he chose the man's service in preference to his own choice.

12. One of those who like carping and have learnt only to mock what is fine would say, possibly, that this story is not worthy of mention. But I have added it to the man's miraculous works not only out of a wish to display the reverence paid him by great men, but also because I think it advantageous to show the sweetness and modesty of his character. Although his virtue was so great in both kind and degree, he did not suppose himself worthy of any honor but refused it as in no way befitting him, and yet again allowed it, as beneficial to those who rendered it.

13. To escape being honored—for he became conspicuous to all and drew to himself through fame the lovers of the good—he finally set out for Mount Sinai with a few of those closer to him, entering no city or village but making passable the impassable desert. They carried on their shoulders the necessary food—I mean bread and salt—and also a cup made from wood and a sponge tied to a piece of string, in order (if ever they found the water too deep) to draw it up with the sponge, squeeze it into the cup, and so drink it. Accordingly, after completing a journey of many days, they reached the mountain they longed for, and having worshiped their own Master passed much time there, thinking the deserted character of the place and tranquillity of soul supreme delight. On this rock, under which Moses the leader of the prophets hid when he was counted worthy to see God, in so far as it is possible to see him, Julian built a church and consecrated an altar of God, which has remained to this day, and so returned to his own wrestling-school.¹⁰

14. On learning of the threats of the emperor who shared his name but not his piety (for he threatened the pious with total destruction as

¹Cf. Jn 13:8–9.   ᵐCf. Mt 3:13–16.

he set out on his expedition against the Persians, and those who shared his convictions gaped after his deprecable return), he thereupon addressed urgent prayer to God and extended it till the tenth day, when he heard a voice saying that the foul and noisome swine had been destroyed.[11] Although his prayer had not yet come to its end, he immediately ended it, and changed petition into hymnody, sending up a hymn of thanksgiving to the One who is saviour of his own and both a patient and powerful enemy of aliens; for he showed long-suffering to the impious man for as long as possible, but when his long-suffering merely trained the wretch for greater madness, he inflicted punishment opportunely. When James had finished his prayer and turned to his brethren, he was manifestly buoyant in his thoughts, for he showed a face beaming with delight. Those who were with him marveled at the novelty of the sight—for though he always appeared stern, on this occasion he was seen to smile—and enquired after the cause. 'The present occasion, my friends,' he replied, 'is one for gladness and delight; for the impious man has ceased (to use the expression of Isaiah),[n] and paid a penalty worthy of his presumption. Having rebelled against the God who is Creator and Saviour, he has justly been slain at the hand of a subject. This is why I am rejoicing, as I see the churches he made war upon exulting, and observe that the miscreant has received no assistance from the demons he honored.' Such was the foreknowledge he enjoyed at the slaying of this impious man.

15. When Valens, who received the reins of the Roman Empire after him,[12] discarded the truth of the evangelical doctrines and embraced the deceitful imposture of Arius, then still greater was the storm stirred up against the Church, with the helmsmen everywhere expelled and certain wreckers and enemies brought in instead. In order not to recount the whole of that tragedy at present, I shall now leave aside the rest and recall one single event that will display distinctly the grace of the divine Spirit that blossomed forth in this Old Man. From Antioch had been expelled the great Meletius, who had been entrusted with shepherding this city by the God of the universe;[13] also expelled from the churches of God were all those enrolled in the sacred clergy who maintained the one divine substance of the Trinity,

[n] Is 26:10 (LXX).

together with the laity of the same conviction. Now they would proceed to the foot of the mountain and hold the sacred assemblies there; now they would make the bank of the river the place of prayer, and at other times the military drill-ground which lies in front of the North Gate, for the enemy did not allow the pious to settle in one place.

16. The nurslings of falsehood sowed and circulated a rumor in this city to the effect that the great Julian—I mean this Old Man—embraced the fellowship of the doctrines they professed. The pious were particularly tormented by the fear this rumor might trick the more simple and naive and entrap them in the nets of the heretics. But those inspired and blessed men Flavian and Diodore, who had merited the priesthood and were in charge of the pious laity, and also Aphrahat, whose life I shall, with God's help, lay before you on its own, persuaded the great Acacius, whom I have already mentioned, to take as companion for the journey the famous Asterius, who had been both Acacius's own teacher and the disciple of this holy old man, and to hasten to that universal ornament of piety and prop of the evangelical teaching, and persuade him to leave his life in the desert and come to the help of the countless number being ruined by deception, and to quench the flame of Arius by the dew of his coming.[14] The divine Acacius made haste. Taking the great Asterius as he had been bidden, he came to the great star of the Church, and made his greeting. 'Tell me, father,' he said: 'why is it with pleasure that you put up with all this toil?' He replied: 'Serving God is for me of more value than body and soul and existence and the whole of life, and I try to offer him, as far as I am able, a ministry pure of stain, and to please him in every way.' 'I can show you,' said Acacius, 'a way in which you will serve him more than now, and I shall tell it not by the use of mere reason but having learnt it from his own teaching. He once asked Peter if he loved him more than the others, and on learning what he knew even before Peter's utterance, "You know, Lord, that I love you", he showed him what to do in order to serve him more: "If you love me," he said, "shepherd my sheep and feed my lambs."º This, father, is what you too should do.[15] The flocks are in danger of being destroyed by wolves, but the one you love loves them exceedingly, and it is characteristic of

ºCf. Jn 21:15–17.

the affectionate to perform those actions that delight those for whom they have affection. Otherwise, there is no small danger that those many and great exertions would be wasted, if you bore to allow by your silence the truth to be hard pressed in war, those devoted to it to be ensnared, and your own name to be the bait for those caught, for the champions of Arius's abomination brag that you share in their impiety.'

17. As soon as the Old Man heard this, he bade goodbye to his solitude for a time and, unalarmed at the unpleasantness of civil tumult, hastened to Antioch. Having completed two or three days' journey through the desert, he reached a certain place as evening overtook him. A woman of the wealthy class, hearing of the arrival of this sacred choir, ran to reap their blessing, and prostrating at their feet begged them to stay at her house; the Old Man consented, although he had been segregated from the sight of women for more than forty years. While this wonderful woman was busy serving these sacred men, a seven year-old child, who alone had as mother the woman emulating the hospitality of Sarah,P in the dark of the evening fell into the well. Naturally enough, this caused a commotion. The mother, on hearing it, told everyone to keep quiet and, putting a cover on the well, kept at her serving. When the table had been laid out for the men of God, the godly Old Man ordered the child of the woman to be summoned to receive his blessing. When the wonderful woman declared he was oppressed by sickness, he persisted in charging him to be brought. When the woman revealed her misfortune, the Old Man left the table, ran to the well and ordered the cover to be removed and light to be brought. He saw the child sitting on the surface of the water, striking the water playfully with his hand and thinking his supposed death a mere children's game. Tying someone with cords and letting him down, they drew up the child, who ran at once to the feet of the Old Man, saying he had seen him carrying him on the water and stopping him drowning. Such was the reward for hospitality that the wonderful woman received from the blessed Old Man.

18. To omit the other occurrences during the journey, they arrived at Antioch, and everyone flocked together from every side, longing to see the man of God and eager, each one of them, to receive some

---

PCf. Gen 18:6.

cure for his disease. He settled in the caves at the foot of the mountain, where the divine apostle, the blessed Paul, is said to have settled and been concealed.[16] But immediately, so that everyone should learn that he was a human being, he had a violent attack of fever. The great Acacius, seeing the assembled crowd, was vexed at this occurrence of sickness, for he thought that those assembled would be dumbfounded if men expecting to find healing at his hands should learn of the disease. 'Do not despair,' replied the Old Man. 'If health is a thing needed, God will grant it instantly.' Immediately after these words he had recourse to prayer: touching the ground with his knees and forehead as usual, he begged to recover health, if this would result in some advantage for those assembled. He had not yet finished his prayer when profuse sweat suddenly broke out and quenched the fire of the fever.

19. After freeing many from all kinds of disease, he proceeded from there to the assembly of the pious. As he passed through the gates of the palace, a beggar who used his buttocks in place of his feet and crawled on the ground, on stretching out his hand and touching the goat's hair cloak, drove out his affliction by faith, and leaping up displayed how he had run before his sickness, doing the same as the lame man whom Peter and John raised up.[q] At this occurrence, all the people of the town assembled, and the military drill-ground became filled with those flocking together; shamefaced were the calumniators and concocters of the lie, totally cheered and delighted the nurslings of piety.

20. From there those in need of healing drew the star of piety into their houses. And a certain man who had been appointed to very great authority and entrusted to control the rudder of the east[17] sent and begged him to come and free him from the sickness that oppressed him. Without delay he attended on him, and praying to the common Master destroyed his affliction with a word, and bade him avow thanks to God.

21. After these and similar achievements he decided to return finally to his ascetic cell. Making his journey through Cyrrhus—this city is two stages from Antioch—, he lodged at the shrine of the victorious martyr Dionysius. The leaders of piety there came together and begged

[q]Cf. Ac 3:1–8.

him to help them as they expected sure destruction; for Asterius, they said, who had been reared in sophistic falsity and then made his way into the church of the heretics, where he received the episcopal ministry,[18] was craftily advocating falsehood and using artifice against the truth. 'And we fear,' they said, 'that covering over his falsehood with a smooth tongue as if with a decoy and spreading out the web of his syllogisms like nets, he may catch many of the inveterate simpletons, for it was for this that he was called in by our opponents.' 'Have confidence,' replied the Old Man, 'and together with us make supplication to God, joining fasting and mortification to prayer.' They entreated God accordingly; and one day before the festival on which the advocate of falsehood and enemy of the truth was going to make an address, he received a blow inflicted by God, and after only one day's illness was deleted from the list of the living, hearing in all likelihood this utterance: 'Fool! this night your soul is required of you; the evil nets and snares you prepared will be for you and not another.'[r]

22. He suffered the same as Balaam, who likewise was called in against God's people; he paid the penalty for giving Balak unholy advice against them by being slain by the hand of an Israelite;[s] and so this man, when he contrived designs against the people of God, was deprived of his life by the people of God. And it was through the prayer of this man that Cyrrhus enjoyed this salvation. The story was transmitted to me by the holy bishop, the great Acacius, who knew accurately everything about him. So he left here and rejoined his disciples; and after living no little time with them,[19] he migrated with real eagerness to the life without old age or sorrow, having practised impassibility in a mortal nature and awaiting the immortality of the body. At this point I shall end the account of this narrative and proceed to another one, begging those saints introduced in the narrative to procure for me through their intercession favor from above.

[r]Cf. Lk 12:20.   [s]Cf. Num 31:8, 16.

NOTES

1. Julian Saba was a famous holy man in the desert of Osrhoene. A series of Syriac hymns on his life, written shortly after his death and included among the works of Ephraem (CSCO 322 & 323), broadly confirms Theodoret's account. He died in 367, having been an ascetic for fifty years. Since his community preceded that of Gindarus (see n.7, below), it must have been founded as early as c.320.
2. A diet of bread, salt, and water appears also at XI.1 and XX.3; it was a traditional ascetic diet in Syria (cp. *Acts of Judas Thomas* 20) and elsewhere (cp. Athanasius, *Life of Antony* 7). For the great value attached to fasting in Syriac Christianity, see Ephrem, *Hymns on Fasting* (CSCO 246-7).
3. Fifty stades is six miles.
4. On the monastic realization of 'prayer without ceasing' (1 Th 5:17), which could be taken more or less literally, see I. Hausherr in *RAM* 32 (1956) 33-58 and 284-297; on p. 35 he cites this passage of the *Rel. Hist.* as a case of 'simultaneous collaboration' as distinct from the 'successive collaboration' most familiar from the Acoemetes at Constantinople, who prayed all day and night in shifts.
5. Here, as regularly in the *Rel. Hist.*, 'hymnody' means 'psalmody'.
6. See IV.8: James, after Julian's death, moved to the monastery of Teleda near Antioch.
7. For a demon in the form of a dragon being routed by the sign of the cross, cp. III.7 and *Life of Antony* 23.
8. Gindarus was thirty miles east of Antioch on the main route from Mesopotamia. Since it was at the monastery here that Acacius (b. 321) was 'trained in the monastic life from boyhood' (Sozomen, VII.28), it must have been founded in c.330.
9. Acacius was born in 321 (see a letter by John of Antioch in C. Lupus, *Opera* VII: 55), entered the monastery at Gindarus in boyhood, gained a reputation at Antioch for keen orthodoxy (see §15 below) and in 378/9, was made bishop of Beroea (Aleppo), where he lived on, amazingly, till 436/7. He was known by Theodoret personally, and was the chief source for his accounts of Julian (see § 22 below) and of Eusebius of Teleda (IV.7). He features repeatedly in Theodoret, *Eccl. Hist.* (IV.24; V.4,8,23,27), and may well have been a key influence in Theodoret's development as ascetical bishop, polemicist and historian.
10. This pilgrimage to Mt Sinai, and the building of a chapel, are also mentioned in the Syriac *Hymns on Julian* XIV.10, XIX.13. Cp. the account at VI.7-12 of Symeon the Elder's pilgrimage to Sinai, with our note *ad loc.*
11. The emperor Julian died during his Persian expedition in June 363. This story of Julian's telepathy is repeated in Theodoret, *Eccl. Hist.* III.24(19) still more graphically. Prescience on the same occasion is attributed to Didymus the Blind in Palladius, *Lausiac History* 4.
12. The brief reign of Jovian (363-4) is omitted.
13. Meletius, bishop of Antioch 360-381, spent most of his episcopate in exile. In question here is his second exile, 365-367.
14. Of the activities of Flavian and Diodore, Theodoret gives a fuller account in *Eccl. Hist.* IV.25(22); for Aphrahat, see ch. VIII below. Julian's visit to Antioch dates to 365; Theodoret, *Eccl. Hist.* IV.27(24) compares it to Antony's visit to Alexandria in 354/5, which had the same motive, viz. to scotch Arian claims that he was on their side (*Life* 69).
15. The same argument for hermits accepting pastoral responsibilities occurs at IV.4.

16. Other sources are ignorant of this cave on Mt Silpius, which is not to be confused with the more famous 'Grotto of St Peter'.
17. The *Comes Orientis*, with authority over both Syria and Egypt. The identity of the *Comes* in 365 is uncertain.
18. This Asterius invites confusion with the better-known Asterius the Sophist who was also an Arian propagandist (see Quasten, *Patrology*, III: 194-7), but the latter had died more than twenty years previously.
19. In fact, as we learn from the sixty century *Chronicle of Edessa*, Julian died in 367, soon after his return to Osrhoene.

III
Marcianus

HOW COULD WE adequately express admiration of the famous Marcianus?[1] Clearly by classing him with Elijah and John and those like them, who 'went about in skins of sheep and goats, destitute, afflicted, ill-treated, of whom the world was not worthy, wandering in deserts and mountains and caves and the holes of the earth.'[a] This man had as his fatherland formerly Cyrrhus, which I mentioned above, and thereafter the desert; and leaving both the one and the other he now has heaven. The one gave birth to him, the other nurtured him and made him victorious, the third received him as one crowned.

2. Despising both the distinction of his family (for he was of noble descent) and an illustrious position at court[2] (for it was there he flowered, receiving great bodily size and beauty from the Creator of nature and having a soul adorned with sagacity), he transferred all this love to God and the things of God. Bidding farewell to all this, he repaired to the heart of the desert, and built a small cell that was not

[a] Heb 11:37-8.

even the size of his body. Surrounding it with another small wall, he was immured continuously and deprived of all human company, while conversing with the Master of the universe and hearkening to that sweet voice, for in reading the divine oracles he held he was enjoying the divine voice, and by praying and making supplication he conversed with the Master. In his constant enjoyment of such delight he refused to experience satiety; for he had heard the divine Spirit chanting through the great David that 'he who meditates on the law of the Lord day and night will be like the tree planted by the outlets of waters, which will give its fruit in its season, and its leaf will not fall.'[b] In his desire for these fruits he embraced this most pleasant labor; psalmody succeeded prayer, prayer succeeded psalmody, and both again were succeeded by reading the divine oracles.

3. His food was bread alone, and this taken according to measure: the measure was such as to satisfy the need not even of a child just separated from the breast, for they say that his pound of bread, divided into four, was distributed over four days, with one portion assigned to each day. He had resolved to eat each day in the evening, and never to experience satiety, but to be always hungry and always thirsty, supplying the body with the bare necessities of life; for he used to say that he who takes food only at several days' interval performs the Master's liturgy in a weak state on days of fast, while on a day when he eats food he naturally takes more and burdens the stomach, and this, weighed down, makes the soul more sluggish at keeping vigil. It was therefore better, he said, to take food each day and never expect satiety, since the true fast is perpetual deficiency. This man of God persevered in laying down this rule; and although he had a very big body, being indeed the biggest and most handsome of all the men of his time, it was with little food that he nourished it.

4. After some time had passed, he admitted two to live with him: Eusebius, who became the inheritor of this sacred cell; and Agapetus, who transplanted this angelic rule to the region of Apamea. There is a large and populous village whose name is Nicerte. In it Agapetus founded two retreats of philosophy, one called after his own name and the other after that of the wondrous Symeon, who was conspicuous in

[b] Ps 1:2–3.

this philosophy for a total of fifty years.[3] In them there are living even today more than four hundred men, athletes of virtue and lovers of piety, purchasing heaven with their labors; the legislators of this way of life were Agapetus and Symeon, who received their laws from the great Marcianus. From these were planted innumerable other ascetic dwellings regulated by these laws, which it is not easy to count; but the planter of them all was this inspired man, for he who provided the finest seed could fairly be called the cause of the good plants.

5. At first, as I said, he lived in this voluntary prison on his own. Then when he admitted these two, he did not have them live with him; for the hut was not adequate for himself alone, being extremely small and causing him, whether sitting or reclining, much discomfort: when standing he was unable to hold himself erect, since the roof made him bend his head and neck; nor when lying down could he stretch out his feet, since the cell did not have a length equal to his body. So he told them to build another one and bade them live there, singing hymns, praying, and reading the divine oracles on their own. When more people needed to share in this benefit, he ordered another dwelling to be built at a distance and bade those who wished live there. Their superior was Eusebius, who transmitted the teaching of the great Marcianus. The great Agapetus, when he had received the necessary training and exercise and learnt well this athletic skill, departed, as I said, and sowed the seeds he had received from that godly soul. He became so notable and celebrated that he was counted worthy of an episcopal see, appointed to the charge of a flock and entrusted with tending his own fatherland.[4]

6. The wonderful Eusebius, while presiding over the flock he had gathered together, took over looking after his teacher as well: he alone was counted worthy to pay him timely visits and enquire if he wanted anything. On one occasion, wishing to see what he did at night, he dared to go up to the window (which was small); and peering in, he saw a light, not of a lamp or made by hands but God-given and of the grace from above, flashing from the teacher's head and revealing the composition of letters in the divine oracles, for he happened to be holding a book and searching out the inviolate treasury of the divine will. Seeing this, the wonderful Eusebius was filled with dread and became full of awe; he was instructed about the grace poured

down upon the divine ministrant and learnt the goodwill of God towards his servants.

7. On another occasion, when the great Marcianus was praying in the forecourt, a serpent crawled up onto the wall facing east, and leant down from the wall gaping and looking grim at the same time, displaying his intention. Standing at a distance, Eusebius, frightened at this terrifying sight and presuming his master did not know of it, indicated it by crying out and begging him to flee. But he rebuked him and told him to cast off his cowardice, saying that this too is a destructive passion, and he made the sign of the cross with his finger and blew with his mouth, intimating the ancient enmity. The serpent, withered and, so to speak, burnt by the breath of his mouth as if by some fire, was dissolved into many fragments like straw that is set ablaze.[5]

8. Therefore examine with me if he did not imitate his Master as a well-disposed servant; for the Master, once when the sea was raging against his disciples' boat and he saw them panic-stricken, did not curb the surge of the sea before he had put an end to the disciples' lack of faith with a rebuke.[c] Taught by that, this wonderful man first dispelled his companion's cowardice and thereafter delivered the beast to punishment.

9. Such was the wisdom of the great Marcianus, his working of miracles and his familiar access to God. Nevertheless, despite receiving such grace and being capable of great miracles, he was keen to hide his power, suspecting the machinations of the thief of virtue, for he sows secretly the passion of arrogance and tries to steal the fruits gathered with toil. Eager to hide the grace given to him, he worked miracles reluctantly, as the splendor of his achievements flashed forth and revealed his hidden power. And indeed there occurred the following miracle. A man of noble family and often appointed to military commands, who originated from Beroea in Syria, had a daughter who for a long time had been delirious and raving, troubled by an evil demon. He repaired to the desert, since, being acquainted with the great Marcianus, he expected to meet him and make entreaty on the ground of their former acquaintance. Being disappointed of his hope

[c] Mt 8:24–6.

and failing to see the servant of God, he besought an old man, who at that time was entrusted with serving the man of God, to take a little flask full of oil and place it by the very door of his cell.[6] The old man, after refusing the commission several times and several times being pressed again, yielded to the request. The great Marcianus, hearing the noise, asked who it was and what he had come for. The old man hid the true reason and pretended he had come to find out if he had some order to give, and on saying this was sent away. The next morning the father of the girl asked for the flask to be returned to him; the old man went off in trepidation as quietly as he could and, stretching out his hand, tried to take the flask without being noticed. The other again asked what he had come for, and when the old man gave the same reason which he had offered in the evening, the man of God was annoyed at the old man's visit taking place contrary to custom and ordered him to tell the truth. The old man, in fear and trembling and unable to deceive the man full of divine grace, said who had come, told of the tragic illness and showed the flask. The other was indignant, as was natural for one not willing to display his power; nevertheless, after threatening that if he dared such a thing again he would be deprived of his company and stripped of his role of service — a great penalty for those who knew the benefit of it —, he sent him away with instructions to return the flask to the giver. As he gave this order, the demon at a distance of four days' journey cried out at the power of the one who was driving him out. Marcianus was effecting in Beroea the work of judges, using as it were executioners against the demon, driving out the miscreant and freeing the girl of his activity.[7] The father of the girl ascertained this exactly. As he was returning and was a few stades' distance from the town, he was met by a servant whom his mistress had sent into the country; on seeing his master he told him the good news of the miracle that had taken place, saying it had taken place four days before. So counting the days and determining the time exactly, he discovered it was that time when the old man brought out the flask.

10. The thought that occurs to me is, what could this great man not have done if he had wanted to work miracles? If he emitted such luster when eager to hide the grace he had received, what prodigies would he not have worked had he wished to? Likewise he did not

display his spiritual wisdom to all, although finally he gave those who wanted it permission to come to him after the festival of the Lord's passion and the Master's resurrection.

11. At this season, of course, all were eager to see him. On one occasion the leading bishops assembled and came to him – the great Flavian, entrusted with shepherding Antioch, the divine Acacius whom I mentioned above, Eusebius of Chalcis, and Isidore, then entrusted with governing Cyrrhus – all of them preeminent in virtue.[8] And with them was Theodotus who held the reins of Hierapolis, glorious for asceticism and gentleness; present too were some councilors and officials possessing the spark of the faith. When they all sat in silence and waited for his sacred utterance, he too sat in silence for a long time, stilling his tongue while exercising his hearing. Then one of those sitting, who was well-acquainted with him through spiritual direction and in addition was glorious in rank, said, 'All the divine fathers are athirst for your teaching and await from you most pleasant streams: so bestow a benefit on all those present and do not hold back the flow of your beneficence'. But he, with a great sigh, replied, 'Each day the God of the universe speaks through creation and discourses through the divine Scriptures, recommends what is necessary and proposes what is advantageous, alarms with threats and encourages with promises, and yet we reap no profit. How then could Marcianus benefit by speaking, when he rejects such benefit along with the rest and is unwilling to find profit therein?' This stimulated much discussion among the fathers, which I have thought superfluous to include in my narrative. Standing up to pray, they wanted to confer on him ordination to the priesthood, but they baulked at the attempt. Each one urged another to do it, but all likewise declined and made their return.

12. I wish to add to this another story to make known his divine understanding. A certain Avitus was the first to set up his ascetic cell in another desert, more northerly than this one and lying a little to the east, under the north wind that is near to the east wind. He was older than Marcianus in both age and labor, a philosopher nurtured in the austere life. Learning that the man's virtue was common talk everywhere and thinking such a sight more advantageous than protracted solitude, he hurried apace to see what he longed for. Learning of his arrival, the great Marcianus opened the door and received him

into his presence. He bade the wonderful Eusebius cook pulses and greens if he had any. When they had had their fill of mutual conversation and had learnt of eath other's virtue, they performed together the liturgy of the ninth hour; and Eusebius came bearing the table and bringing loaves. The great Marcianus said to the inspired Avitus, 'Come over here, my best of friends, and let us share this table.' But he said, 'I do not know that I have ever taken food before the evening, and I often continue without food for two or three days together'. The great Marcianus replied, 'Change your habit today, at least for my sake. Being in a weak bodily state I cannot wait till the evening'. When these words did not persuade the wondrous Avitus, he is related to have sighed and said, 'I am utterly discouraged and cut to the heart at this: after undergoing such labor in order to see a laborious man and philosopher, you have been disappointed of your hope, and have seen instead of a philosopher a tavern-keeper and profligate'. This distressed the most divine Avitus, who said that, rather than hear such words, he would be glad to take meat.[9] The great Marcianus continued, 'We too, my friend, lead the same life as you and embrace the same profession, honor labors before repose and prefer fasting to nourishment, and take it only after nightfall. But we know that charity is a thing more to be prized than fasting, since the one is a work laid down by divine law, while the other depends on our own authority. It is right to count the divine laws as far more to be prized than our own.' After conversing with each other in this way and partaking of slight nourishment, singing hymns to God and spending three days with each other, they parted, seeing each other again only in spirit.

13. Who then would not wonder at this man's wisdom, governed by which he knew the time for fasting and the time for brotherly love, and knew the distinction between the parts of virtue, and which ought to yield to which, and which be given the victory at the proper time?

14. I have another story to make known his perfection in the things of God. There came to him from his fatherland his sister with her son, now a man and a leading citizen of Cyrrhus; she brought a lavish supply of the necessities he needed. He did not consent to see his sister,[10] but received his nephew, since it was the time laid down for meeting people. When they begged him to accept what they had brought, he asked, 'Through how many monasteries have you come?

To which of them did you give some of this?' When his nephew replied that they had given to none, he said: 'Go away with what you have brought, for we do not need any of it, nor if we did would we accept it. For you have done us this kindness out of consideration for physical relationship but not for the service of God; for if it was not only closeness of kinship that you valued, you would not have apportioned what you brought to us alone.' With these words he dismissed his nephew with his sister, after giving orders that not even a little of what they had brought was to be accepted.

15. In this way he transcended nature and crossed over into the life of heaven. How could one produce a clearer proof than this that he was worthy of God, according to the utterance of God himself, who says, 'He who does not leave father and mother and brothers and sisters and wife and children is not worthy of me?'[d] If he who does not leave them is unworthy, he who leaves them and practises so strict a perfection is clearly most worthy.

16. I myself, in addition to this, admire also his strictness over the divine doctrines. For he abhorred the madness of Arius, which at that time was being kindled by imperial authority; he abominated the folly of Apollinarius; he fought nobly against those of Sabellius's persuasion, who lump the three hypostases into one; and he rejected utterly those called Euchites, who hide under a monastic disguise the disease of the Manichees.[11]

17. So fervent was his zeal for the doctrines of the Church that he engaged in a just battle with a man who was wonderful and godly. In that desert there was a certain old man called Abraham, a man hoary in hair and hoarier still in thought, glorious in every virtue and always shedding tears of compunction. At the beginning, misled by a certain simplicity, he presumed to celebrate Easter as previously, in apparent ignorance of the rule laid down on this matter by the fathers at Nicaea, preferring to be tied to the ancient custom—many others at this time suffered from the same ignorance.[12] But the great Marcianus used many arguments on many occasions to try and lead Old Man Abraham—for so the local people called him—back into the harmony of the Church, and on seeing him obstinate, he publicly separated

---

[d]Cf. Mt 10:37, Lk 14:26.

himself from communion with him. But when time had passed, that inspired man cast off this reproach and embraced the harmony of the divine festival, chanting in truth, 'Blessed are those without reproach on the way, who journey in the law of the Lord.'[e] And this was the achievement of the teaching of the great Marcianus.

18. Many everywhere built him burial shrines—in Cyrrhus his nephew Alypius, in Chalcis a certain Zenobiana, glorious in birth, preeminent in virtue and flourishing in abundance of wealth, and not a few others did the same thing, in competition to carry off this victorious athlete. Knowing this, the man of God adjured that wonderful Eusebius, imposing on him oaths fraught with every terror, to bury his body in that spot and inform no one of his grave, save two of his more intimate companions, until a great number of years had passed.[13] That wonderful man carried out this oath: when the end of the victor had come and the choir of angels transferred that sacred and godly soul into the abodes of heaven, he did not announce his death until, with the two companions most close to him, he had dug the grave, buried the body, and leveled the surface of the ground. Fifty years or more passed by, a countless number hastened along and searched for the body; yet the grave remained undetected. When each of the shrines mentioned above had received remains, one of Apostles and the other of martyrs, the heirs of his earthly tent and teaching were now reassured. Having prepared a stone coffin two years earlier, they placed in it the remains of his precious body, once one man—for he alone of the three was left—had pointed out the tomb.

19. Having become an emulator of his virtue, the wonderful Eusebius continued to wear away his body by still more labors. Although wearing one hundred and twenty pounds of iron, he laid on himself the other fifty of the most godly Agapetus and also added the eighty of the great Marcianus. He had as his oratory and dwelling a certain cistern that lacked water, living in this way for a total of three years.[14] I have made this digression wishing to show for how many others the great Marcianus was the cause of great achievements.

20. His philosophy also profited the wonderful Basil who a long time later built his monastic dwelling near Seleucobelus—it is a city of

[e]Ps 119:1.

Syria[15] — and who, while glorious in many other forms of virtue, was especially glorious in the possession, dear to God, of charity and in the divine work of hospitality. Indeed, who could number with ease those whom, in the words of the Apostle, he presented to God as workmen with no need to be ashamed, rightly handling the word of truth?[f]

21. Omitting at present the others, who though worthy of eulogy would cause lengthiness in the account, I shall mention only one of them. There was a disciple of this man, named Sabinus, who expended his body on innumerable labors. He took neither bread nor anything cooked; his food was meal soaked in water. It was his custom to prepare together all the food for the month in such a way that it went mouldy and emitted a great stench. The character of such food was intended to blunt his bodily appetites, and by the stench of the food extinguish pleasure. While living in this way on his own, if ever one of his acquaintance came, he would partake in simplicity of everything that was served.

22. He had received such grace from God that a woman of the nobility, distinguished in birth and wealth, hastened to him from Antioch and begged him to help her daughter who was beset by a demon: 'I had a dream,' she said, 'that bade me hasten here and get healing for my daughter from the head of the monastery.' The monk who gave answers replied that it was not the custom for the superior to speak with women. When the woman persisted, weeping and wailing and imploring bitterly, the superior of the monastery came out. But the woman said it was not he but another — ruddy and with spots on his face — who had been indicated to her. When they realized whom she was seeking — the third in the monastery, not the first —, they persuaded him to come to the woman, and immediately she recognized his face. The evil demon cried out and departed from the girl.

23. Such were the achievements of the disciples of disciples of the great Marcianus; such were the plants that the excellent planter planted everywhere. I myself again, after bringing this account to an end, beg and entreat through the intercession of them all to obtain the help of God.

[f]Cf. 2 Tm 2:15.

NOTES

1. Marcianus was an ascetic of the region of Chalcis, living about sixty miles from Beroea (see §9); we may deduce from §18 tht he died in the 380s. Both he and other ascetics mentioned in this chapter—Agapetus, Symeon, Avitus, Abraham—are listed in Theodoret, *Eccl. Hist.* IV.28(25) under the reign of Valens (364-378), though Marcianus may well have entered on his labors some time earlier.

2. The meaning is probably that Marcianus at a young age received the honor of nominal membership of the senate of Constantinople, with the style *clarissimus*.

3. Theodoret himself had been a monk of one of these monasteries at Nicerte, prior to becoming a bishop in 423. Symeon is presumably the 'priest and monk of the territory of Apamea' who was an ally of John Chrysostom and received an extant letter from him (*ep.* 55) in *c*.405.

4. Agapetus was made bishop of Apamea in *c*.388.

5. For a demon in the form of a dragon being routed by the sign of the cross cp. II.6 above and *Life of Antony* 23.

6. Cp. XXIV.7 and XXVI.20 for the great power attributed to oil blessed by a holy man. Theodoret is clearly tolerant, but some bishops, such as Rabbula of Edessa († 437), saw this as a threat to the sacramental power of the ordained clergy.

7. To this *actio in distans* cp. *Life of Antony* 58, 61.

8. This visit probably dates to 381, the very year of Flavian's ordination (Garnier, PG 84: 247A). Flavian's position was insecure, in that there was a rival orthodox bishop at Antioch (Paulinus, recognized by Egypt and the West) and he therefore had special need of monastic support. In any case, the story illustrates both Marcianus's reputation and the trouble bishops took to maintain close relations with holy men, who might otherwise be rival centers of authority. Doubtless, the bishops' idea of ordaining Marcianus priest (see end of paragraph) was motivated by a desire to place his spiritual authority firmly under the aegis of his bishop; see XIII, note 3, below.

9. The force of the remark lies in the fact that many monks never ate meat; see Athanasius on Antony's diet: 'Of meat and wine it is superfluous to speak, since neither with other earnest men was anything of the kind to be found' (*Life* 7).

10. Monks naturally avoided meeting women, even close relatives: cp. VIII.13 and XXVI, note 14, and §21.

11. The emperor Valens (364-378) tried to impose Arianism. Apollinarius's extreme monophysite Christology was most keenly debated between 373 and 381. The monks of the Chalcis region were particularly concerned to uphold the Trinitarian 'three hypostases' formula in the late 370s (see J. Kelly, *Jerome*, 32-36). For Theodoret on the Euchites or Messalians see *Eccl. Hist.* IV.10, and *Epitome of Heretical Myths* IV.11. They were wandering ascetics who, in contrast to the sobriety and humility of mainstream monasticism, laid claim to every grace and perfection (see A. Guillaumont in *Dictionnaire de Spiritualité* 10: 1074-83). This polemical streak in Marcianus suggests, but does not prove, that he is the Marcian who wrote some surviving ascetical and controversial fragments; see A. van Roey in *Studia Patristica XII*: 160-177.

12. At Antioch, and in several neighboring provinces, Easter was traditionally celebrated in immediate proximity to the Jewish Passover, a practice that was condemned in 325 at the Council of Nicaea. But the older custom continued to have its adherents, who were excommunicated by the Antiochene Council of 341 and are the objects of attack in an anonymous homily of 387 (published in *Sources Chrétiennes*, vol. 48).

13. The dying St Antony likewise instructed his two companions to tell no one where they buried him; his body was only 'discovered' in the sixth century. For a holy man insisting on being buried where he died rather than translated to a prestigious shrine, cp. XV.5 and XXI.30.

14. For a hermit living in a disused cistern, cp. XIII.2, XXVI.6.

15. Seleucobolus was a town near Apamea.

IV
Eusebius
(of Teleda)

WHICH FRUITS ARE OFFERED to God by the fruitless desert, ripe and mature and precious, dear to the gardener and beloved and thrice desired by men of good judgment—these we have displayed in the narratives we have already written. But lest anyone should suppose that virtue is circumscribed in place and that only the desert is suitable for the production of such a yield, let us now in our account pass to inhabited land, and show that it does not offer the least hindrance to the attainment of virtue.[1]

2. Lying east of Antioch and west of Beroea, there is a high mountain that rises above the neighbouring mountains and imitates at its topmost summit the shape of a cone. It derives its name from its height, for the local inhabitants are accustomed to calling it Koryphê (Summit). On its very peak there was a precinct of demons much revered by those in the neighborhood. To the south stretches out a plain curved in shape,[2] surrounded on either side by not very high lines of hill; these extend to the road for horses and admit paths from either side that cut from south to north. In this plain have been built villages both small and great, adjoining the hills on either side. At the

very skirts of the high mountain there is a large and well-populated village, which in the local speech they call Teleda. Above the mountain-foot there is a dale not very steep but sloping gently towards that plain and facing the south wind. Here one Ammianus built a philosophical retreat,³ a man glorious in many other forms of virtue but surpassing others in his total modesty of spirit. There is proof of this; for while well able to teach not only his own disciples but even twice that number, he often hastened to the great Eusebius,⁴ begging to get a helper, and a trainer and teacher of the wrestling-school founded by him.

3. He was twenty-five stades distant,⁵ immured in a tiny dwelling that did not even have windows. He was guided into this form of virtue by his uncle Marianus, a faithful servant of God—to say so much is sufficient, since the Master honored the great Moses with this title.[a] This Marianus, having tasted divine love, was not willing to luxuriate in good things on his own, but made many others his fellow-lovers. He captured the great Eusebius and also his brother, who was his brother too in his mode of life, for he did not think it sensible to capture for virtue those who were quite unrelated to him while leaving his nephews uncaught. Immuring them both in a small cell, he taught them the evangelical way of life. The brother, however, caught a disease that cut short his course. Death followed on the disease, for he survived his departure from there only a few days before coming to the end of his life.

4. During the entire life of his uncle the great Eusebius continued neither speaking to anyone nor seeing the light but uninterruptedly immured; and after his death he embraced this life until the wonderful Ammianus won him over, bewitching him with much entreaty. 'Tell me, my friend,' he said to him, 'whom do you think to please by having adopted this laborious and austere life?' He, of course, as was natural, replied: God, the teacher and lawgiver of virtue. 'So since you love him,' continued Ammianus, 'I shall show you a way by which you will both kindle your love the more and serve the Beloved. Restricting all one's care to oneself would not escape, I think, the charge of self-love, for the divine law prescribes loving one's neighbor as oneself. Admitting many to a share of one's wealth

---

[a] Cf. Heb 3:5.

is characteristic of the virtue of charity, and it is charity that the inspired Paul called 'fulfilment of the law'.[b] He exclaims again, 'The whole law and the prophets are summed up in the following saying, in "You will love your neighbor as yourself."'[c] And the Lord in the holy Gospels tells Peter, who had professed to love him more than the others, to tend his sheep;[d] accusing those who had not done this, he exclaims through the prophet, 'O shepherds, do the shepherds feed themselves? Do they not pasture the sheep?'[e] It was because of this that he also ordered the great Elijah, who pursued this life, to go about in the midst of the impious; and he sent the second Elijah, the famous John, who embraced the desert, to the banks of the Jordan, bidding him baptize and preach there. So since you too are a fervent lover of the God who has created and saved, make many others as well his lovers; for this is specially welcome to the common Master. This is why he called Ezekiel "watchman" and charged him to warn sinners,[f] and ordered Jonah to hasten to Nineveh and since he was unwilling sent him as a prisoner.'6 With these and like words he charmed the divine man; digging through his voluntary prison, he led him out and away, and entrusted to him care of the brethren.

5. I myself do not know which to admire the more, the modesty of the one or the amenability of the other; for the one fled being superior and preferred to be one of the subjects, fearing the danger of leadership; and the great Eusebius, despite his aversion to life with others, yielded none the less and, caught in the nets of charity, accepted care of the flock and led the choir. He did not need many words to teach them, since his mere appearance was sufficient to make the most slothful eager in the race for virtue. Those who have seen him say that his face was always grave and was enough to instil awe into those who saw him. He took food every three or four days, but ordered his companions to partake every day. He charged them to have intercourse with God continually and leave no opportunity free from this activity, but to perform the appointed offices in common and in the intermediate portions of the day entreat God and beg for salvation each one on his own, whether in the shade of a tree or by some rock or wherever he might enjoy solitude, either standing

[b]Rom 13:10. [c]Cf. Rom 13:9. [d]Cf. Jn 21:16. [e]Ezk 34:2. [f]Ezk 3:17–19.

or lying on the ground. He had so taught virtue to each of the parts of his body that they performed what reason alone enjoined.

6. To make this clear to all, I shall recall one of the stories about him. He and the wonderful Ammianus were sitting on a rock. One of them read aloud the history of the divine Gospels, while the other explained the meaning of the more obscure passages. Some farmworkers were ploughing up the land in the plain below, and the great Eusebius was attracted to this sight. When the inspired Ammianus had read out the Gospel passage and was seeking its interpretation, the great Eusebius told him to repeat the reading. When the other replied, 'In your delight over the ploughmen you were doubtless not listening', he made a rule that his eyes were never to look at that plain nor feast upon the beauty of the heavens or the choir of the stars; but using a very narrow path, whose breadth is said to have been a span, to get to the house of prayer, he did not thereafter allow himself to step outside it. They say that he lived on for more than forty years after making this rule. In order that, in addition to this resolve, some duress should compel him to this, he bound his waist with an iron belt and attached a very heavy collar to his neck and then used a further chain to connect the belt to the collar, so that bent down in this way he would be forced uninterruptedly to stoop to the ground. Such was the penalty he imposed on himself for looking at those farm-workers.

7. I was told this by many who had known him and were exactly informed about him; this same story was recounted by the old man, the great Acacius, whom we mentioned above in relation to other stories. He said too that once when he saw him bent double he asked what profit he reaped from not allowing himself to look at the sky or see that plain stretched beneath or walk outside that narrow path. The other answered that he contrived this against the devices of the evil demon. 'To prevent him,' he said, 'making war on me in things of importance — attempting to steal my self-control and righteousness, arming anger and kindling desire, making me swollen and puffed up with vanity, and contriving all the other things of this kind against my soul — I try to transfer the war to these unimportant things, where even if he wins he works no great injury, while if he loses he becomes all the more ridiculous, as unable to overcome even in little things. So because I know that this war is less dangerous — for a man smitten

here suffers no great penalty, for what harm is there in seeing the plain or raising one's eyes to the sky?–, I make him adopt this form of opposition. For here he can neither smite nor kill, for these darts are not mortal, since they lack those points of iron.' The great Acacius said it was this he had heard, and that he admired his wisdom and marveled at his courage and experience in war. Because of this he used to communicate this story too, as admirable and memorable, to those who wished to learn such things.

8. This renown of his spread everywhere and drew all the lovers of virtue to him. Among those who came to him were the rams of the excellent flock of the most godly Julian the Old Man, whose story we proceeded through above. When that inspired man reached the end of his lifespan and passsed to the better life, James the Persian[7] and Agrippa, the leaders of the flock, hastened to the great Eusebius, thinking it better to be well led than to rule. As for James (whom I have already mentioned above, telling of his virtue in summary) now too I shall display distinct proof of his consummate philosophy. When the divine Eusebius, on making his departure from here, bade him preside over the flock, he refused this charge and yet was unable to persuade those who desired this tending; so he departed to another flock, preferring to be ruled than to rule. And it was thus that, having lived on a very long time, he ended this life. So Agrippa succeeded to his post of superior, a man flourishing with many other good qualities but specially with purity of soul, through which he continually enjoyed contemplation of the divine beauty, and consumed by the firebrand of that love wet his cheeks with continual tears.

9. For a long time Agrippa shepherded law-abidingly this elect and godly flock. When he departed from life, the godly David, the sight of whom I myself enjoyed, received the post of superior, a man who had in real fact, in the words of the godly Apostle, mortified his limbs upon earth.[g] He so profited from the teaching of the great Eusebius that, while living forty-five years in this retreat, he lived out all this time without wrath and anger. Nor after he became superior did anyone ever see him overcome by this passion, even though there were doubtless innumerable incitements to it. One hundred and fifty

[g]Cf. Col 3:5.

men were shepherded by his hand, some consummate in virtue and imitating the life in heaven, but others just fledged and learning to spring and fly above the earth. Nevertheless, although there were so many being instructed in the things of God and doubtless transgressing somewhat—for it is not easy for one starting his schooling to get everything right—, that holy man remained unmoved, like a bodiless being, for no inducement could stir him to anger.

10. This I ascertained not only by report but also by experience. I once conceived the desire to see this godly flock, and arrived with others who embraced the same life as myself as companions for the journey.[8] During the entire cycle of a week that we spent with this man of God, we saw his face remain without any change, not now relaxed and now contracted with sternness. Likewise his look was not at times grim and cheerful at others, but his eyes always preserved the same orderliness; they were sufficient proof of the calm of his soul. But perhaps someone may suppose that he looked like this because there was nothing to stir him: because of this I am compelled to narrate something that happened in our presence. This holy man was sitting beside us, stimulating discussion on philosophy and searching out the summit of the evangelical life. In the middle of this discussion one Olympius, by race a Roman, himself admirable in his way of life, honored with the priesthood and exercising the second position of authority there, came up to us exclaiming against the godly David, calling his forbearance a general injury, saying that his gentleness was harmful to everyone and calling his consummate philosophy not forbearance but folly. But the other took these words as if he had a soul of steel: he was not stung by words of a nature to sting, nor did he alter his expression, nor did he break off the discussion in hand, but in a gentle voice and with words that revealed his serenity of soul, he sent that old man away, urging him to attend to what he chose. 'I,' he said, 'am conversing, as you see, with these visitors of ours, since I think this service a necessary one.'

11. How could one give a better proof of gentleness of soul? That, although entrusted with this leadership, he should be treated with such insolence by one in second place, specially when strangers were present and heard the abuse, and yet feel no surge or stirring of anger— what greater manliness and endurance is possible? Certainly the holy

Apostle, out of regard for the weakness of human nature, adapted his rule-giving to fit nature: 'Be angry,' he said, 'but do not sin; do not let the sun go down on your wrath'.ʰ For knowing that movements of anger are of nature not of will, he does not presume to lay down what is certainly burdensome and perhaps even impossible, but he determines that a day is to be the measure for the stirring of nature and the surge of anger, ordering reason to apply the restraint and discipline of the bit, and not allowing progression beyond the set limit. But this man of God strove to surpass the rules laid down and overleapt the boundary; so far from allowing his anger to be stirred until evening, he did not permit it to be stirred at all. In this way did he too profit from the company of the great Eusebius.

12. I saw in his cell many other lovers and emulators of this philosophy, some in their bodily prime, others in advanced old age. Men who had lived for more than ninety years were not willing to abandon the laborious life but were conspicuous with the sweat of youth, as all day and all night they entreated God and performed those holy liturgies, and partook of their frugal food every other day. To pass by the others, who deserve not silence but eulogy and every kind of praise, but not to make the account long beyond measure, there was in that godly place a man—they call him Abba—who, although grown from Ishmaelite stock, had not like his ancestor been expelled from the household of Abraham, but shared with Isaac the paternal inheritance,ⁱ or rather grasped the very kingdom of heaven. He first entered on this ascetic life with one who at that time lived in the desert, an excellent gymnast of this kind—his name was Marôsas⁹—; afterwards the latter as well, leaving rule over others, entered this flock together with Abba, and lived on for no short time, and after striving gloriously and becoming celebrated departed from life. The other has now spent thirty-eight years there.¹⁰ His eagerness for labor is as if he had just now begun to labor. For right up to today he has never covered his feet with shoes; during frost he sits in the shade, in flaming heat he takes the sun and welcomes its flames as if it were a westerly breeze. During all this time he has refused to take water, despite not eating those things that are customarily taken by those practising

ʰEph 4:26.   ⁱCf. Gen 21:10.

not drinking (they are wont to feed on food that is more moist); instead, it is while feeding on the same food as the others—and eating little, just enough to provide slight strength—that he thinks using water superfluous. Though girt round his waist with a heavy chain, he rarely sits down; for the greater part of night and day, either standing or down on his knees, he offers the liturgy of prayer to the Master. He has totally rejected the need to lie down: no one right up to today has ever seen him lying down, but since being made leader of the choir and attaining the post of superior, he bears all this toil readily, setting himself up as a model of philosophy for all his subjects.

13. Such victorious contestants did the divine Eusebius, the gymnastic trainer of all these contests, offer to God. There are very many others who he formed like this and sent to be teachers in other wrestling-schools, who have filled all that holy mountain with these divine and fragrant pastures.[11] While he set up his original ascetic cell in the east, offshoots of his philosophy are to be seen in the west and the south, like stars in a choir round the moon, hymning the Creator, some in Greek, others in the local language. But I am attempting the impossible in desiring to proceed through all the achievements of this godly soul, therefore it is necessary to bring this account to an end, and switch to another one and apply the benefit therefrom in turn, after begging to receive the blessing of these great men.

NOTES

1. Cp. Maesymas (XIV.2) and Abraham (XVII.4), who combined asceticism with being village priests, and the numerous ascetic bishops (see I, note 5). But the typical habitat of Theodoret's holy men was neither town nor desert but the intermediate region of the fringe of inhabited areas. This followed naturally from the nature of the terrain; see P. Brown, 'The Rise and Function of the Holy Man'. 110-1.

2. This is the plain of Dana, on the limestone ridge in the east of the territory of Antioch; it is dominated by Mt Barakat, on which had stood the great shrine of the Semitic deities Zeus Malbachos and Salamanes. On the plain and its monasteries, see G. Tchalenko, *Villages antiques de la Syrie du Nord*, I: 103-182.

3. The monastery of Téleda, which became the greatest monastery of the Antiochene region and the center of a remarkable coenobitic expansion (§13), was already outstanding by 367 (§8), so its foundation may be presumed to go back to c.350. It has left notable ruins, on which see Tchalenko, I: 154-5, and III, pl. CLXVIII.1; they appear to date to the late fifth or early sixth century, the period of the monastery's apogee. Theodoret himself once spent a week at the monastery (§10), probably between 410 and 415. Doubtless, the material in this chapter largely derives from what he learnt then. He also mentions (§7) Acacius of Beroea as an informant (on whom see II, note 9).

4. Both Eusebius and two other holy men who feature in this chapter, Ammianus and Marianus, are listed in Theodoret, *Eccl. Hist.* IV.28(25) as among the major ascetic figures of the late fourth century.

5. Twenty-five stades is three miles.

6. Cp. the argument used by Acacius to persuade Julian Saba to visit Antioch (II.16), with its fuller use of Jn 21.

7. For James see II.6. Julian Saba died in 367 (see II.27 with note *ad loc.*).

8. On Theodoret at this time (early 410s), see Introduction, xii.

9. Marosas is mentioned by Sozomen, *Eccl. Hist.* VI.34, where he is described as a native of 'Nechilis', which Tchalenko (I: 134, 153) identifies tentatively with the 'Neghaule' of sixth century monastic lists, lying about twelve miles from the plain of Dana.

10. Our date of 440 for the *Rel. Hist.* (see Introduction, section II) implies 402 for the date of Abba's entering the monastery.

11. XXVI.4 mentions the foundation of a further monastery at Teleda by two disciples of Eusebius, Eusebonas and Abibion. From 350 to 600 there was an enormous monastic expansion in the hinterland of Antioch. Some extant texts of the 560s list thirty monasteries in the plain of Dana (see n.2) alone (Tchalenko, I: 150).

V
PUBLIUS

AT THIS SAME TIME there lived a certain Publius,[1] who was both good-looking in physique and possessed a soul that matched his physique, or rather displayed one far more wondrous than his body. He originated from the curial order, while his city was where the celebrated Xerxes, marching against Greece and eager to cross the river Euphrates with his army, assembled a large number of ships, yoked them to each other and in this way bridged the river; he called the place Zeugma, giving it a name from the event. Originating from here and stemming from such a family, he repaired to a high place not more than thirty stades distant from the town. Here he built a small hut and gave away everything he had inherited from his father—I mean home, property, herds, clothing, vessels of silver and bronze, and anything else that went with them.

2. After distributing these, according to divine law, to those who needed them, and freeing himself from every worldly care, he took on one care to replace them all, the service of the One who had called him, and turning this over in his soul, continued night and day considering and examining how to increase it. For this reason his toil

increased continually and was intensified each day; yet it was sweet and full of pleasure, driving satiety far away. For no one ever saw him taking a rest for even a small part of the day, but psalmody was succeeded by prayer, prayer by psalmody, and both by the reading of the divine oracles; then came attending to visitors, and then some other of the necessary tasks.

3. Spending his life in these pursuits, and exposed as a model of virtue for those who wished to emulate him, like some singing bird he drew many of his fellows into this trap of salvation. At the beginning, however, he would not have anyone to live with him; building small adjacent cells, he ordered each of those who assembled to live separately, while he continually inspected and examined the cells to prevent their containing something stored away in excess of need. They say that he even carried scales with which to examine closely the weight of the bread, and that if he found more than had been laid down, he was angry and called those who did this gluttons. He ordered them to expect satiety in neither their eating nor their drinking, but to take that quantity which was sufficient to assure life to the body, and if ever he saw meal separated from bran, he would rail at those who had done this for feeding on sybaritic fare. At night he would come to each door suddenly, and if he found someone awake and hymning God, he would depart again in silence; but if he perceived someone fast asleep, he would knock on the door with his hand and rebuke the sleeper with his tongue for giving the body more than it needed.

4. On witnessing this labor of his, some of the like-minded proposed the building of one dwelling for all. They said that those who were now scattered would live more strictly and that he would be released from a great anxiety. The wise man accepted this suggestion: gathering all together, he demolished those small cells, and for those brought together he built a single one. He told them to live in common and stir each other on—one was to imitate the gentleness of another, who in his turn was to mix gentleness with the zeal of the first, while yet another, while giving a lesson in keeping vigils, would receive a lesson in fasting. 'It is by so getting what we lack from others' he said, 'that we shall achieve the most perfect virtue. Just as in city markets one sells bread, another vegetables, one trades in clothes while another makes shoes, and so supplying their needs from each

other they live more contentedly – the one who provides a piece of clothing receives a pair of shoes in exchange, while the one who buys vegetables supplies bread –, so it is right that we should supply each other with the precious components of virtue.'[2]

5. While those of the same tongue trained and strove in this way and hymned God in the Greek language, desire for this same way of life also seized those who used the local language. Some came together and begged to join the flock and gain a share in his sacred teaching. He accepted the request, remembering the law which the Master issued to the sacred Apostles when he said, 'Go and make disciples of all nations'.[a] By the first dwelling he built a further one and told them to live there; and he constructed a church of God, in which he told both groups to assemble at the beginning and close of the day, in order to offer the evening and morning hymnody to God; this they were to do divided into two and each using their own language, while sending up their song in turn.[3]

6. This form of life has continued even till today: neither time, which is eager to change things of this kind, nor those who inherited this man's charge have been induced to change anything of the rules he laid down, and this although not two or three but many have become superior. As soon as he had completed his contest and departed from this life and crossed to that life without sorrow, Theotecnus became superior over the Greek-speakers and Aphthonius over the Syriac-speakers, both of whom were living statues and images of his virtue. They prevented both their brethren and visitors from outside from being aware of his death by making themselves impresses of his mode of life. But the divine Theotecnus lived on only a short time and passed on the post of superior to Theodotus; Aphthonius continued for a long period to look after the flock and direct it according to the rules in force.

7. This Theodotus, originating from Armenia, beheld this ascetic company and was at first enrolled among the subjects, obeying the government of the great Theotecnus. When, as I said, the latter made his departure, he received the leadership, and abounded in such good qualities as almost to obscure the fame of his predecessors; for divine

[a] Mt 28:19.

Publius

longing so worked on him, and wounded him with darts so great in kind and number, that night and day he poured forth tears of compunction. He was full of such spiritual grace that when he prayed all those present simply listened in silence to his sacred words, thinking the listening to be an earnest prayer. For who, while these words were being offered so sincerely, was so made of steel as not to be bewitched in soul and to make soft what was hard and unyielding in it and transfer this to the service of God? Thus increasing his wealth each day and making his inviolate treasury full of such good things, after shepherding the sheep for twenty-five years, he was gathered to his fathers, reared to a fine old age, in the words of divine Scripture,[b] and handed over the reins to Theotecnus, his nephew in birth and brother in character.

8. That divine Aphthonius, after presiding over the choir for more than forty years, received the episcopal see, but without changing either his rough ascetic cloak or his tunic made from goat's hair; and he ate the same food as before his episcopate. Despite taking on this charge he did not tend that flock any less, but spent most of his days there, now resolving the strife of those quarreling, now exercising care of those wronged by anyone, at other times addressing exhortation to his disciples; and he performed each of these tasks while, in between, stitching the rags of his companions or cleaning lentils or washing grain or doing something else of the kind. After having thereby adorned his episcopate and increased his virtue, he repaired with this cargo to the divine harbor.

9. And what should one say about Theotecnus and his successor Gregory? The former acquired in his youth every form of philosophy and departed with the fame of his predecessor, while the latter still labors in profound old age as in a body in full vigor, for he has persevered in entirely refusing the fruit of the vine and not even taking vinegar or raisins, nor milk whether freshly drawn or curdled — for this mode of life was laid down by the great Publius. As for oil, they share in using it during the season of Eastertide, but refuse a share of it afterwards.

10. Such is what I have learnt of the great Publius — of which some came to me by hearsay, and some by my seeing his disciples, recognizing

[b]Cf. Gen 15:15.

the teacher in his disciples and discovering the trainer through his athletes. Therefore, thinking it unjust, even malicious, to leave something so beneficial in silence, I have set out this narrative for those who do not know it, gaining for them its benefit and procuring for myself the profit that comes from recalling it. For I have attended to the saying of the Lord, 'Everyone who acknowledges me before men I too shall acknowledge before my Father who is in heaven'.[c] And I know clearly that, through communicating to mankind the memory of these men, I shall enjoy being remembered by them in the presence of the God of the universe.

[c]Mt 10:32.

NOTES

1. Publius was a monk and monastic founder three miles outside Zeugma in Euphratensis. He is listed in Theodoret, *Eccl. Hist.* IV.28(25) among the monks of around the time of Valens (364-378), and is here described as Eusebius's contemporary (see IV.2 with notes 3-4). His immediate successor Aphthonius, who was abbot for 'more than forty years' (§8), received letters from John Chrysostom in 406 (*epp.* 70, 93). This all suggests that Publius founded his monastery *c.*350.

2. For this theme of the coenobitic life's enabling mutual assistance, see St Basil, *Longer Rules* 7.

3. Cp. the funeral of St Paula (in 404), where psalms were chanted in Greek Syriac, and Latin (Jerome, *ep.* 108.29). That Greek was the language of Publius's first disciples, as well as his own curial origins (§1), shows that monasticism originated here among the educated, Hellenized class.

VI
Symeon the Elder

IF ONE WERE DELIBERATELY to omit Symeon the Old Man[1] and consign the memory of his philosophy to oblivion, one would doubtless not escape a charge of injustice and malice, as neither being willing to praise what is worthy of praise nor offering what is worthy of love for imitation to those wishing to benefit; I myself not from fear of accusation but through desire to praise shall make the narration of this man's mode of life. He persevered for the greatest possible length of time in embracing the eremetical life and dwelling in a tiny cave; he enjoyed no solace from men, for he chose to live alone, but discoursed persistently with the God of the universe. It was edible plants that he made his food.

2. This toil won him also the gift of rich grace from above, even to the extent of exercising authority over the most bold and fearsome of wild animals. And this was manifest not only to the pious but also to unbelieving Jews. Because of some need they were journeying to one of the forts that lie outside our own inhabited region. There came torrential rain, a fierce storm beat down, and they lost their way, being unable to see ahead; they wandered in the desert, finding neither village

nor cave nor traveller. Storm-tossed on mid-continent like those on board ship, they came upon, as on some harbor, the cave of the godly Symeon and caught sight of a man dirty and filthy and wearing on his shoulders a ragged goat's hair cloak. As soon as he saw them, he greeted them—for he was courteous—and asked the cause of their visit. They recounted everything and asked to be told the road leading to the fort. 'Wait,' he said, 'and I shall give you guides immediately to show you the road you want.' They did as he bid and took a rest. While they were sitting down, there arrived two lions, not looking ferocious but as if fawning on a master and intimating their servitude; with a gesture he ordered them to escort the men and lead them to the road which they had left when they lost their way.[2]

3. Let no one think this story a myth, for I have as witnesses to its truth the common enemies of the truth—for it is those who benefited from this good deed who persisted in celebrating it. This was recounted to me by the great James, who said he had been present when they recounted the miracle to the inspired Maron.[3] If someone disbelieved Jews witnessing to a Christian miracle, how would he not be called with good reason more unbelieving than Jews—if, while those who are even hostile are worsted none the less and yield to the rays of the truth, those who are thought to be well-disposed and to share the faith do not even believe their enemies when they testify to the power of grace?

4. As a result of such miracles this man of God became famous and attracted many of the neighboring barbarians—this desert is inhabited by those who boast of Ishmael as their ancestor. In his desire for quiet he was compelled to leave his cave.[4] At the end of a long journey he reached the mountain called Amanus; this mountain, previously burdened with much polytheist madness, he cultivated with many miracles of every kind and planted the piety that is now practised on it.

5. But to recount them all would be extremely laborious and for me perhaps impossible. I shall mention just one, offering it as an image of the way he worked miracles like the Apostles and Prophets, and leave it to my readers to form a notion therefrom of the strength of the grace he had received. It was summer and harvest-time, and the sheaves were being carried to the threshing-floor. A certain man,

dissatisfied with the lawful fruits of his toil and coveting those of another, stole from the sheaves of his neighbor and tried with these to increase his own heap. But immediately the Godhead declared sentence against the theft: lightning struck and the threshing-floor went up in flames. This wretch repaired to the man of God, who dwelt not far from the village, and recounted the disaster, while trying to hide the theft. But when ordered to tell the truth, he confessed the theft—for the misfortune compelled him to accuse himself—and this man of God commanded him to end the punishment by ending the injustice. 'For if,' he said, 'you repay those sheaves, this fire sent by God will be extinguished'. And so you could see the man running and presenting the stolen ears to the man he had wronged, and the fire being quenched without water by the prayer and intercession of the godly old man.

6. This event not only filled the local inhabitants with awe, but also made the whole city hasten there—I mean Antioch, for to this city the place is subject—as one person begged to be freed from demonic fury, another for an end to a fever, another for a cure to some other trouble. Without stinting he applied the streams of the grace that dwelt in him.

7. Longing for quiet yet again, however, he conceived the desire to repair to Mount Sinai.[5] On learning this, many excellent men who pursued the same philosophy assembled together in their desire to share the journey with him. After traveling for many days, when they reached the desert of Sodom, they saw from a distance the hands of a man stretching upwards out of the depths, and at first they suspected a demonic deception; but when after earnest prayer they still saw the same thing, they set off to the spot, and observed a tiny hole such as foxes are wont to make when they contrive dens for themselves. But they saw no one appear there. Hearing the sound of feet, the man who had his hands stretched out had hidden away within the den.

8. The old man leant down and besought him at length to let himself be seen, if he had a human nature and it was not some deceptive demon who contrived this appearance. 'For we,' he said, 'in our pursuit of the ascetic life and longing for quiet are wandering in this desert, wishing to adore the God of all things on Mount Sinai, on which he made his own epiphany to give the tablets of the Law to his servant Moses—not that we think that the Godhead has been circumscribed

in place (for we hear him saying, "I fill heaven and earth, says the Lord,"[a] and "he contains the circle of the earth, and the inhabitants in it as grasshoppers"[b]) – but since to those who love fervently not only are their beloved thrice desired, but lovable too are the places that have been graced by their presence and frequenting.'

9. While the old man spoke to this effect, the man who had hidden raised himself from the den. He was wild to look at, with unkempt hair, shriveled face, the limbs of his body reduced to a skeleton, dressed in some dirty rags sewn together with palm shoots. After having welcomed them and given the greeting of peace, he asked who they were, where they had come from and where they were going. The old man replied to his questioning and asked in turn where he had come from and why he had chosen this mode of life. 'I too had the same longing,' he said, 'that makes you depart. I had made a friend share this journey who was like-minded and had the same goal as I did; we had bound each other with an oath to let not even death break up our fellowship. Now it happened that he came to the end of life on the journey, in this place. Bound by the oath, I dug as well as I could, and committed his body to burial; by this grave I dug another tomb for myself, and here I await the end of life and offer to the Master the customary liturgy. I have as food the dates which a certain brother was detailed to bring to me by my Protector.'

10. While this was being said, there appeared at a distance a lion. Those with the old man were filled with alarm; but when the man sitting on the den saw it, he stood up and gestured to the lion to go across to the other side. It immediately obeyed and came up carrying the bunch of dates. It then turned and went back again and at a distance from the men lay down and went to sleep. So he distributed the dates among all of them, and joined with them in prayer and psalmody; at the end of the liturgy at break of day he took leave of them, and sent them on their way awe-struck at this novel spectacle.

11. If anyone does not believe what I have said, let him remember the life of the great Elijah, and the ministering of the crows who were regular in bringing him bread in the morning and meat in the evening.[c] It is easy for the Creator of the universe to contrive all kinds of ways to

[a] Jer 23:24.   [b] Is 40:22.   [c] Cf. 1 Kgs 17:6.

look after his own: so he protected Jonah for three nights and days in the belly of the whale,^d rendered the lions in the pit awe-struck at Daniel,^e and made the lifeless fire act rationally in illuminating those within while burning those without.^f But I am doing something superfluous in offering proofs of God's power.

12. It is related that, when they reached the mountain they desired, this wonderful old man, on the very spot where Moses was counted worthy to see God and beheld him as far as was possible for human nature, knelt down and did not get up until he heard a divine voice announcing to him the Master's favor. He had spent the whole cycle of a week bent double in this way and taking not a scrap of food when the voice sounded and bade him take what was offered him and eat it willingly. Stretching out his hand he found three apples; and on taking his fill of them, as their giver had enjoined, he recovered all his strength and, naturally enough, greeted his companions with gladness of heart. So he returned home rejoicing and exulting at having heard a divine voice and enjoyed food that was likewise a gift from God.

13. On his return he built two philosophic retreats: one on the ridge of the mountain we mentioned above, the other on the very skirts of the mountain-foot beneath. He assembled athletes of virtue in each, and was the gymnastic trainer of both groups — teaching the assaults of the adversary and enemy, promising the favor of the Umpire, urging them to be confident, filling them with spirit, and telling them to be modest towards their fellow-men, while bidding them show self-assurance towards the enemy.

14. Such were his teaching and life, and such the miracles he wrought, as he emitted effulgence of every kind, when he came to the end of his life of labor and migrated to the life without old age or sorrow, leaving behind unquenchable glory and a memory lasting for ever. His blessing, while he was still alive, was enjoyed by my blessed and thrice-blessed mother, who often related to me many of the stories about him. And I myself now beg to gain his powerful intercession, and know that I shall gain it; for he will assuredly grant my request, in imitation of the Master's love for men.

---

^d Cf. Jon 1:17.   ^e Cf. Dan 6:22.   ^f Cf. Dan 3:22–5.

NOTES

1. Symeon the Elder was at first a hermit in the desert to the east of Cyrrhus (§2), and then moved to Mt Amanus (just north of Antioch), which he converted to Christianity, and where he eventually founded two monasteries (§13). Towards the end of his life he used to bless Theodoret's mother, but apparently died before he could do the same to the infant Theodoret (§14). This establishes c. 390 as his date of death. Since witnesses to a miracle he performed before moving to Mt Amanus were still alive and active in the 390s (see §3, with note 3 below), his move to this district would have occurred around 370. He is listed in Theodoret, *Eccl. Hist.* IV.28(25) as among the holy men of the Antiochene region in the time of the emperor Valens (364-378).

2. To the tame lions here and at §10, cp. *History of the Monks in Egypt* IX.6 (serpents guarding the cell of Amoun), XII.7-9 (Abba Helle using a crocodile as a ferry across the Nile), with the comments of B. Ward on p. 43f. of the English edition (*The Lives of The Desert Fathers*, trans. N. Russell, Cistercian Studies 34): the stories amount to a return to man's state before the Fall, when Adam enjoyed full authority over the animal kingdom.

3. James (XXI) lived with Maron (XVI) for a few years in the 390s (see XXI, note 1), which dates the Jews' recounting of the story.

4. For the Ishmaelites, see XXVI.13ff., with note *ad loc*. It emerges from Theodoret's account that Symeon settled on the southern slopes of Mt Amanus, within easy reach of Antioch: manifestly 'desire for quiet' cannot have been the reason for his move; it is more likely to have been the desire to evangelize a still pagan district.

5. Cp. the pilgrimage to Sinai of Julian Saba (II.13). A pilgrim to Sinai exactly contemporary to Symeon was Egeria, whose detailed account survives (J. Wilkinson, ed., *Egeria's Travels*, 91ff). Sinai was already a standard place of pilgrimage, with a great number of spots precisely identified as the locations of stories in Exodus, and with local monks acting as guides.

VII
PALLADIUS

THE CELEBRATED PALLADIUS[1] was of the same date and way of life as Symeon, and his familiar and friend; in frequenting each other, it is said, they enjoyed mutual benefit, stimulating and stirring each other on to holy rivalry. He was immured in a cell near a large and well-populated village which has the name Imma. The man's endurance, fasting, vigils, and perpetual prayer I think superfluous to narrate, since in them he bore the same yoke as the godly Symeon.

2. But I have judged it useful to relate the miracle, still celebrated today, that occurred by means of his voice and hand. There was a gathering for a fair in the foresaid village, drawing traders from all around and attracting an innumerable throng. At this fair was a trader who, having sold what he had brought and amassed money, decided to depart during the night. A murderer, seeing the money that had been collected, and filled with some onset of frenzy, drove sleep from his eyelids and watched for this man's departure. At cockcrow he set off in good heart; the other, who had set out in advance and reached a spot suitable for an ambush, made a sudden attack, delivered the

blow and perpetrated the murder. To this crime he added a further impiety: taking the money, he dumped the dead body at the door of the great Palladius.

3. When day came and the news circulated and the whole fair talked of the event, all hastened together, broke down the door and called on the godly Palladius to answer for the murder; one of those who did this was the actual perpetrator of the murder. Surrounded by such a crowd, the wonderful man, looking up to heaven and passing beyond it in his thought, besought the Master to expose the falsehood of the calumny and make the hidden truth manifest. After this prayer, he took the right hand of the outstretched man: 'Tell us, young man,' he said, 'who struck you this blow? Point out the perpetrator of the crime and free the innocent from this wicked calumny.' Word responded to word, gesture to gesture: the man sat up, looked round the people present, and pointed with his finger at the murderer. A cry went up from everyone, astounded at the miracle and deploring the calumny that had been committed; stripping the murderer, they even found the knife, still red with blood, and also the money that had caused the murder. The godly Palladius, who was already remarkable, naturally became, as a result of this, still more remarkable, for the miracle was sufficient to show the man's familiar access to God.

4. Of the same company was the wonderful Abraham, who, while dwelling in a place called Paratomus, emitted flashes of virtue in every direction.[2] To the splendor of his life bear witness the miracles performed after his death: even today his tomb pours forth cures of every kind—the witnesses are those who through faith draw them forth in abundance there. May I too share in assistance from these men, having sanctified my tongue by recalling them.

NOTES

1. Palladius was a hermit near Imma, a large village twenty-five miles to the east of Antioch. His friendship with Symeon, and listing in Theodoret, *Eccl. Hist.* IV.28(25), establish the 370s and 380s as his *floruit*.

2. Abraham is listed with Palladius in *Eccl. Hist.* IV.28(25), under the reign of Valens (364-378). His being 'of the same company' as Palladius does not imply (as Festugière, *Antioche*, 314, supposes) that they ever lived together in a coenobitic community, but simply that they were both hermits at the same time and in the same region.

VIII
APHRAHAT

THAT THE NATURE of all men is one and that it is simple for those who wish to practise philosophy, whether they are Greeks or barbarians, is easy to learn from many other examples. Aphrahat[1] on his own, however, is sufficient to show this clearly; for this man, though born and bred among the lawless Persians,[2] stemming from such parents and educated in their customs, advanced to such virtue as to eclipse those who have been born of pious parents and have received a pious education from childhood. First of all, thinking nothing of his family, although it was distinguished and illustrious, he hastened to worship the Master, in imitation of his forebears the Magi; then, in disgust at the impiety of his kin, he chose a foreign country in preference to his own, and repaired to Edessa, a city large and well-populated and exceptionally illustrious in piety.[3] Finding a hovel outside the city-walls and immuring himself, he tended his own soul, pulling out, like an excellent cultivator, the thorns of the passions by the roots, weeding the divine crop, and offering to the Master the seasonal fruits from the seeds of the Gospel.

2. From there he repaired to Antioch, which was being severely shaken by the storm of heresy.⁴ Settling in a philosophic retreat in front of the town and knowing just a few phrases of the Greek language, he drew vast numbers to hear the divine oracles; using a language that was semi-barbarous, he brought forth the offspring of his thought, receiving such streams from the grace of the holy Spirit. Who of those who plume themselves on their eloquence, knit their eyebrows, speak pompously, and embark with zest on syllogistic traps, has ever surpassed the voice of this uneducated barbarian? With arguments he overcame arguments, with divine words the words of the philosophers, exclaiming with the great Paul, 'Even if unskilled in speaking, I am not in knowledge.'[a] In this manner, he always persevered, in accord with the apostolic saying, in 'destroying arguments and every high thing raised up against the knowledge of God, and taking every thought captive for obedience to Christ'.[b] One could observe hastening together councilors and officials, those with some military rank and manual laborers, in a word civilians and soldiers, the educated and the uninitiated in learning, those inured to poverty and those flourishing in wealth, those who accepted what he offered in silence and those who asked questions and inquired and provided an occasion for discourse.

3. Despite taking on such great labor he would never consent to take a companion, and preferred doing things himself to the assistance offered him by others. Holding these conversations at the outer door, he himself opened the door to those coming in and escorted those leaving. He never accepted anything from anyone, neither bread nor prepared food nor clothing, but a single one of his friends supplied him with bread; on attaining extreme old age he also took greens after sunset.

4. It is related that Anthemius (who later became perfect and consul), when he had made his journey to Persia on being made ambassador,⁵ brought him a tunic woven by the Persians and said, 'Father, knowing that to every human being his own homeland is sweet and the fruits produced there most pleasant, I have brought you from

[a] 2 Co 11:16.   [b] 2 Co 10:5.

your homeland this tunic, and I beg you to accept it in exchange for your blessing'. The other told him, first of all, to put it on the bench, and then, after conversation on other topics, professed to be at a loss, with his mind torn in two directions. On Anthemius asking the reason he replied: 'I have always chosen to live with a single companion, and I have imposed a rule on myself to refuse totally to live with two. For sixteen years someone has been living with me who is agreeable: and now there has arrived a compatriot of mine who wants to live with me and demands to be granted this. My mind is torn over this: I will not consent to have two at the same time; I welcome my compatriot as a compatriot, but to expel my earlier companion when he has become dear to me is something I think both distressing and unjust.' 'And with good reason, father,' replied the other; 'for it is not right to dismiss as unsuitable the one who has served you for so long a time, and to accept the one who has not yet given proof of his character simply on account of his country of origin.' At this the godly Aphrahat continued, 'In that case, my excellent friend, I will not accept this tunic: for I will not consent to have two, and the one that has served me for so long a time is pleasanter in my opinion and superior in yours.' By thus outwitting Anthemius and exhibiting a miracle of shrewdness, he induced him to utter no further word to him about the tunic. I have told this in full out of a wish to demonstrate two things at the same time: that he received the care that sufficed for his body from one garment alone, and that he was full of such wisdom as to make the person who begged him accept decide that he should not accept.

5. But leaving this and such matters aside, I shall relate what is of greater importance. When the accursed Julian had paid the penalty for his impiety on barbarian soil, the nurslings of piety enjoyed a brief calm once Jovian had received the helm of sovereignty; when he came to the end of his life after a very short reign, and Valens succeeded to the sovereignty of the East, hurricanes and tempests stirred up the sea around us, a dangerous swell arose and enormous waves from all sides assailed the ship.[6] What made the storm yet more dangerous was the lack of pilots, for these had been forced by an emperor brave against piety alone to live beyond the frontier. Despite practising such lawlessness, he could not satiate his impiety, but dispersed the whole assembly of the pious, eager like a wild beast to

scatter the flock; because of this he drove them out not only from every church but also from the skirts of the mountain, from the banks of the river and from the military drill-ground—for they constantly switched between all these places, making additional work for the military arm. While the Scythians and other barbarians ravaged with impunity the whole of Thrace from the Danube to the Propontis, he himself with stopped ears, as the saying is, could not bear even to hear of them,⁷ but used his weapons against his compatriots and subjects and those illustrious in piety.

6. The people of God, lamenting these unseasonable ills, sang the psalm of David, 'By the rivers of Babylon, there we sat down and wept when we remembered Sion'.ᶜ But the rest of the song no longer applied to them; for Aphrahat, Flavian, and Diodore⁸ would not allow the harps of teaching to be hung up on the willows, nor permit them to say, 'How shall we sing the Lord's song in an alien land?'ᵈ Instead, on the hills and on the plains, in the city and in the suburbs, in their homes and in the squares they sang the Lord's song continually. For they had learnt from David that 'the earth is the Lord's and the fulness thereof, the world and those who dwell therein.'ᵉ Again they had heard the same prophet saying, 'Bless the Lord, all his works, in every place of his dominion'.ᶠ They had also heard the inspired Paul urging 'that in every place the men should pray, lifting holy hands without anger and quarreling'.ᵍ And the Master himself, speaking with the Samaritan woman, had made distinctly the following prophecy: 'Amen, I say to you, woman,' he said, 'that the hour is coming and now is, when neither in this place nor in Jerusalem but in every place will they worship the Father'.ʰ After this teaching, they persevered in bearing witness both at home and in the square, 'in public and from house to house,' in the apostolic phrase,ⁱ and, like excellent generals, in arming their own men and shooting down their opponents.

7. That the great Flavian and the godly Diodore, as assistant shepherds at this time and honored with the second place, acted as I have related, is wondrous and worthy of praise; nevertheless, they did this as generals at the front, following the rules of generalship. But the

ᶜPs 137:1. ᵈPs 137:4. ᵉPs 24:1. ᶠPs 103:22. ᵍ1 Tm 2:8. ʰJn 4:21.
ⁱAc 20:20.

most wise Aphrahat leapt into these combats as a volunteer. Though he had been reared in solitude and had chosen to live on his own, sitting quietly outside the range of missiles, as the saying is, when he observed the fierceness of the war, he did not cherish his own safety, but, bidding goodbye for a time to solitude, became a champion in the army of the pious, delivering blows by means of his life, words, and miracles, but never himself receiving a blow.

8. On one occasion the utterly senseless emperor saw him going out to the military drill-ground—for it was there that the adherents of the Trinity happened then to be assembling—and as he was walking along the bank of the river someone pointed him out to the emperor who was peering out from the palace.[9] He asked him where he was setting out to so hurriedly. When he replied that he was on his way to make prayers on behalf of the world and his reign, the emperor again asked him, 'Why, when you profess the solitary life, are you walking without scruple in the public square, deserting your solitude?' The other, who was wont in imitation of the Master to reason in parables, replied, 'Tell me this, O emperor: if I had been a girl shut away in some inner room and saw a fire attack my father's house, what would you have advised me to do on seeing the flames kindled and the house on fire? Sit indoors and let the house be burnt down? In that case I myself would have become a casualty of the conflagration. If you say that I ought to have dashed to fetch water and run up and down and extinguished the flames, do not blame me, O emperor, for doing this very thing. It is what you would have recommended to the girl in the inner room that I am compelled to do, despite my profession of the solitary life. If you blame me for deserting my solitude, blame yourself for having cast these flames into the house of God and not me for being compelled to extinguish them. For you yourself have agreed that it is certainly right to bring assistance to one's father's house on fire; and it is obvious to everyone, even the utterly unitiated in divine things, that God is more truly our father than fathers on earth. Therefore we are doing nothing wide of the mark or contrary to our original commitment, O emperor, in assembling and pasturing the nurslings of piety and providing them with the divine fodder.' At these words, the emperor, out-argued by the justice of this defence, expressed approval by silence.[10]

9. One of those who count as neither men nor women but who have been deprived of in time becoming fathers, and for this reason are thought to 'please' an emperor, and derive their name from this,[11] one of these repeatedly abused the man of God, even to the extent of threatening him with death; but it was not long before he paid the penalty for his insolence. The emperor chose to treat his body with a bath, and so the wretch went to the bath to see if it was well mixed; deprived of his wits, he jumped into the pool, which contained unmixed hot water, and since no one rescued him — for he had gone in alone to see if it was ready — he went on gradually being boiled to death. Since time was meanwhile stretching out, the emperor sent someone else to call him: he found no one in any of the rooms, and so reported to the emperor. After this a number of people dashed in and made a search of all the baths, and coming finally to the one in question saw that he had fallen in and lost his life. As a hubbub arose, with everyone lamenting, some drained out the hot water, while others lifted up the poor body.

10. As a result fear fell on the emperor and on all those in arms against piety; the story echoed throughout the city of how that wretch had paid the penalty for his insolence against Aphrahat, and all continued to hymn the God of Aphrahat. This prevented the man of God being exiled, despite the pressure of his enemies; for in his terror the emperor rejected those who advised this and held the man in awe.

11. He learnt of the man's power from another incident as well. A certain horse of good breed and trained to be an excellent mount was particularly dear to the emperor. To the great distress of the emperor it caught a disease: its secretion of urine was blocked. Those trained in the skill were summoned to tend it; but to the distress of the emperor and the grief of the man entrusted with the care of the horses, their skill was defeated. Being pious and strong in faith, he repaired at midday to the dwelling of the great Aphrahat. After mentioning the disease and declaring his faith, he besought him to dispel the complaint by prayer. Without delaying for a moment but instantly beseeching God, he ordered water to be drawn from the well, and making on this the sign of the cross of salvation gave instructions for it to be given to the horse, which, contrary to its habit, drank it. Then consecrating oil by the invocation of the divine blessing, he anointed the

horse's belly: at the touch of his hand the disease immediately departed and at once natural secretion took place. In great joy the man took the horse and ran back to the stable.

12. In the evening the emperor, who was in the habit of visiting the stable at this time, came and asked how the horse was. When the man told of his good health and led the horse out, vigorous, prancing, neighing, and holding his neck up proudly, he inquired after the cause of health. After evading reply several times—for he feared to indicate the doctor, knowing the enmity of the questioner—he was finally forced to tell the truth and told of the manner of cure. The emperor was astonished and agreed that the man was remarkable. However, he was not freed of his earlier madness, but persisted in raging against the Only-begotten until he became a casualty of a fire lit by barbarians and did not even receive a burial like servants or beggars.[12]

13. The divine Aphrahat both displayed his power in this storm and at the coming of calm continued to perform similar acts; he worked innumerable other miracles, of which I shall recall one or two. A woman of noble family, who shared the yoke of marriage with a debauched husband, came to this blessed man bewailing her misfortune. She told how her husband, in his attachment to a concubine, had been bewitched by some magical enchantment and became hostile towards the wife yoked to him in lawful wedlock. The woman told this standing in front of the outer door—for he was not accustomed to make conversation with the female sex, and never admitted any woman inside the door.[13] On this occasion taking pity on the woman as she implored loudly, he quenched the power of the magic by prayer, and blessing by divine invocation a flask of oil she had brought told her to anoint herself with it. Following these instructions, the woman transferred to herself her husband's love, and induced him to prefer the lawful bed to the unlawful one.

14. It is related how, on an occasion when locusts suddenly attacked the land and like a fire consumed crops, plants, marshlands, woods, and meadows, a pious man came to him begging him to help one who had but a single farm from which to support himself, wife, children, and household, and in addition pay the imperial taxes.[14] Again imitating the Master's love for men, he ordered a gallon of water to be brought to him. When the petitioner had brought the

gallon, he placed his hand over it and besought God to fill the water with divine power; then on finishing the prayer he told the man to sprinkle the water round the boundaries of his property. The man took it and did as instructed, and it served as an invincible and inviolable defence for those fields, for the locusts, while crawling or flying like armies up to this boundary, retreated backwards in fear at the blessing placed upon it, restrained as it were by a curb and prevented from advancing forwards.

15. What need is there to set out all the works performed by this blessed soul? These suffice to indicate the splendor of the grace that dwelt in him. I myself saw him and reaped the blessing of that holy hand when still an adolescent[15] and accompanying my mother on a journey to the man. Half-opening the door to her, according to his wont, he honored her with conversation and blessing; but me he received within and gave me a share in the wealth of his prayer. May I enjoy it even now, since I believe him to be alive, to belong to the choir of the angels, and to possess familiar access to God even more than before; for at that time it was measured out according to the mortality of the body, lest greater access might be the occasion of presumption; but now that he has shed the burden of the passions, he enjoys as a victorious athlete familiar access to the Umpire. Because of this I pray to gain his intercession as well.

NOTES

1. Aphrahat was a hermit of Persian origin, who after a period at Edessa (§1) moved to Antioch (§2), where he distinguished himself by his resolute opposition to Arianism. His arrival at Antioch can be dated to 360/1 (see n. 3, below). He lived long enough to know Theodoret as an adolescent but not apparently as a young man (§15): this dates his death to between 407 and 413. For his place of burial see X.8.
2. Christianity was in fact well rooted in Persia by this time: see I.4, and Eusebius, *Life of Constantine* IV.13. It was doubtless Theodoret rather than Aphrahat who could not conceive proper Christianity outside the borders of the Christian empire.
3. Edessa, already entirely Christian by the time of Eusebius of Caesarea (*Eccl. Hist.* II.1.7), was the greatest center of Syriac Christianity, and had a native tradition of asceticism.
4. The reference, if exact, must be to Constantius II's measures against the Nicene party at Antioch, which date to 360/1; see Theodoret, *Eccl. Hist.* II.31(27).
5. On Anthemius, see *Prosopography of the Later Roman Empire*, II: 93–5, which gives 383 as a possible date for his Persian mission. Festugière, *Antioche*, 268, proposes a date between 375 and 378.
6. Julian the Apostate died during his Persian expedition in 363; his successor Jovian died in 364, to be succeeded as eastern emperor by Valens. Valens' persecution of the Nicene party extended from 365 till 377.
7. The Gothic ravaging of Thrace in question here cannot be that of 377, as supposed by Festugière and Canivet, since this coincided with the end, not the beginning, of Valens's persecution. The reference is rather to the less famous ravaging of Thrace of 364–6, which coincided with the start of the persecution in 365.
8. For Flavian and Diodore, see II.16: they led the Nicene party at Antioch during the lengthy exiles of bishop Meletius (II.15).
9. The imperial palace at Antioch lay at the north-west corner of the city, with the military drill-ground just beyond it; see Theodoret, *Eccl. Hist.* IV.26(23), where the story told here is repeated with greater topographical precision. The date must be the period of Meletius's third exile (371–7), since during his second exile (365–7) Valens was not at Antioch.
10. To Aphrahat's boldness in rebuking Valens, cp. Theodoret, *Eccl. Hist.* IV.34(31): Isaac of Constantinople prophesied to Valens' face in 378 that he and his army would be destroyed by the Goths unless he ended his campaign against the Nicenes (which, in fact, he had just done). After the event, many monks and laymen claimed to have rebuked Valens. This must cast doubt on the historicity of the story told here, even though Aphrahat was a consistent Nicene and a realistic setting is provided.
11. Theodoret artificially connects *eunouchos* (eunuch) with *eunoëin* (to please).
12. Valens perished at the disastrous defeat of the Roman army at the hands of the Goths on 9 August 378 near Adrianople. On the exact manner of his death, see the contemporary treatment in Ammianus Marcellinus XXXI.13.12–16; one account related that he was burnt to death in a cottage in which he had taken refuge. The 'strange manner' of Valens' death (so Eunapius, *Lives of the Philosophers*, 480) was made much of by both his Christian and his pagan enemies.
13. For the regular exclusion of women from monastic enclosures, cp. III.14 and XXVI, note 14.
14. This peasant is not a *colonus*, or serf, but a small freeholder. For the survival of this class in the region of Antioch in this period, see W. Liebeschuetz, *Antioch*, 67–69.
15. Theodoret's adolescence began around 407, which dates this story.

IX
PETER
(the Galatian)

WE HEAR OF THE GALATIANS in Europe, those of the West, and we know of those in Asia, their ancestors, who had settled by the Euxine Sea; it was from the latter that stemmed the blessed Peter,[1] thrice and many times blessed. Reared by his parents for seven years, they say, from the time of his birth, he spent the whole of the rest of his life in the contests of philosophy. He is said to have died after living ninety-nine years. Who could adequately express admiration for one who strove for ninety-two years and through every day and night pursued his victorious path? What tongue could suffice to narrate the laborious achievements of the child, boy, adolescent, adult, middle-aged man, elderly man, and ancient man? Who could measure his sweat? Who could number the combats that took place during so long a time? What account could attain to either the seeds he sowed or the sheaves he garnered? Who is so elevated in thought as accurately to survey the abundance he amassed from so excellent a commerce? I know the ocean of his achievements, and therefore fear to embark on historical narration, lest the account become submerged. Because of this I shall walk along the shore, and admire and narrate that which is beside the land on the near side of the ocean; the deep sea I shall leave to one who, in the scriptural phrase,[a] searches the depths and knows secrets.

2. At first, therefore, he contended in Galatia; from there for the sake of sightseeing he made his way to Palestine,[2] to see the places where occurred the sufferings of salvation and to worship in them the God who saved us—not that He is circumscribed in place (for he knew the lack of circumscription in His nature)—, but in order to feast his eyes with seeing what he desired and so that the eyes of the soul should not through faith enjoy spiritual delight on their own, without the sense of sight. It is somehow natural for those who are lovingly inclined to someone not only to reap delight from seeing him but also to gaze in great joy at his home and clothing and footwear. It is with this love for the bridegroom that the bride mentioned in the Song of Song exclaims, 'As an apple-tree among the trees of the wood, so is my beloved among the sons; in his shadow I yearned and sat, and his fruit was sweet in my mouth.'[b] So this divine man did nothing unreasonable when he fell in love with the same bridegroom and used the words of the bride, 'I am wounded with love'.[c] Out of a desire to behold as if a shadow of the bridegroom, he set out to see the places which had poured forth for all men the streams of salvation.

3. After enjoying what he desired, he settled at Antioch; observing the city's love of God he preferred the foreign city to his homeland, counting as fellow-citizens not those of the same race and family but those of the same convictions, sharing the faith and bearing the same yoke of piety.[3] Having fallen in love with this life, he did not pitch a tent or set up a cell or erect a hut, but spent all his time in the tomb of another; it had an upper story and projecting balcony, to which a ladder was attached to admit those who wanted to ascend.[4] He continued immured in this for an immensely long time, using cold water, eating only bread, and this not every day; remaining one day without food, he would take food on the next.

4. There came to him a raving maniac, full of the action of the evil demon. He cleansed him through prayer and freed him from that diabolical frenzy. Since he had no wish to go away, but begged to give

---

[a]Cf. 1 Co 2:10.   [b]Sg 2:3.   [c]Sg 5:8.

his services in return for this cure, he made him his companion. I knew this man as well. I remember the miracle and witnessed how he paid for the cure. And I heard them conversing about me: Daniel—this was his name—said that I too would share in this noble service of him; but that inspired man did not agree that this would happen, adducing in argument the love my parents had for me. He often sat me on his knees and fed me with grapes and bread; my mother, who had had experience of his spiritual grace, ordered me to reap his blessing once each week.

5. He had become known to her from the following cause. A disease that afflicted one of her eyes appeared to be beyond medical knowledge, for there was no remedy, either recorded by the ancients or discovered by their successors, that had not been applied to the disease. When it defeated them all and showed them to be of no avail, one of her friends came to inform her of the man of God and to tell of a miracle he had performed: she related that the wife of the man who at that time held the rudder of the East—he was Pergamius[5]— had been a victim of this same complaint, and that he had cured her by means of prayer and the sign of the cross.

6. No sooner had my mother heard this than she immediately rushed to the man of God. She was wearing ear-rings, necklaces, and other golden jewelry, and an elaborate dress woven from silk thread, for she had not yet tasted the more perfect virtue; she was at the flower of age, and was content with the adornment of youth. So when this inspired person saw this, he first cured the weakness of love of adornment by means of the following words: 'Tell me, child,' he said (I shall use his own words and not alter the speech of this holy tongue), 'if some painter, well trained in his art, painted a portrait as the rules of the art prescribe and exhibited it to those who wanted to view it, and someone else, who had no accurate knowledge of the art but dashed off according to his fancy whatever he chose to paint, came along and criticized the artistic painting, and then added longer lines to the eyebrows and eyelashes, made the face whiter, and put red coloring on the cheeks—, does it not seem to you that the first painter would rightly be indignant at his skill being grossly insulted and undergoing useless additions by an unskilled hand? And so (he continued) believe too that the maker of the universe, the sculptor

and painter of our nature, is rightly indignant at your accusing his ineffable wisdom of a lack of skill. For you would not have poured on red, white, and black coloring if you had not thought you needed this addition: by supposing your body to require them, you condemn the Creator for deficiency. But one ought to recognize that he has power corresponding to his will, for, as David says, the Lord "has done whatever he chose".[d] Devising beforehand what will benefit every being, he gives nothing that is harmful. Therefore do not ruin the image of God, or try to add what he has wisely not given, or devise this spurious beauty which harms even modest women by laying snares for the beholder.'[6]

7. When the excellent woman heard this, she immediately entered the net of Peter, for he too, like his namesake, was a fisherman.[e] Seizing his feet and imploring loudly, she begged to be granted a cure for her eye. He protested that he was a man with the same nature as her and carrying a great burden of sins which deprived him of familiar access to God. When my mother besought him with tears and declared she would not go away without obtaining the cure, he replied that it was God who heals these things and always grants the petitions of those who believe: 'So now too,' he said, 'will he grant it, not showing favor to me but recognizing your faith: so if you have faith pure and unmixed and free of all doubt, then, bidding farewell to doctors and medicines, accept this medicine given by God.' Saying this, he placed his hand on her eye and forming the sign of the saving cross drove out the disease.

8. On thence returning home, she washed off her make-up and, rejecting all extraneous ornament, now lived according to the rules laid down by her doctor, neither wearing elaborate dress nor decking herself with gold jewelry—and this even though she was very much in her young prime of life: she was in her twenty-third year from birth, and not yet a mother; it was after a further seven years of life that she underwent the pangs of my birth, her first and only ones.[7] So great was the profit she drew from the teaching of the great Peter, receiving a double cure: in quest of healing for the body, she obtained in addition the health of the soul. This is how he operated through words and prevailed through prayers.

[d] Ps 115:3.   [e] Cf. Mt 4:18–19.

9. On another occasion, she brought along a cook of her household, who was troubled by an evil demon, and begged to receive his help. After praying, the man of God ordered the demon to tell the cause of his power over one of God's creatures, like some murderer or burglar standing before the judge's seat and ordered to say what he had done; so he proceeded through everything, compelled by fear to tell the truth, contrary to his wont. He declared that in Heliopolis,[8] when the master of this domestic was once ill and the mistress was sitting by her husband because of his illness, the maidservants of the mistress of the house where they were staying were recounting the life of the monks practising philosophy at Antioch and how much strength they have against demons, and then these servants, as girls who enjoyed play, acted the part of raving demoniacs, while this domestic, putting on a goat's hair cloak, exorcised them like a monk. 'While this was being performed,' continued the demon, 'I was standing at the door. Finding these boastful remarks about monks unbearable, I decided to learn by experiment the power these servants bragged of them possessing. For this reason, leaving the maidservants, I intruded myself into this man, wanting to find out how I would be driven out by the monks. And now (he concluded) I have found out and need no further proof: at your command I shall immediately depart.' Saying this, he darted away, and the domestic recovered his freedom.

10. Another rustic possessed by a demon was brought along by my maternal grandmother, my nurse, who begged the adversary of evil to help him. He again asked where he came from and what gave him power against one of God's creatures. Since the other stood there in silence making no answer, he knelt down to pray and besought God to show the miscreant the power of his servants; he stood up again, and again the other resisted in silence, and this continued till the ninth hour. When he had addressed to the Master still more zealous and fervent prayer, he stood up and said to the miscreant, 'It is not Peter who is ordering you, but Peter's God. So give answer, compelled by his power'. The avenging spirit, despite his shamelessness, felt compunction at the holy man's modesty, and with a great voice cried out, 'I haunt Mount Amanus, and seeing on the road this man drawing water from a spring and drinking it, I made him my abode'. 'But depart from him,' said the man of God, 'since he who was crucified on

behalf of the world gives you this order.' On hearing this he fled, and the rustic was restored to my nurse freed of his frenzy.

11. Although I have innumerable other stories of this kind to tell about this blessed soul, I shall omit most of them, out of fear at the weakness of ordinary men. Taking themselves as the standard, they disbelieve the miracles of the men of God. But I shall recount one or two before passing on to another contestant.

12. There was a certain debauchee, formerly a general. An unmarried girl of marriageable age, who had him as master, left behind her mother and family and fled to a convent that contained a company of athletes—for there are women who compete like men and enter the racecourse of virtue.[9] On discovering her flight, the general had the mother whipped and strung up, and did not free her from bonds till she had revealed the convent of pious women. Impelled by his own fury, he snatched the girl away from there and took her back home, hoping, the wretch, to satisfy his lechery. But He who tried Pharaoh with great and grievous trials because of Sarah the wife of Abraham, and guarded her chastity unsullied,[f] and who struck the Sodomites with blindness when they tried to outrage angels they took for strangers,[g] struck the eyes of this man too with blindness, and so made the quarry escape out of the midst of the nets; for as he entered the chamber, the girl, under guard within, immediately dashed out and disappeared, and made her way to her thrice-desired convent. This taught the senseless man that he would not get the better of one who had chosen the divine suitor; he was forced to remain quiet and give up hunting for one who, though captured, had escaped through the power of God.

13. After time had passed, the girl fell victim to a grave illness. The disease was cancer, and as her breast swelled out the pain too increased. At the height of the pain she called for the great Peter; and she used to relate how, as soon as his sacred voice struck her ears, all that pain was lulled and she got not even a slight unpleasant sensation from it. Because of this she used to send for him repeatedly, and enjoy relief, for she used to say that all the time he was present her pains totally ceased. After she had contended in this way, he sent her forth from this life with the praises for victory.

[f]Cf. Gen 12:17.   [g]Cf. Gen 19:11.

14. Yet again, when after my birth my mother was at the gates of death, in response to earnest entreaty by my nurse he came and snatched her out of the hands of death. While the doctors had given her up, and her household in tears were expecting the end, she was lying, they say, with her eyes closed, possessed by a violent fever, recognizing none of her intimates. On the arrival of the one counted worthy of the name and grace of the Apostle, and his saying to her, 'Peace be with you, child' – for this was his mode of greeting –, she is said immediately to have opened her eyes, looked straight at him and asked for the fruit of his blessing. When the crowd of women broke into a shriek – for despair and confidence were mixed together – and uttered this cry, the godly man bade them all join with him in prayer; for so, he said, had Tabitha obtained healing, while the widows wailed and the great Peter offered their tears to God.[h] They made supplication as he bade them, and were rewarded as he had foretold; the end of their prayer marked the end of the disease as well. Sweat suddenly poured from her whole body, the fever was extinguished, and the signs of health reappeared.

15. Such are the miracles that in our times too the Master works through the prayers of his servants. Even the skin of this man, acting through his clothes, had a similar power, as in the case of the most godly Paul.[i] I have stated this without any exaggeration and in agreement with the truth. For cutting his girdle in two – it was broad and long, of thick twined flax – he put one half of it round his own waist and the other half round mine. My mother often put it on me when I was ill and often on my father, and thereby expelled disease; and she herself used this remedy as a means to health.[10] Many of her acquaintance who had discovered this constantly took the girdle to help the sick; and it everywhere gave proof of the power of his grace. Consequently, someone who took it stole it from the givers, showing no consideration to his benefactors. In this way we were deprived of the gift.

16. After thus blazing forth and illuminating Antioch with his rays, he passed from the contest, awaiting the crown laid up for victors. I myself, who enjoyed his blessing when he was alive, beg also to enjoy it now, and so bring this account also to an end.

[h]Cf. Ac 9:36–40.   [i]Cf. Ac 19:11–12.

NOTES

1. Peter was a hermit first in Galatia and later at Antioch. He knew Theodoret when he was a child (§5) but apparently not later, which dates his death to *c*.403. If he indeed lived to the age of ninety-nine, as Theodoret relates (§1), this implies a date of birth of *c*.304 and a start of his ascetic labors in *c*.311. He is listed in Theodoret. *Eccl. Hist.* IV.28(25) as one of the ascetics on Mt Silpius, just south of Antioch, together with Romanus (XI), Zeno (XII) and others; Macedonis (XIII) belongs to the same group.
2. Peter could have been one of the pilgrims who visited the Holy Land even before the Constantinian development of the holy places; see E.D. Hunt, *Holy Land Pilgrimages in the Later Roman Empire*, 4.
3. Antioch was more Christian than Peter's native Galatia (see Harnack, *The Mission and Expansion of Christianity*, II: 216–220).
4. Zeno also settled in a tomb on Mt Silpius (XII.2). The reason is likely to have been merely practical, in contrast to Antony of Egypt, who chose a pagan tomb in order to expose himself to demonic assault (*Life of Antony* 8–10).
5. Pergamius was *Comes Orientis*, the highest official resident at Antioch. The date must be 385/6 (see n.7 below).
6. Cp. Clement of Alexandria, *Paedagogus* II.8 and III.2, and John Chrysostom, *8 Catéchèses Baptismale* I.34–8, for the condemnation of cosmetics, fine dress, and jewelry by high-minded Christians.
7. This dates the conversion of Theodoret's mother to the devout life to 386.
8. Heliopolis is the modern Baalbek, not far north of Damascus.
9. See XXX.4–6 for convents of women in Syria. The only reference to one in Antioch itself appears to be Theodoret, *Eccl. Hist.* III.14 – a community of virgins at the time of the emperor Julian (361–3).
10. Cp, XXI.16 – the protective power of James's old cloak – or the Bohairic *Life of Shenute* of Atripe (Upper Egypt) 106–8 – a holy man's belt securing victory for the general who wore it.

X
Theodosius

RHÔSUS IS A CILICIAN CITY, on the right as one sails into the Cilician Gulf. South and east of it is a high mountain, thickly grown and shaded; it teems with wild beasts in its thickets. Finding here a dale sloping towards the sea, the great and celebrated Theodosius,[1] building a small cell, embraced the evangelical life in solitude. A man originating from Antioch, distinguished for the luster of his family,[2] he nevertheless abandoned home, family, and all the rest, in order, in the Gospel phrase, to buy the pearl of great price.[a]

2. About his fasting, sleeping on the ground, and hair clothing it is superfluous to speak to those who have seen his followers and disciples and beheld in them this way of life. It was, however, in an exceptional manner that he observed these practices, in that he offered himself as an example to those under his direction. To these practices he added a load of iron on his neck, his loins, and both his hands. He wore his hair unkempt and stretching down to his feet and even further, and for this reason had it tied round his waist. By continual recourse to

[a] Cf. Mt 13:46.

prayer and hymnody he put to sleep desire, anger, pride, and all the other wild beasts of the soul. Always adding toil to toil, he also practised manual labor, now weaving what are called creels and mats, now ploughing small fields in the dale, sowing seed and gathering therefrom sufficient food.

3. When with the passing of time his fame circulated everywhere, many hastened from all sides, wishing to share his dwelling, labors, and way of life; these he welcomed and guided in this life. One could observe some weaving sails, others hair coats, some plaiting mats or creels, other assigned agriculture. And since the place was on the sea, he later built a landing-place which he used for the needs of merchandise, exporting the products of the brethren and importing what was needed. He remembered the apostolic utterance which runs, 'Working night and day, that we might not burden any of you',[b] and, 'These hands assisted both myself and those with me'.[c] And so he both labored himself and urged his companions to add to the labors of the soul exertion of the body: 'While those engaged in life toil and labor to support children and wives, and in addition pay taxes and are dunned for tribute, and also offer the first-fruits to God and supply the needs of beggars as far as they are able, it would be absurd for us not to supply our essential needs from labor—especially since we use scanty and simple food and simple dress—, but to sit indoors with our arms crossed, reaping the handiwork of others.' By this and similar remarks he stimulated them to work, performing at the proper times the divine liturgies that are customary everywhere and allotting the time in between to work.³

4. Not least did he attend to looking after guests, entrusting this charge to men adorned with gentleness and modesty of spirit and possessing love for their neighbor. He himself examined everything minutely, checking to see if each detail was carried out in accordance with the rules laid down. He became so famous as a result of all this that sailors even more than a thousand stades away invoked in danger the God of Theodosius and by naming Theodosius lulled the surge of the sea.

5. He was respected even by the audacious and savage enemies who plundered and enslaved most of the East—who of those who

[b] 2 Thess 3:8.   [c] Cf. Ac 20:34.

live in our part of the world has not heard of the misfortunes that occurred at this time because of those formerly called Solymi and now Isaurians?⁴ Nevertheless, men who spared neither city nor village, but plundered and burnt all those they could seize, showed respect to his philosophy, and after merely asking for bread and requesting prayers, left that ascetic dwelling unharmed; and this they did not once but even twice.

6. However, the leaders of the churches conceived a fear that the devil might inspire love of money in these barbarians and make this great luminary a captive—for it was likely that a huge ransom for him would be sent to them from all sides by those who honor the things of God—and so they persuaded him by entreaty to make his way to Antioch. For they had already taken two church leaders captive, and treated them with every attention, and after receiving fourteen thousand gold pieces for them, then allowed them to return wherever they might wish. When he arrived at Antioch, he settled in an abode beside the river, and attracted to himself all who knew how to gather such a harvest.

[7. Carried away by the flow of the account, I have omitted to relate a miracle performed by this inspired man, which, although to the many it will seem perhaps incredible, yet continues even now to confirm the account, and to show what favor and familiar access with God was possessed by this wonderful man. A precipitous rock overhangs the retreat which he had built; it had hitherto been completely dry and moistureless. Here he made a conduit, leading from the summit to the monastery, as if the production of water was in his power. Full of trust in God, clearly confident that he had won God's goodwill, and with unwavering faith, he rose in the night and went up to the top of the conduit before rousing his disciples for the customery prayers. After entreating God in prayer, with confidence in the One who does the will of those who fear him, he struck the rock with the staff with which he happened to be supporting himself. Water burst forth and poured out like a river; entering the monastery by the conduit and abundantly serving every need, it is evacuated into the sea nearby, and to this day is manifested the operation of the grace, like that of Moses,ᵈ

ᵈCf. Ex 17:6.

of the great Theodosius. This story on its own suffices to manifest the man's familiar access to God.]⁵

8. After living on a short time, he migrated to the angelic choir. His sacred body was carried through the middle of the city, adorned with that famous iron as if with gold chaplets, and escorted by everyone, including those entrusted with the great offices. There was strife and dispute round the bier, as everyone pressed eagerly to carry it, in their desire for blessing therefrom. So borne along, he was buried in the shrine of the holy martyrs, obtaining the same abode and roof as Julian the victorious contestant in piety; the same tomb received him that received also the inspired and blessed Aphrahat.⁶

9. To the leadership of the flock succeeded the wonderful Helladius, who continued for sixty years in that place, and then received from God the first see of Cilicia, not abandoning his earlier philosophy but each day adding to those labors the exertions of the episcopal office.⁷ The blessed Romulus, who had been his disciple, was made leader of a huge flock, and his choir has continued to this day loyal to the same mode of life. (By the retreat lies a village called in Syriac Marato.) I myself, having brought the account to this termination, beg to receive his blessing as well.

NOTES

1. Theodosius, a native of Antioch, set up a hermitage, and then a monastery, on Mt Amanus in south-east Cilicia. His successor as superior, Helladius, was a monk there for sixty years (§9) before becoming bishop of Tarsus, where we hear of him in the 430s. This establishes 370 as the *terminus ante quem* for the monastery's foundation. This chapter contains two indications of Theodosius's date of death: the Isaurian raids that shortly preceded it (§5-8) started in 403 (see n.4 below); and Aphrahat, whose tomb Theodosius shared (§8), died c.410 (see n.6 below).

2. Theodoret means that Theodosius belonged to one of the great curial families of Antioch and enjoyed the honorary rank of *clarissimus* (implying membership of the senatorial order. Cp. III.2 with note *ad loc.*).

3. This, and XXX.4,6, are the only references to monastic manual labor in the whole of the *Rel. Hist.* It was normal in coenobitic communities (see John Chrysostom, *On priesthood* VI.6, and *Homilies on the Statues* XIX.2, and Rabbula of Edessa, *Monastic Canons* 15) and was practised by many hermits (e.g. Jerome when a monk in Syria, *ep* 17.2), though other hermits lived on alms (XIII.3, XXVI.8). Generally, Syrian monasticism, unlike Egyptian, did not attribute spiritual value to manual labor.

4. The reference must be to the Isaurian raids that started in 403, were at their height in 404-5 and continued at least till 408: see Tillemont, *Histoire des Empereurs*, V: 473-5.

5. Cp. John Moschus, *The Spiritual Meadow* 80 (describing a visit to this monastery in the sixty century): 'The fathers of this monastery led us up above the monastery, to a distance of one arrow-shot. And as they showed us, they said, "This extremely fine and great spring we have from God; it is not natural, but given us by God. Often did our holy father, the great Theodosius, fast and shed tears with many genuflexions, that God might grant us the enjoyment of this water. . . . Before, our fathers used to draw their fill from the watercourse, but God, who always does the will of those who fear him, accorded us the blessing of this water through the prayers of our father" (PG 87: 2937CD). Canivet argues that the inclusion of this story in the *Rel. Hist.* is an interpolation: first, it is misplaced, since where it stands it would relate to a monastery in Antioch; secondly, it is lacking in several manuscripts. The first objection is groundless, since the writer himself says that, 'carried away by the flow of the account', he has inserted the story out of order; but the second objection has considerable weight. Stylistically, one suspicious element is the use, twice in this paragraph, of the word *monasterion*, elsewhere consistently avoided in the *Rel. Hist.* (in favor of 'philosophical retreat' or 'dwelling') as unclassical, save once in direct speech (III.14).

6. Aphrahat died between 407 and 413 (see VIII, note 1, above). About ten years later the hermit Macedonius was buried in the same shrine (XIII.19).

7. Helladius became bishop of Tarsus, and as such played a role in the controversies that followed the Council of Ephesus (431).

XI
ROMANUS

THE GREAT THEODOSIUS, while originating from Antioch and contending in the mountains of Rhôsus, returned to the city of Antioch to finish his life there. In contrast, the godly Romanus, both born and first reared at Rhôsus, took up the contests of virtue in Antioch; he pitched his tent outside the circuit of the city by the foot of the mountain, and lived all the time in someone else's house, and this a tiny one.¹ He continued into old age neither using fire nor accepting the light of a lamp; his food was bread and salt and his drink spring-water. His hair was like that of the great Theodosius, as likewise his dress and irons.

2. He surpassed him, however, in simplicity of character, gentleness of behavior, and modesty of spirit. Because of this he emitted the radiance of divine grace; for, 'On whom,' says the Lord, 'will I look except on the man who is gentle and quiet and trembles at my words?'[a] And again he said to his own disciples, 'Learn from me, for I am meek and lowly in heart, and you will find rest for your souls',[b] and again, 'Blessed are the meek, for they shall inherit the earth'.[c] And this was

[a]Is 66:2. [b]Mt 11:29. [c]Mt 5:5.

the distinguishing feature of the achievements of Moses the lawgiver: 'Moses,' he says, 'was very meek, more than all men that were on earth.'[d] The all-holy Spirit bore witness of this in the case also of the prophet David: 'Lord, remember David and all his meekness.'[e] And concerning the patriarch Jacob we have learnt that he 'was a quiet man, dwelling at home'.[f]

3. Gathering these virtues like a bee from the divine meadows, he made the true honey of philosophy. But he did not enjoy these labors in solitude; also to those outside there flowed from him most pleasant streams. Speaking gently and sweetly to those who visited him, he addressed many exhortations on fraternal love, many on harmony and peace. Many he made lovers of the things of God simply by being seen; for who would not have been overwhelmed with admiration on seeing an old man who was worn away in body, put up with long hair, chose to wear as much iron as possible, used clothing made of hair, and took food sufficient only to prevent death from hunger?

4. In addition to the greatness and number of his labors the bloom of grace induced all to admire and honor him. From many he often drove out serious diseases, to many sterile women he gave the gift of children. But although he had received such power from the divine Spirit, he called himself a pauper and beggar.

5. He continued his whole life long, by his presence and words, to shower with benefits all who visited him. On his departure from here and transference into the angelic choir, he left behind a memory not buried with the body but flowering, flourishing, abiding inextinguisable for ever, sufficing to profit those who wish. And so after gaining blessing therefrom, I shall recount, as far as possible, the facts about the other athletes.

[d]Num 12:3.   [e]Ps 132:1 (LXX).   [f]Gen 25:27.

NOTES

1. Romanus is listed in Theodoret, *Eccl. Hist.* IV.28(25) as one of the hermits on Mt Silpius, near Antioch, in around the time of Valens (364–378). He clearly died before the young Theodoret could visit him or, indeed, gather more precise information about him. It is solely his birthplace, Rhôbus, that wins him mention here (to balance Theodosius), in an account that is otherwise a mere tissue of clichés.

XII
ZENO

NOT MANY KNOW of the wonderful Zeno,[1] but those who do cannot adequately express admiration of him. After renouncing exceptionally plentiful wealth in his native land — it was Pontus —, he benefited, as he used to tell, from the streams of his neighbor the great Basil, watering the land of Cappadocia, and yielded fruits worthy of the watering.[2]

2. Immediately after the violent death of the emperor Valens, he lay aside the military girdle — he had been enrolled among those who carry swiftly the letters of the emperor.[3] Darting from the palace into a tomb (for the mountain near Antioch contains many), he lived alone; purifying his soul and constantly cleansing its eye, he perceived the vision of God, 'placing in his heart the highways' of God,[a] yearning to have 'wings like a dove' and desiring to 'fly away and be at rest' in God.[b] For this reason he had neither bed nor lamp nor hearth nor jar nor flask nor chest nor book nor anything else, but he used to wear old rags and likewise shoes that needed straps, since the pieces of leather had come apart.

[a]Ps 84:5.   [b]Ps 55:6.

3. By one alone of his acquaintances was he brought the food he needed; this was one piece of bread provided for two days. As for water, he himself brought it, drawing it at a distance. On one occasion someone saw him heavy-loaded and asked to relieve him of the labor. He at first refused, explaining that he could not bear to take water brought by someone else. On failing to persuade him, he gave him the jars, for he was carrying two in his two hands. But when he entered his outer door, he poured out and spilt the water, and hastened back to the stream, having confirmed his words by action.

4. I too, when I first conceived the desire to find out about him and went up the mountain, saw him holding the jars in his hands.[4] I then asked where the dwelling of the wonderful Zeno was; he replied that he had no knowledge of a monk called by that name. Taking the modesty of his words as proof, I guessed it was he, and so I followed. When I got inside the door, I saw a couch made of hay and another heap strewn on the stones so that those who sat on them would not derive any discomfort. When we had held a long conversation on philosophy — I myself set questions and he solved them for us —, it was now necessary to return home, and I begged him to give me his blessing for the journey. He refused, saying it was we who lawfully performed prayer and calling himself a civilian and us soldiers — I happened at that time to be a reader of the sacred books for the people of God.[5] When we adduced our youth and our immature age (for we had only just experienced a slight growth of down) and swore we would not come again if we were now forced to perform it, he was belatedly and reluctantly won over by repeated entreaty and offered up intercession to God. He made a lengthy apology for his intercession, saying he had performed it out of charity and amenability; and we heard him praying, since we were just by him.

5. Who could adequately express admiration for an old man who had completed forty years in asceticism, preserving at such a summit of philosophy such modesty of spirit? What eulogy could one make consonant with such greatness? Having obtained such wealth of virtue, while living in the depth of poverty, he would come each Sunday to the church of God together with the multitude — listening to the divine oracles, lending his ear to the teachers and partaking of the mystic table[6] —, and then would return to that novel dwelling. He had no

key or bar, and left no guard, for it was inaccessible to malefactors and utterly inviolable since he possessed only that heap of hay. He would borrow one book from his friends, read it all and first return it before borrowing another one.[7]

6. Although he had no bars and used no bolts, he was, however, protected by grace from on high; and this we learnt clearly from experience itself. When a band of Isaurians captured the citadel at night, they ran down at dawn to the foot of the mountain and cruelly shot down many men and many women who practised the ascetic life.[8] Then this divine man, seeing the massacre of the others, obscured the vision of the Isaurians by means of prayer; passing by his door, they did not see the entrance. As he declared, calling truth to witness, he saw distinctly three youths repelling all their band, as God gave clear proof of his favor. What kind of life this divine man led and what favor he received from God, these facts suffice to demonstrate.

7. But it is necessary to add to them the following. He was greatly distressed and tormented at still having possessions and not having sold and distributed them according to the Gospel rule.[c] The reason for this was the immature age of his brothers. The real and liquid estate was held in common, and so, while unwilling to go himself to carry out the distribution, he was afraid to sell his part of the property, lest the purchasers defraud his nephews and so expose him to slander. Turning these considerations over in his mind, he postponed the sale for a long time. But he later sold everything to one of his innumerable acquaintances and distributed most of it; and in the meantime an illness that struck him forced him to make up his mind about the rest. So he sent for the bishop of the city – it was the great Alexander, the ornament of piety, the model of virtue, the exact image of philosophy[9] –, and said to him, 'Come now, you whom I know to be a godly person, become an excellent steward of this money too, distributing it according to God's purpose, knowing you will render accounts to that judge. I myself dealt with the rest and gave it round as I thought best, and I intended to disburse the rest in the same manner; but since I am bid pass over from this life, I appoint you steward over it, since you are a bishop and live a life worthy of the episcopal

[c]Cf. Mt 19:21.

office.' He handed the money over as to a divine paymaster. He himself did not survive for long, but departed like some Olympic victor from the place of contest, receiving praise not only from men but also from angels. I myself, after begging him as well to intercede for me with God, shall turn to another narration.

NOTES

1. Zeno, like Peter (IX), Romanus (XI), and Macedonius (XIII), was a hermit on Mt Silpius, and is listed as such in Theodoret, *Eccl. Hist.* IV.28(25). In his case an exact date is provided for entry into asceticism (§2): 378. The mention of bishop Alexander of Antioch in §7 dates his death to the middle or late 410s.
2. St Basil was, until his death in 379, the leading ascetic writer of Asia Minor. He can scarcely have exerted a decisive influence on Zeno's choice of vocation, since he was emphatic on the preferability of the coenobitic to the eremitical life (*Longer Rules* 7).
3. Valens died in 378 (see VIII.12, with note *ad loc.*). Theodoret means that Zeno was one of the *agentes in rebus*, a corps of civil servants with a special responsibility for the public post; but as a junior member of the service he will indeed have been employed carrying despatches (A.H.M. Jones, *The Later Empire*, 578).
4. The date will be the early 410s, when the young Theodoret visited many of the holy men of the region (see Introduction, p. xii).
5. The lectorate was often bestowed on young boys destined for the clerical state; though a lector would indeed read in church, he had often no regular duties.
6. For a hermit coming regularly to church, cp. Domnina (XXX.1); contrast Macedonius (XIII.4) and Maris (XX.4), who clearly did not. The special mention here gives the impression that attendance at church was unusual. Some early Syriac writing develops the theme that hermits, as temples of the Holy Spirit, offer a spiritual sacrifice equivalent to the eucharist, or that hermits, though bodily distant from the Church's worship, are spiritually present (E. Beck, in *Il Monachesimo Orientale*, 1958, p. 359f.).
7. No deduction can be made as to the general educational level of hermits: Zeno was of an upper-class background. Still, his wants were modest compared to those of Jerome, who took with him into the desert of Chalcis a library and team of copyists (J. Kelly, *Jerome*, 49).
8. The Isaurian raids into Syria were at their height in 404-5; see Tillemont, *Histoire des Empereurs*, V: 473-5.
9. Alexander was bishop of Antioch in the middle and late 410s.

XIII
MACEDONIUS

MACEDONIUS,[1] called the Barley-eater—for this food won him the name—, is known by all, Phoenicians, Syrians, and Cilicians, and known too by the neighbors bordering on them, of whom some were eyewitnesses of the man's miracles, while others heard reports that celebrated and circulated them. Not all know everything, however, but some have learnt this and others that, and naturally they admire only what they know. I, who possess more accurate knowledge than others concerning this to me sacred person—for I had many incentives to go to him and go often—, shall relate each point as I may be able. I have reserved this position for him and placed his story after many others, not because he was second to the others in virtue—for he was a match for the perfect and first—but because, having lived an especially long time, he came to the end of his life after those whom I have recalled already.

2. He had as his wrestling-ground and stadium the tops of mountains; he did not settle in one place, but now dwelt in this one and then transferred to that. This he did not through dislike of the places, but to escape from the crowds of those who visited him and flocked

from all sides. He continued living in this way for forty-five years, using neither tent nor hut, but making his stops in a deep hole, whence some called him Goubâ, a word which, translated from the Syriac into the Greek language, means 'pit'. At the end of this time, now an elderly man, he yielded to those who besought him, and set up a hut; later, at the entreaty of his friends, he made use of cottages that were not his own but belonged to others. He continued living in the hut and the cottages for twenty-five years, so that the time of his contests came together to seventy years.

3. As food he used neither bread nor pulses, but ground barley, merely soaked in water; it was this food that my mother, who became his friend, supplied him with for a very long time.[2] On one occasion, visiting her when she was unwell and learning that she refused to take the food appropriate for her illness—for she herself already embraced the ascetic life—, he urged her to yield to her doctors and consider such food a medicine, since it was being offered her not for the sake of luxury but because of need. 'I myself,' he said, 'after using only barley, as you know, for forty years, when yesterday I felt some weakness, told my companion to ask for a small piece of bread for me and bring it. For a thought had occurred to me that, were I to die, I would have to answer for my death before the just judge, as having fled from the contest and run away from the labors of servitude. Even though it was possible with a little food to prevent death and to cling to this life in toil and hardship, amassing the wealth therefrom, I would have adjudged death from hunger preferable to the philosophic life. Filled with alarm at this, and wishing to blunt the pricks of reflection, I both had bread asked for and ate it when it was brought; and I bid you supply me no longer with barley but with bread.' So we heard from that tongue incapable of deceit that for forty years he had made barley his food. This itself is sufficient evidence of the man's asceticism and love of labor.

4. The innocence and simplicity of his character we shall show from other instances. When the great Flavian had been appointed to shepherd the great flock of God, and learnt of this man's virtue—for praise of him circulated in the mouths of all—, he got him down from the mountain-top by pretending that a charge had been made against him; while the mystic liturgy was being offered up, he led him to the

altar and enrolled him among the priests.³ When at the end of the liturgy someone informed him of this – for he was completely ignorant of what had happened –, at first he was full of reproaches and assailed everyone with words. Then, taking his stick (because of old age he was wont to walk with support), he pursued the bishop himself and all those present, for he supposed that the ordination would deprive him of the mountain-top and the life he loved. On this occasion some of his friends with difficulty calmed his indignation. But when at the end of the weekly cycle the day of the Master's feast came round again, the great Flavian sent for him a second time, bidding him join them for the festival. He replied to those who came, 'Are you not satisfied with what has been done already, but want to appoint me priest again?' Although they told him that no one man could receive the same ordination twice, he did not consent to come until with time his friends had often assured him of this.

5. I know that to many this story will not seem admirable. I have recorded it because I think it worthy of mention as sufficient proof of his simplicity of thought and purity of soul. It was to such men that the Master promised the kingdom of heaven: 'Amen, I say to you,' he said, 'unless you turn and become like these children, you will never enter the kingdom of heaven.'ᵃ Now that we have shown the stamp of his soul in summary, let us show the frankness of speech that resulted from his virtue.

6. A certain general who loved coursing went up the mountain to hunt. He was accompanied by dogs and soldiers and whatever is needed for a hunt. On seeing the man from a distance and learning from his companions who it was, he immediately leapt from his horse, went up and spoke to him, and asked him what he did, living there. He replied, 'What have you come here to do?' When the general told him it was to hunt, he said, 'I too am hunting my God. I yearn to catch him, I long to behold him, and I shall not give up this noble hunt.' After hearing this, the general departed, naturally struck with admiration.

7. On another occasion, when the city was driven insane by some evil demon and vented its frenzy against the imperial statues, the

---

ᵃMt 18:3.

supreme generals arrived with a verdict of total destruction against the city.⁴ He descended from the mountain and stopped the two generals as they were crossing the square; on learning who it was, they leapt down from their horses, clasped his hands and knees, and asked for his salutation. He charged them to tell the emperor that he was a man, with the same nature as those who had acted outrageously, that while anger ought to be proportionate to one's nature, he had given rein to anger that was out of proportion: because of his own images he was consigning to execution the images of God, and for the sake of bronze statues delivering bodies to death. 'It is easy and simple for us,' he continued, 'to remould and refashion bronze figures, but it is impossible for you, even though you are emperor, to bring back to life bodies you have slaughtered. And why do I say bodies? You cannot refashion over a single hair.' He said this in Syriac; and while the interpreter translated it into Greek, the generals shuddered as they listened, and promised to convey this message to the emperor.⁵

8. I think that everyone would agree that these words came from the grace of the holy Spirit. How else could they have been spoken by a man who had had no education and a rustic upbringing, dwelt on mountain-tops, possessed in his soul complete simplicity and had not even devoted his time to the divine oracles? This is why it is after having displayed his spiritual wisdom and the frankness of speech appropriate to a righteous man⁶ – for 'the righteous man has the confidence of a lion'ᵇ – that I shall now proceed to his miracles.

9. The wife of a nobleman fell ill of morbid gluttony; some called the illness a demonic attack, others thought it a sickness of the body. Whether the former or the latter, it was like this: they used to relate how, though eating thirty chickens a day, she could not by surfeit extinguish her appetite but hungered for still more of them. While their substance was being thus exhausted on her, her relatives took pity on her and made supplication to the man of God. He came and offered prayers, and by placing his hand over water, tracing the sign of salvation, and telling her to drink, healed the disease. And so completely did he blunt the excess of her appetite that thereafter a small piece of chicken each day satisfied her need for food. Such was the cure this illness received.

ᵇPr 28:1.

10. A girl still kept at home was suddenly possessed by the action of an evil demon. Her father hastened to the godly man with loud and clamorous entreaty, begging that his daughter be cured. Having prayed, he ordered the demon to depart from the girl immediately. He replied that he had not entered her willingly but under the compulsion of magic spells; he even told the name of the man who had compelled him, and revealed that love was the cause of the enchantment.

11. On hearing this, the father did not contain the onrush of his anger or wait for his child's cure, but repairing to the official over the chief officials, presiding over several provinces, he brought a charge against the man and related the crime.[7] On appearing before the court, the man denied the charge and called it a false accusation. The father, having no other witness to call except the demon who had served the magic, begged the judge to hasten to the man of God and receive the evidence of the demon. When the judge replied that it was in accordance with neither secular nor divine law to carry out a judicial interrogation in a place of asceticism, the father of the girl promised to bring the godly Macedonius to the courtroom. He hastened to him, persuaded him, and brought him. The judge, by taking his seat outside his residence, became not a judge but a spectator; the role of judges was performed by the great Macedonius, who used the power within him to order the demon to leave off his usual deceit and give a true account of the whole tragedy of the affair.[8] Under the pressure of the greatest duress, the demon pointed out the man who had compelled him by magical charms and also the maidservant who had administered the potion to the girl. But when he was pressing on to tell of further things he had done under the compulsion of certain others – how he burnt the house of one man, destroyed the property of another, and injured someone else in some other way –, the man of God ordered him to keep silence and to depart somewhere far from the girl and from the city. As if obeying an enactment of the Master, he did what was ordered and rushed away at once.

12. Thus freeing the girl from this frenzy, the man of God also rescued the wretch from the charge and prevented the judge's sentence of death, saying it was not right to inflict the death penalty on the evidence provided by the demon, but rather to grant him the preservation earned by repentance. This miracle is itself sufficient to

show the abundance of divine power supplied to him. I shall, however, relate others as well.

13. A woman of the very wealthiest of the nobility – she was called Astrion – lost her wits; she could recognize none of her household, and could not bear to take food or drink. She continued delirious for a very long time. The others called it the action of a demon, while the doctors named it a disease of the brain. When all skill had been expended and no help came from it, the woman's husband – he was Ovodianus, a curial of the highest rank – hastened to this godly person, described his wife's affliction and begged to obtain a cure. The inspired man consented, went to the house and addressed earnest supplication to God. On completing his prayer, he bade water be brought, traced the sign of salvation and bade her drink it. When the doctors objected, saying that drinking cold water would increase the disease, the husband dismissed the whole company of them and gave his wife the drink. As she drank, she came to herself and became sane: totally freed of her affliction, she recognized the man of God, and begging to take his hand placed it on her eyes and moved it to her mouth. From then on she continued to have a sound mind.

14. While he was embracing the mountain life, a shepherd looking for lost sheep came to the spot where the man of God was. It was the dead of night, and thick snow was falling. He saw, as he related, a great fire lit just by him and two figures clothed in white supplying wood for the fire, for, contributing his zeal, he enjoyed divine aid.

15. He had also received the gift of prophecy. On one occasion there came to him a general distinguished for piety – who is ignorant of the virtue of Lupicinus?[9] He was worried, he said, about some men who were bringing him provisions by sea from the imperial city. Fifty days had passed, he declared, since they put out from harbor, and yet he had received no word of them. Without hesitation the other replied, 'One ship, my friend, is lost, but the other will reach the harbor of Seleucia tomorrow.' This he heard the holy tongue say, and he learnt from experience the truth of the words.

16. To omit the rest, I shall recount what involved ourselves. My mother lived with my father for thirteen years without becoming the mother of children, for she was sterile and prevented by nature from bearing fruit. This did not greatly trouble her, for, instructed in the

things of God, she had faith that this was advantageous. But childlessness greatly distressed my father, who went round everywhere, begging the servants of God to ask for children for him from God. The others promised to pray and bade him acquiesce in the divine will; but this man of God gave an explicit assurance that he would ask for a single son from the Creator of the universe, and promised to obtain his petition. When three years had passed and the assurance had not been fulfilled, my father hastened again to demand what had been promised. The other told him to send his wife. When my mother arrived, the man of God said he would ask for a child and obtain one, and that it would be fitting to give the child back to the one who gave it. When my mother begged to receive only spiritual salvation and escape from hellfire, he replied: 'In addition to that the munificent one will also give you a son, for to those who ask sincerely he grants their petitions twofold'. My mother returned form there bearing away the blessing contained in his assurance. And in the fourth year of the promise she conceived and bore a burden in her womb; she went to the holy man to show the sheaves of the seeds of his blessing.[10]

17. In the faith month of her pregnancy there occurred a danger of miscarriage. She again sent to her new Elisha[c] — her affliction prevented her from hastening herself —, to remind him that she had not wanted to become the mother of children and to confront him with his promises. Seeing from a distance the coming of the messenger, he recognized him and knew the cause, for during the night the Master had revealed to him both the affliction and the cure. So taking his stick, he arrived with this support; on entering the house, he gave, as usual, the greeting of peace. 'Have confidence,' he said, 'and do not fear; for the giver will not rescind the gift, unless you transgress the agreements made. You promised to give back what will be given you and to consecrate it to God's service.' 'That,' replied my mother, 'is how I both wish and pray to give birth, for I think failure in giving birth preferable to rearing the child otherwise.'[11] 'Then drink this water,' said the man of God, 'and you will feel God's help.' So she drank as he had directed, and the danger of a miscarriage vanished. Such were the miracles of our Elisha.

[c]Cf. 2 Kgs 4:16.

18. I myself often enjoyed his blessing and teaching. To exhort me he often said: 'You were born, my child, with much toil: I spent many nights begging this alone of God, that your parents should earn the name they received after your birth. So live a life worthy of this toil. Before you were born, you were offered up in promise. Offerings to God are revered by all, and are not to be touched by the multitude: so it is fitting that you do not admit the base impulses of the soul, but perform, speak, and desire those things alone that serve God, the giver of the laws of virtue.' Such was the exhortation that the godly man always continued to give me; I remember his words and have been taught the gift of God. But since I do not display his exhortation in my actions, I beg to receive God's help through his prayer, and to live the remainder of my life according to his instructions.

19. The type of man he was and the labors by which he attracted divine grace, these stories are sufficient to demonstrate. Even in this life the close of his labors received due honor. All the citizens and aliens, and those entrusted to administer the great offices, bearing the sacred bier on their shoulders, conveyed it to the shrine of the victorious martyrs, and buried the holy body, dear to God, with those godly men, Aphrahat and Theodosius.[12] His fame has remained inextinguishable, and no length of time will be able to obliterate it. We, on bringing this narrative to an end, have reaped the fragrance that comes from narrating it.

NOTES

1. Macedonius was a hermit on Mt Silpius near Antioch for a total of seventy years (§2). He was already in 'old age' when ordained priest by Flavian of Antioch in the 380s (see n.3 below), but he outlived Zeno (§1), who died in the middle or late 410s (see XII, note 1). A chronology that would reconcile the data must run as follows: born *c.*330, an ascetic from *c.*350, ordained *c.*385, died *c.*420. See also the following note.
2. For the conversion of Theodoret's mother to the devout life see IX.8; the date was 386. Canivet, *Le monachisme syrien*, 162, deduces therefrom a chronology for Macedonius: if he lived on barley for forty years till a change of diet at the very time of the first visit paid him by Theodoret's mother soon after her conversion, then Macedonius will have entered on his ascetic labors *c.*346. But what in fact we read here is that she had been Macedonius's friend and supplying him with barley for 'a very long time' before his change of diet. This implies a somewhat later chronology, and is compatible with the one proposed in the preceding note.
3. Flavian was bishop of Antioch from 381 to 404, but Theodoret implies that Macedonius's ordination occurred in the earlier part of this period. Cp. the similar ordinations of Acepsimas (XV.4) and Salamanes (XIX.2). This honorary ordination of holy men was doubtless partly motivated by a desire to place their charisms firmly under the aegis of the established ecclesiastical hierarchy. Ordination of this kind, involving no pastoral charge, was declared invalid by the sixth Canon of the Council of Chalcedon (451).
4. This is the celebrated Riot of the Statues in 387, which occasioned John Chrysostom's *Homilies on the Statues* and several orations by Libanius (Loeb *Selected Works*, II: 237–407); see too Theodoret, *Eccl. Hist.* V.19. Tension in the city, due to high taxation, erupted into a riot in which statues of the imperial family were overturned and insulted. Two imperial commissioners arrived to investigate the affair and discipline the city: Ellebichus, *magister militum per Orientem* (Commander-in-Chief of the eastern armies) and Caesarius, *magister officiorum* (head of the civil service). The Antiochenes supposed they had come to order the destruction of the city; the massacre at Thessalonica in 390 is evidence that this fear was not irrational. In fact, the city was treated comparatively mildly, after effective intercession by bishop Flavian, the rhetorician Libanius — and the monks.
5. John Chrysostom, *Homily on the Statues* XVII, gives the following version of Macedonius's words to the commissioners: 'The statues which have been overturned have been set up again and resumed their appearance, and what was done has been rapidly set right; but if you kill the image of God, how will you be able to revoke your offence? How revive those destroyed, and restore their souls to their bodies?' The contrast between this 'frankness of speech' and the obsequious groveling of Chrysostom and Libanius is notable. The holy man could speak in such forthright terms because of his God-given authority; and in situations of conflict, it could be convenient for both sides to yield to this authority. See further R. Price, 'Holy Men's Letters of Rebuke', *Studia Patristica* xvi: 56–59.
6. P. Brown, 'The Rise and Function of the Holy Man,' nn.7–8, notes that Macedonius's freedom to rebuke high military officials had been earned by his already befriending such officials (§6, 15). Alexander the Acoemete (d. 430) rebuked officials and got no thanks for his pains, for he did not deign to befriend them beforehand (see *Life of Alexander*, PO VI: 643ff.).

Macedonius

7. For the judicial role of this official, the *Comes Orientis*, see W. Liebeschuetz, *Antioch*, 110-2. On magic in the Late Antique world, see P. Brown in *Religion and Society in the Age of St Augustine*, 119-146.

8. Canivet (note *ad loc.*) supposes that the governor coopted Macedonius onto the bench as an assessor, but Theodoret's account is not to be read so literally. By consenting to hear the demon only outside the courtroom, the judge treated Macedonius's evidence as judicially inadmissable.

9. Lupicinus was *magister equitum* (commander of the cavalry) in the East from 364 to 367 (see *Prosopography of the Later Roman Empire*, I: 520). He was a devout Christian, but is criticized by the historian Ammianus (XX.1.2) for arrogance, avarice, and cruelty. He is the recipient of Theodoret, *ep.* 90.

10. For the piety of Theodoret's mother, and his own birth in 393, see Introduction, p. xi.

11. For a mother, in gratitude for the gift of a son, dedicating him to the Lord from his birth, see *Life of Daniel the Stylite* 2-4.

12. See, above, X.8.

XIV
MAËSYMAS

I KNOW THAT MANY other luminaries of piety have been conspicuous near Antioch: Severus the Great, Peter the Egyptian, Eutychius, Cyril, Moses, and Malchus, and very many others who trod the same path;[1] but if we were to try to record the life of them all, limitless time would not be enough for us. In any case, the reading of a long account is for most people tedious. Judging therefore the lives of those omitted from those recorded, let everyone praise and emulate them, and reap benefit. I myself shall pass over to the meadows of Cyrrhus, and display, as far as is possible, the bloom of fragrant and beautiful flowers therein.

2. In the times before our own there was a certain Maësymas,[2] who was Syrian in his language, had had a rustic upbringing and manifested every form of virtue. Having been conspicuous in the solitary life, he was entrusted with the care of a village. Acting as priest and pasturing the divine flock, he spoke and performed those things which the divine law prescribes. It is said that for a very long time he did not change either his tunic or his goat's hair cloak, but sewed other rags on to the tears that occurred in them and in this way

looked after his old age. So zealously did he attend to the care of strangers and the poor that he threw open his doors to all who came. He is said to have had two jars, one of grain and the other of oil, out of which he always supplied those in need, and which he always had full, since the blessing given to the widow of Zarephath[a] had been attached to these jars as well: 'the same Lord is of all, rich for all who call upon him',[b] and just as he ordered her jar and cruse to pour forth, providing the sheaves of the seeds of her hospitality, so he gave to this wonderful man an abundance to equal his zeal.

3. He received from the God of the universe much grace also to perform miracles. I shall recall one or two miracles, but omit the rest, in my haste to proceed to other ascetics. A certain woman adorned both in birth and faith had a son, very young, who fell victim to an illness, and whom she showed to numerous physicians. When their art was defeated and the physicians had written him off and said explicitly that the child would die, the woman did not abandon her better hopes, but emulating the Shunnamite woman[c] had her carriage attached to mules. Placing in it herself and her child, she repaired to the godly man, and showing by tears her natural distress begged for his aid. Taking the child in his hands and placing it at the foot of the altar, he lay face downwards as he entreated the Physician of souls and bodies. Gaining his request, he restored the son in good health to his mother. I myself heard this from the very woman who witnessed the miracle and obtained the healing of her son.

4. The story is told that the master of this village once made a visit – he was Letoius, preeminent in the council of Antioch, but engulfed in the darkness of impiety.[3] He demanded crops from the peasants with more severity than was needed. The man of God advised and exhorted him to show kindness, and expatiated on pity and mercy. But he remained implacable, until he learnt by experience the penalty for obstinacy. When he had to depart, and his carriage was ready and, taking his seat, he ordered the muleteer to urge on the mules, they pulled with all their strength, in eager haste to pull the carriage-pole, yet the wheels were as if fastened with iron and lead. When all the peasants together tried to move the wheels with bars

[a] Cf. 1 Kgs 17:9-16.   [b] Rom 10:12.   [c] Cf. 2 Kgs 4:22.

and achieved nothing more, one of Letoius' well-wishers, who was seated next to him, indicated the cause, telling how the holy old man was imprecating a curse and that it was right to conciliate him.[4] Accordingly, leaping from the carriage, he entreated the one he had insulted, and falling prostrate at his feet and clasping his dirty rags begged him to relax his anger. The other, accepting the petition and transmitting it to the Master, freed the wheels from their invisible bonds and made the chariot move as usual.

5. Many other stories of this kind are told about this godly person. One can learn from them that those who choose to practise philosophy are harmed not at all by life in towns and villages; for this man and those like him responsible for the service of God have shown that it is possible even for those who go about among many to attain the very summit of the virtues.[5] May I ascend a short way the foot-hills at least of this summit, aided by their prayers.

NOTES

1. Severus, Peter the Egyptian, Moses, and Malchus are likewise listed in Theodoret, *Eccl. Hist.* IV.28(25) as monks on Mt Silpius during the latter part of the fourth century.
2. Maësymas was an ascetic village priest in the region of Cyrrhus. There is a single, and vague, chronological indication: Theodoret, in dating him to 'the times before our own', means that he died before Theodoret became bishop of Cyrrhus in 423.
3. The Letoii were one of the greatest curial families of Antioch. the best known Letoius was elderly in 364, so the one referred to here is more likely to have been a descendant or relative of a generation or two later. See P. Petit, *Libanius*, 349, 399. It is evidence of the religious independence of rural Syria that this village was a Christian one, with a resident priest, although it belonged to the estates of a pagan urban family.
4. Cp. the sudden illness and death of a curial of Antioch who was oppressing the tanners and rejected the pleas on their behalf made by Symeon Stylites (*Syriac Life* 92).
5. Cp. IV.1 and XXV.1 for this theme.

XV
ACEPSIMAS

AT THE SAME TIME lived Acepsimas,[1] whose fame extends throughout the East. Immuring himself in a cell, he persevered for sixty years neither being seen nor speaking. Turning into himself and contemplating God, he received consolation from this, in accordance with the prophecy that says, 'Take delight in the Lord, and may he grant you the requests of your heart'.[a] He received the food that was brought to him by stretching his hand through a small hole. To prevent his being exposed to those who wished to see him, the hole was not dug straight through the thickness of the wall, but obliquely, being made in the shape of a curve. (The food brought him was lentils soaked in water.)

2. Once a week he came out at night to draw sufficient water from the nearby spring. On one occasion a shepherd pasturing his animals at a distance, when it was dark, saw him move. Presuming it was a wolf—for he walked bent double, laden with a quantity of iron—he got his sling ready to shoot a stone. But when his hand lost

[a] Ps 37:4.

all movement for a long time and could not launch the stone, until the man of God had drawn the water and returned, he realized his mistake, and after daybreak repaired to the retreat of virtue, related what had happened and begged forgiveness. He received the remission of his sin, not by hearing a voice speak but learning of his goodwill from the gestures of his hand.

3. Someone else, wishing out of malign curiosity to discover what he spent all his time doing, had the presumption to climb up a plane-tree that grew alongside the enclosure. But he immediately reaped the fruits of his presumption: with half his body paralysed, from the crown of his head to his feet, he became a suppliant accusing himself of his sin. The other predicted that his health would be restored by the cutting down of the plane-tree – for to prevent another doing the same deed and suffering the same penalty, he ordered the tree to be cut down immediately. The cutting down of the tree was followed by the remission of the punishment. Such was the self-control this inspired man exercised; such was the grace he had received from the Umpire.

4. When about to set out on his migration from here, he foretold that he would come to the end of life after fifty days, and received everyone who wished to see him. The leader of the Church, on his arrival, pressed him to accept the yoke of a priest. 'I know, father,' he said, 'both the elevation of your philosophy and the excess of my poverty, but entrusted as I am with the episcopal office, it is in virtue of the latter not of the former that I perform ordinations. Accept then (he continued) the gift of the priesthood, a gift to which my hand ministers, but which is supplied by the grace of the all-holy Spirit.' To this he is said to have replied, 'Since I am emigrating from here in a few days, I shall not quarrel about this. If I were going to live for a long time, I would utterly have fled from the heavy and fearful burden of the priesthood, terrified at answering for the deposit. But since in no long time I shall depart and leave what is here, I shall accept obediently what you command.' And so at once, without any compulsion, the one awaited the grace on bended knee, and the other laying on his hand ministered to the Spirit.[2]

5. After surviving the priesthood for a few days, he exchanged one life for another, and took up the one without old age or sorrow in place of the one full of anxiety. Everyone wished to seize his body

and proposed to carry it off to his own village, but someone resolved the dispute by revealing the oaths of the saint, saying the saint had extracted oaths to commit it to burial in this same place.

6. Thus it was that the citizens of heaven attended to frugality even after death; neither when alive could they endure to entertain haughty thoughts, nor after death did they grasp at honor from men. Instead, they transferred all their love to the Bridegroom, like modest women who are eager to be loved and praised by their spouses but despise adulation from others. Because of this the Bridegroom made them celebrated even against their will, and gave them an abundant share of renown among men; for whenever someone pursues the things of God and asks for the things of heaven, he adds to these things innumerable others, granting their requests many times over. This he enacted when he said, 'Ask for the kingdom of God and his righteousness, and all the rest shall be added to you'.[b] And again, 'He who leaves father and mother and brothers and wife and children, for my sake and for the Gospel, in this age will receive a hundredfold, and in the age to come will inherit eternal life'.[c] This he both declared and accomplished. May we, instructed by word and example and supported by the prayers of these men, be able to 'press on toward the goal for the prize of the upward call in Christ Jesus our Lord'.[d]

[b] Mt 6:33.   [c] Mt 19:29.   [d] Phil 3:14.

NOTES

1. Acepsimas is mentioned in Theodoret, *Eccl. Hist.* IV.28(25) as a recluse for sixty years in the region of Cyrrhus, in the second half of the fourth century. It is clear from §4 that he died before Theodoret became bishop of Cyrrhus in 423.
2. For this honorary ordination of holy men, cp. XIII.4, with note *ad loc.*

XVI
MARON

AFTER HIM I SHALL RECALL Maron,[1] for he too adorned the godly choir of the saints. Embracing the open-air life, he repaired to a hill-top formerly honored by the impious.[2] Consecrating to God the precinct of demons on it, he lived there, pitching a small tent which he seldom used. He practised not only the usual labors, but devised others as well, heaping up the wealth of philosophy.

2. The Umpire measured out grace according to his labors: so the munificent one gave in abundance the gift of healing, with the result that his fame circulated everywhere, attracted everyone from every side and taught by experience the truth of the report. One could see fevers quenched by the dew of his blessing, shivering quieted, demons put to flight, and varied diseases of every kind cured by a single remedy; the progeny of physicians apply to each disease the appropriate remedy, but the prayer of the saint is a common antidote for every distress.

3. He cured not only infirmities of the body, but applied suitable treatment to souls as well, healing this man's greed and that man's anger, to this man supplying teaching in self-control and to that providing

lessons in justice, correcting this man's intemperance and shaking up another man's sloth. Applying this mode of cultivation, he produced many plants of philosophy, and it was he who planted for God the garden that now flourishes in the region of Cyrrhus. A product of his planting was the great James, to whom one could reasonably apply the prophetic utterance, 'the righteous man will flower as the palm tree, and be multiplied like the cedar of Lebanon',[a] and also all the others whom, with God's help, I shall recall individually.

4. Attending in this way to the divine cultivation and treating souls and bodies alike, he himself underwent a short illness, so that we might learn the weakness of nature and the manliness of resolution, and departed from life. A bitter war over his body arose between his neighbors. One of the adjacent villages that was well-populated came out in mass, drove off the others and seized this thrice desired treasure;[3] building a great shrine, they reap benefit therefrom even to this day, honoring this victor with a public festival. We ourselves reap his blessing even at a distance; for sufficient for us instead of his tomb is his memory.

[a]Ps 92:12.

NOTES

1. Maron, while professing himself the disciple of Zebinas (XXIV.2) emerges from the *Rel. Hist.* as the first influential hermit of the region of Cyrrhus. His pattern of life in the open air, exposed to the extremes of the climate, was imitated by many — James (XXI), Limnaeus (XXII), and others (XXIII) — and gave the asceticism of Cyrrhestica a distinctive character, for elsewhere hermits normally lived in cells or caves. Since his disciple James entered on his labors in 402 (see XXI, note 1), Maron must still have been alive then; but he must have died before Theodoret came to Cyrrhus in 423, since it appears that they never met. It is surprising, in view of Maron's importance, that this chapter is so brief and sketchy. A partial explanation is provided by the fact that Maron's fame was eclipsed by that of his disciple James (XXI.3). Maron is also mentioned at VI.3, XXII.2, XXIV.2, XXX.1. He may be the 'Maron priest and monk' who received a letter from John Chrysostom (*ep.* 36) between 404 and 407, but he is not to be identified with Maron of Apamea.

2. The identification of this hill-top with Qalᶜat Kalota, six miles east of Telanissus, recently proposed by Pena and others, *Les reclus syriens*, 34, must be rejected, since this locality lay within the territory of Antioch, while Maron lived in that of Cyrrhus.

3. Maron himself wished to be buried with the hermit Zebinas (XXIV.2). For other instances of competiton to secure the bodies (dying or dead) of holy men, cp. X.8, XVII.10, XXI.9. When Symeon Stylites died, Antioch sent a whole convoy of notables and soldiers to seize his body from the local inhabitants and bring it into the city (Antony, *Life of Symeon* 29, in Festugière, *Antioche*, 374).

XVII
ABRAHAM

NOR WOULD IT BE PIOUS to pass over the memory of the wondrous Abraham[1], using as a pretext the fact that after the solitary life he adorned the episcopal chair; for because of this he would with good reason deserve to be remembered surely all the more, in that, when compelled to change his position in life, he did not alter his mode of life, but brought with him the hardships of asceticism, and completed his course of life beset simultaneously with the labors of a monk and the cares of a bishop.

2. This man too was a fruit of the region of Cyrrhus, for it was born and reared there that he gathered the wealth of ascetic virtue. Those who were with him say that he tamed his body with such vigils, standing, and fasting that for a long time he remained without movement, quite unable to walk. Freed of this weakness by divine providence, he resolved to run the risks of piety as the price of divine favor, and repaired to the Lebanon, where, he had heard, a large village was engulfed in the darkness of impiety. Hiding his monastic character under the mask of a trader, he with his companions brought along sacks as if coming to buy nuts—for this was the main produce

of the village. Renting a house, for which he paid the owners a small sum in advance, he kept quiet for three or four days. Then, little by little, he began in a soft voice to perform the divine liturgy. When they heard the singing of psalms, the public crier called out to summon everyone together. Men, children, and women assembled; they walled up the doors from outside, and heaping up a great pile of earth poured it down from the roof above. But when they saw them being suffocated and buried, and willing to do or say nothing apart from addressing prayer to God, they ceased from their frenzy, at the suggestion of their elders. Then opening the doors and pulling them out from the mass of earth, they told them to depart immediately.

3. At this very moment, however, collectors arrived to compel them to pay their taxes; some they bound, others they maltreated. But the man of God, oblivious of what had happened to them, and imitating the Master who when nailed to the cross showed concern for those who had done it, begged these collectors to carry out their work leniently. When they demanded guarantors, he voluntarily accepted the call, and promised to pay them a hundred gold pieces in a few days. Those who had performed so terrible a deed were overwhelmed with admiration at the man's benevolence; begging forgiveness for their outrage, they invited him to become their patron – for the village did not have a master; they themselves were both cultivators and masters.[2] He went to the city (it was Emesa), and finding some of his friends negotiated a loan for the hundred gold pieces; then returning to the village he fulfilled his promise on the appointed day.

4. On observing his zeal, they addressed their invitation to him still more zealously. When he promised his consent if they undertook to build a church, they begged him to start operations at once, and conducted the blessed man round, showing him the more appropriate sites, one recommending this one, another that. Having chosen the best one and laid the foundations, in a short time he put the roof on, and now that the building was ready bade them appoint a priest. When they said they would not choose anyone else and begged to take him as their father and shepherd, he received the grace of the priesthood. After spending three years with them and guiding them well towards the things of God, he got another of his companions appointed in his place and went back to his monastic dwelling.

5. Not to make the narrative long by narrating all he did—after gaining fame among them, he received the see of Carrhae, a city which was steeped in the sottishness of impiety and had given itself up to the frenzy of the demons. But after being honored by his cultivation and receiving the fire of his teaching, it has remained free of its former thorns, and abounds now in the crops of the Spirit, offering to God sheaves of ripe ears.³ The man of God did not perform this cultivation without labor; with innumerable labors and imitating the art of those entrusted with the treatment of bodies—in some cases sweetening by fomentation, in others contracting by astringent medicines, in others again applying surgery and cautery—he effected this sound state of health. His teaching and other attentions found support in the luster of his life. Illuminated by this, they hearkened to what he said and gladly welcomed what he did.

6. All the time of his episcopacy, bread was for him superfluous, water superfluous, a bed useless, and use of fire superfluous.⁴ At night he chanted forty psalms antiphonally, doubling the length of the prayers that occur in between; the rest of the night he sat on a chair, allowing a brief rest to his eyelids. That 'man will not live on bread alone' had been said by Moses the lawgiver,[a] and the Master recalled this utterance when he rejected the invitation of the devil;[b] but that living without water is among the things possible, we have nowhere been taught in the divine Scripture—even the great Elijah first satisfied this need from the brook, and then on going to the widow of Zarephath first told her to bring him water and then likewise asked for bread.[c] But this wonderful man throughout the time of his episcopacy took neither bread nor pulses nor greens cooked by fire and not even water, which is considered by those reputed clever about these things to be the first of the elements in utility; but it was lettuce, chicory, celery, and all plants of the kind that he made his food and drink, rendering superfluous the skills of baking and cooking. In the fruit-season fruit supplemented his needs. His food he took after the evening liturgy.

7. While wearing down his body with such labors, he was inexhaustible in the services he rendered others. For strangers who came

[a]Deut 8:3.   [b]Cf. Mt 4:4.   [c]Cf. 1 Kgs 17:6–11.

a bed was ready, glistening and select rolls were offered, wine of a fine bouquet, fish and vegetables and all the other things that go with them; he himself at midday sat with the diners, offering to each portions of the fare provided, giving goblets to all and bidding them drink, in imitation of his great namesake – I mean the Patriarch – who served his guests but did not dine with them.[d]

8. Spending the whole day on the lawsuits of those in dispute, some he would persuade to be reconciled with each other, while to those who would not obey his gentle teaching he applied compulsion.[5] No wrongdoer went away victorious over justice through audacity; to the wronged party he always accorded the just man's portion, making him invincible and stronger than the one who wanted to wrong him. He was like an excellent physician who always prevents the excess of the humors and contrives the equilibrium of the elements.

9. Even the emperor desired to see him, for fame has wings and easily publishes everything, good and bad. He summoned him, and when he arrived embraced him, and considered his rustic goat's hair cloak more honorable than his own purple robe. The choir of the empresses clasped his hands and knees; and they made supplication to a man who did not even understand Greek.[6]

10. And so for emperors and all men philosophy is a thing worthy of respect; and when they die its lovers and adherents win still greater renown. This can be learnt from all sorts of examples, but not least from the case of this inspired man. For when he died and the emperor learnt of it, he wanted to bury him in one of the sacred shrines, but realizing that it would be right to restore to the sheep the body of the shepherd, he himself escorted it at the front of the procession, followed by the choir of empresses, all the governors and governed, soldiers and civilians.[7] With the same zeal the city of Antioch received him, and the cities after it, until he reached the great river. Along the bank of the Euphrates there hastened townspeople and foreigners. Everyone both of the country and of the adjoining region pressed forward to enjoy his blessing; many rod-bearers accompanied the bier, to deter through fear of blows those who tried to strip the body of its clothing or who wanted to take pieces therefrom. One

[d]Cf. Gen 18:8.

could hear some singing psalms, others dirges; one woman with sighs called him patron, another foster-father, another shepherd and teacher; one man in tears named him father, another helper and protector. With such eulogy and lament did they entrust to the tomb this holy and sacred body.

11. I myself, out of admiration at the way he did not alter his mode of life when changing his position in life, and did not as bishop love a relaxed regime but increased his ascetic labors, have listed him in the history of the monks, and have not separated him from the company he loved, in my desire to receive blessing from this source as well.

NOTES

1. Abraham was an ascetic, originally of Cyrrhus, famous for his missionary work. He was active as far afield as Phoenicia (§2-4), and was finally made bishop of the largely pagan city of Carrhae in Mesopotamia (§5). He died at Constantinople, during a visit to the imperial family (§9-10). This visit is to be dated to the 420s: the reference to 'empresses' (§9) implies a *terminus post quem* of 421, when Theodosius II married Eudocia.

2. Peasants, whether freeholders or tenants, badly needed patrons to protect them against oppression by landowners or officials. This is the theme of Libanius, *Oration* XLVII, *De patrociniis* (Loeb *Selected Works*, II: 500ff). Holy men could be active in this work; cp. XIV.4, and XXVI, note 33 below. They were popular patrons, both because of their influence and because they were disinterested: lay patrons had to be materially rewarded and sometimes reduced their clients to virtual serfs (e.g. Libanius, *Or*. XXXIX.10-11). P. Brown, 'The Rise and Function of the Holy Man', 115-129, is fundamental for this topic, though he exaggerates the extent to which holy men because involved in this work.

3. But we learn from Procopius, *History of the Wars* III.13.7 that Carrhae was still largely pagan as late as the sixth century.

4. For ascetic bishops, see I, note 5, above.

5. For episcopal jurisdiction, which took up a great deal of bishops' time, see A.H.M. Jones, *The Later Roman Empire*, 480, and P. Brown, *Augustine of Hippo*, 195-6.

6. The emperor is Theodosius II (408-450), the empresses his sister Pulcheria and wife Eudocia. For Pulcheria's exceptional piety, and her veneration for holy men and relics, see K. Holum, *Theodosian Empresses*, 91-146.

7. Evidently, the imperial family would simply have attended the initial ceremony at Constantinople. For this *adventus* (solemn translation) of relics, cp. the reinterment of the relics of John Chrysostom at Constantinople in 438, attended by Theodosius and Pulcheria (Theodoret, *Eccl. Hist.* V.36; Holum, 184-5), or the conveying, in a huge procession, of the body of Symeon Stylites from Telanissus to Antioch (Festugière, *Antioche*, 369-375). See too, P. Brown, *The Cult of the Saints*, 98-100.

XVIII
EUSEBIUS
(of Asikha)

TO THE SAINTS described above I shall add the great Eusebius, who died a short time ago.¹ During a lifespan of very many years he endured labor equal to this time, accumulated virtue equal to this labor, and carried off therefrom a profit many times greater, for the Umpire surpasses the contests in the munificence of his gifts in return. Entrusting the care of himself at first to others, he followed where they led, for they too were men of God, athletes, and gymnasts of virtue. After passing time with them, and well and truly acquiring knowledge of philosophy, he embraced the solitary life. Repairing to a mountain ridge—adjacent to it is a large village which they call Asikhâ—and using a mere enclosure whose stones he did not even join together with clay, he continued for the rest of his life to endure the hardship of the open air, covered in clothing of skins, feeding on chick-peas and beans soaked in water; and sometimes he ate dried figs, trying thereby in some way to support the weakness of his body. When he reached extreme old age, such that he lost most of his teeth, he changed neither his food nor his lodging. Frozen in winter and burnt in summer, he bore with endurance the contrasting temperatures of the air, his face shriveled up and all the limbs of his body wasted away. He so exhausted his body with many labors that his belt could not even stay on his waist, but slipped downwards, since there was nothing to hinder it; for his buttocks and hips had been worn away and provided an easy downward passage for the belt. He therefore contrived to keep his belt up by sewing it to his tunic.

2. Intercourse with the multitude exhausted him completely; for perceiving the vision of God continuously, he was not willing to draw his mind away from it. Nevertheless, despite the fervor of his love, he allowed a few of his friends to unblock the doorway and pass within; offering them the nourishment of the divine oracles, he ordered them, when they departed again, to block up the doorway with clay. After judging it better to avoid meeting these few, he walled up the entrance completely, fixing in the doorway a huge stone. Through a hole he spoke with a few of his friends, but without being seen, for so was it contrived; and through it too he received his meagre food. And when again he refused everyone his conversation, he honored me alone with that sweet voice dear to God; and when I wanted to leave, he would keep me for a long time while he discoursed on the things of heaven.[2]

3. Many visited him to ask for the gift of his blessing, and he was extremely vexed at the disturbance they caused. So without thinking of his old age or reflecting on the weakness that oppressed him, he climbed over the enclosure—though hard to scale even for those in full vigor—and replied to the nearby community of ascetics. Using again a small enclosure at the angle of the wall, he pursued the contest by means of his usual labors.[3]

4. The superior of this flock, a man full of every virtue, said that Eusebius would take fifteen dried figs to get through the seven weeks of the holy fast. This contest he maintained during a life of more than ninety years, although worn away with indescribable weakness. But stronger than his weakness was his zeal, and his yearning for God made everything smooth and easy. Dripping with these exertions, he reached the finishing-post of his course, beholding the Umpire and eager for the crowns. I myself request the intercession which I enjoyed when he was alive; for I am confident that he is living and has a still purer access to God.

NOTES

1. Eusebius of Asikha was another ascetic of the region of Cyrrhus. He combined reclusion with the open-air life by living within an unroofed enclosure, like Marana and Cyra (XXIX.2). He died 'a short time ago'—i.e. in the 430s. The figure of ninety years for his lifespan (§4) may be merely conventional (cp. XX.3). Theodoret knew him personally (§2).

2. For other recluses unblocking their doors to admit Theodoret, as their bishop, see XX.3, XXII.2, XXV.2, XXIX.5.

3. For archaeological evidence of towers attached to monasteries that housed recluses, see Lassus, *Sanctuaires Chrétiens*, 280, and Pena and others, *Les reclus syriens*, 165-254.

XIX
Salamanes

SINCE I THINK I would be wronging virtue if I were not also to make known to posterity the life of the wonderful Salamanes,[1] but allow it to be buried by oblivion, I shall, in summary, make the narration. To the west of the river Euphrates, lying on the very bank, is a village called Capersana. Originating from this village, he embraced the quiet life. Finding a small hut in the village on the opposite bank, he immured himself, leaving neither door nor window. Once a year he would dig a hole at ground level and receive his food for the whole year, never speaking to anyone; and he continued in this way not for a short time but for the longest possible.

2. The bishop of the city to which the village belonged, learning of the man's virtue, came with the intention of giving him the gift of the priesthood; getting in by digging through a part of the hut, he laid on his hand and performed the prayer, and spoke to him at length, explaining the grace resulting. Without hearing any speech he departed, after ordering the hole to be walled up again.

3. On another occasion the inhabitants of his village of origin, crossing the bridge of the river[2] by night and digging through his cell,

seized and carried him, neither resisting nor ordering it, along to their own village, where at daybreak they built a similar hut, where they immediately immured him. He maintained silence as before, saying nothing to anyone. But after a few days the inhabitants of the village on the other side, also coming by night and digging through the cell, led him back to themselves, while he made no protest, neither struggling to remain nor returning back eagerly. Thus had he made himself totally dead to this life, and could utter truthfully the apostolic saying, 'I have been crucified with Christ; I no longer live, but Christ lives in me; and the life I now live in the flesh I live by faith in the Son of God, who loved me and gave himself for me'.[a] Such was this man; for these particulars suffice to show the whole purpose of his life. I myself, after reaping thence a blessing, shall proceed to give an account of the others.

[a] Gal 2:20-21.

NOTES

1. Salamanes was a recluse in a village on the east bank of the Euphrates; it lay opposite Capersana, a village north of Zeugma. His dates are unknown.
2. Possibly simply 'the *ford* of the river' (the Greek *poros* is ambiguous); but a bridge across the Euphrates at Capersana is mentioned by Ammianus Marcellinus, XVIII.8.1.

XX
Maris

THERE IS A VILLAGE called by us Omêros. Here the inspired Maris[1] built a small hut and continued immured in it for thirty-seven years. It received much rain from the neighboring mountain; in the winter season it even poured out streams of water. Both townsmen and countrymen are aware what harm this causes bodies; to the peasants are manifest the diseases that are produced thereby. Nevertheless, not even this induced this sacred person to change his cell, but he maintained his endurance until he had accomplished his course.

2. He passed the earlier part of his life in the labors of virtue, whence he preserved purity in both body and soul. This he told me plainly, informing me that his body had remained chaste, just as it had left his mother's womb, and this although he had taken part in many festivals of martyrs when young,[2] and captivated the crowds with the beauty of his voice—for he continued for a long time to be a cantor, and was radiant in bloom of body. Nevertheless, neither his bodily beauty nor his brilliance of voice nor his mixing with the multitude injured his beauty of soul, but living like recluses he looked after his own soul, and then increased his virtue through the labors of reclusion.

3. I often enjoyed his company: he would tell me to unblock the door, embrace me as I entered and make extended discourses on philosophy. He was remarkable too for his simplicity, and utterly abhorred subtlety of character; and he loved poverty more than the greatest wealth. During a life of ninety years he wore clothing made of goat's hair; bread and a little salt supplied his need for food.

4. Having desired for a long time to witness a celebration of the spiritual and mystical sacrifice, he asked for the offering of the divine gift to be made there. I consented gladly. Bidding the divine vessels be brought – the place was not distant – and using the hands of deacons as an altar, I offered the divine and saving sacrifice. He was filled with every spiritual joy and thought he was seeing heaven, and said that he had never experienced such delight.[3] I myself, whom he loved so warmly, thought I would be wronging him if I did not eulogize him even after death, and that I would be wronging others if I did not put forward this excellent philosophy for imitation. And now, after begging to receive help from him, I shall bring this account to an end.

NOTES

1. Maris, again of the region of Cyrrhus, became an ascetic in his youth, and lived on for around seventy years (§3), the last thirty-seven of which were spent in strict reclusion (§1). Theodoret knew him personally (§3).

2. At festivals of the saints 'the greatest cleavage of all in late-antique urban society was bridged: for a delightful and perilous moment, the compartments segregating the sexes in public broke down' P. Brown, *The Cult of the Saints*, 43. Annual concourse round the graves of martyrs can be traced back to the second century (*Martyrdom of Polycarp* 18), and became of major social importance in the fourth and fifth centuries, replacing the old pagan festivals.

3. For the frequency or infrequency of hermits receiving communion, cp. XII.5, with note *ad loc.* The unusual mode of celebrating the eucharist described here was the subject of later canonical legislation in Syria; see Canivet, *Le monachisme syrien*, 232.

XXI
JAMES
(of Cyrrhestica)

NOW THAT WE HAVE PROCEEDED through the contests of the athletes of virtue described above, narrating in summary their laborious exercises, their exertions in the contests and their most glorious and splendid victories, let us now record, and leave to posterity as a profitable memorial, the way of life of those still living, who contend magnificently and strive to surpass their predecessors in exertion. For just as the life of the conspicuous saints of the past brought the greatest benefit to their successors, so the accounts of these men will become models for those after us.

2. At the head of these I shall place the great James,[1] for he has precedence over the others both in time and in labor, and it is by emulating him that his emulators do wondrous and extraordinary things. It has turned out, I know not how, that this name has come at the head of both the departed and those still alive; for in recounting the life of the former I placed at the head the divine James who scattered the Persian army by prayer and, when the surrounding walls of the town fell down, both refused to allow the capture of the city and forced the enemy to flee by sending against them gnats and mosquitoes.[2]

Therefore let the man with the same name and the same ways come at the head of the company of the contestants still alive, not for the reason that he shares the name, but because he also emulated his virtue and became himself a model of philosophy for others.

3. A companion of the great Maron and a recipient of his divine teaching, he has eclipsed his teacher by greater labors.[3] For Maron had a precinct of the ancient imposture as enclosure, pitched a tent of hairy skins, and used this to ward off the assaults of rain and snow. But this man, bidding farewell to all these things, tent and hut and enclosure, has the sky for roof, and lets in all the contrasting assaults of the air, as he is now inundated by torrential rain, now frozen by frost and snow, at other times burnt and consumed by the rays of the sun, and exercises endurance over everything. Competing as if in the body of another, and striving with zeal to overcome the nature of the body—for clad in this mortal and passible one he lives as in an impassible one—, and practising in a body the life without a body, he exclaims with the inspired Paul, 'Though walking in the flesh, we do not wage war according to the flesh, for our weapons are not fleshly but mighty through God for the destruction of strongholds, as we destroy arguments and every high thing exalted against the knowledge of God, and take every thought captive for obedience to Christ'.[a]

4. For these contests that surpass nature he rehearsed by means of lesser labors: it was by earlier immuring himself in a small cell, freeing his soul from the tumults outside and nailing his mind to the thought of God that he engaged in the rehearsal of complete virtue. After training himself perfectly and accustoming his soul to excellent labors, he dared greater contests. Repairing to that mountain which is thirty stades distant from this town,[4] he has made it distinguished and revered, although formerly it was totally undistinguished and sterile. So great is the blessing it is confidently believed to have now received that the soil on it has been quite exhausted by those coming from all sides to carry it off for their benefit.

5. Living in this place he is observed by all comers, since he has, as I said, no cave or tent or hut or enclosure or obstructing wall; but he is to be seen praying or resting, standing or sitting, in health or in the

[a] 2 Co 10:3-5.

grip of some infirmity, so that it is unceasingly under the eyes of spectators that he strives in combat and repels the necessities of nature — nor are other men who have had a respectable upbringing ready to evacuate excrement in the presence of strangers, let alone a man trained in the highest philosophy. And I mention this, not having learnt it from another, but having myself been a witness. Fourteen years ago,[5] a grave illness came upon him which caused him a condition to be expected in one with a mortal body. It was the height of summer, and the heat of the sun's rays was kindled more intensely, with a lulling of the winds and the air remaining motionless. The disease was a flux of bile moving downwards, hurting the guts, causing pressure and forcing one to run outside. It was then that I witnessed the great endurance of this man. For while very many men of the country had assembled with the intention of seizing the victorious body, he sat there torn by contrary impulses: while nature pressed him to go and evacuate, shame before the attendant crowd compelled him to stay in the same position. Noticing this, I addressed many exhortations to those who had come, and many threats, ordering them to go away. Finally I applied to them my episcopal authority, and in the evening, with great effort, sent them away. But even after their departure the man of God was not defeated by nature, but maintained his endurance until the dead of night set in and compelled everyone to go home.

6. Coming to him again on the next day, I saw that the burning heat had become still more intense and that the fever that beset him was nourished and increased by the fire without; so alleging a headache, I said that the impact of the sun's rays was causing me discomfort, and asked him to improvise for me some slight shade by him. He gave the order, and by fixing three stakes and putting two cloaks on them we contrived some shade. When he bid me go inside, I replied, 'It would be disgraceful, father, for me, who am young and strong, to obtain this relief, while you, who are beset by a violent fever and need such solace, sit outside, receiving the impact of the sun's rays. Therefore (I continued) if you want me to enjoy the shade, come and share with me this scanty tent; for I wish to stay beside you, but am hindered by the rays.' On hearing this plea he consented, and chose to render me service.

7. When we were enjoying the shade together, I started on another plea, and said I needed to lie down, since my hip found sitting

painful. Again he begged me to lie down, and heard in reply that I could not bear to lie down and see him seated: 'Therefore,' I said, 'if you want me to enjoy this rest as well, let us lie down together, father, for I will not have the embarrassment of lying down alone.' By this plea I outwitted his endurance and gave him the relief of lying down.

8. Now that he was stretched out on the ground, I made agreeable remarks to him, to make his soul more cheerful; and putting my hand inside his clothing, I tried gently to rub his back. It was then that I perceived the great load of iron that bound his waist and his neck; and other chains, two in front and two behind, extending obliquely from the circle round his neck to the circle below, and forming the shape of the letter X, connected the two circles to each other, both in front and behind; and beneath his clothing his arms bore other bonds of this kind round his elbows. On perceiving this tremendously heavy load, I begged him to assist his sick body, which could not bear at the same time both the voluntary load and the involuntary infirmity. 'At the moment, father,' I said, 'the fever is doing the work of the iron; when it abates, let us at that stage impose on the body again the labor from the iron.' He yielded to this as well, bewitched by these many words of enchantment.

9. On this occasion he recovered easily after a few days of illness; but at a later time he fell ill of a more serious disease. As many came together from all sides to seize his body, all the men of the town, when they heard of it, hastened together, soldiers and civilians, some taking up military equipment, others using whatever weapons lay to hand. Forming up in close order, they fought by shooting arrows and slinging stones—not to wound, but simply to instill fear. Having thus driven off the local inhabitants, they placed the all-round contestant on a litter, while he was quite unconscious of what was happening—he was not even conscious of his hair being plucked out by the peasants—, and set off to the city.[6]

10. Arriving at the shrine of the Prophet,[7] they placed the litter in the retreat adjoining it. Someone came to Beroea, where I happened to be, to tell what had happened and bring the news of his death; immediately I made haste and spent the whole night traveling, and just after daybreak reached the man of God, who was neither speaking nor able to recognize any of those present. But when I addressed him

to tell him that the great Acacius[8] sent his respects, he instantly opened his eyes, asked how he was, and inquired when I had come. When I had answered these questions, he shut his eyes again. After three days had passed, in the evening, he asked where he was; on being told, he was extremely vexed, and demanded to be taken back at once to the mountain. In my wish to serve him in everything, I gave immediate instructions for his litter to be brought and to be carried to the desired spot.

11. It was then that I witnessed the lack of vanity in this, to me venerable, person. On the next day I brought him some barley gruel, which I had cooled – since he refused to take anything hot, having renounced entirely the use of fire. Since he was unwilling to partake, I said, 'Show consideration, father, for all of us, for we think your health to be preservation for all. For not only are you set before us as a model that is of benefit, but you also help us by your prayers and procure us God's favor. If the disruption of your habits torments you, father (I continued), endure this as well, for this too is a form of philosophy. Just as when in health and desiring food you overcame appetite by endurance, so now when you have no appetite show endurance by taking food.' While I was saying this, the man of God Polychronius was also present, who, to support my plea, volunteered to be the first to take food, although it was morning and he often fed his body at seven day intervals. Worsted by this reasoning, he swallowed one cup of the gruel with his eyes shut, just as we normally do with bitter drinks. I think it useful to reveal as well the following example of the philosophy of his soul, which occurred after we induced him to wet with water the feet that out of debility had lost the ability to walk. The cup was lying nearby, and one of the attendants tried to cover it with a basket so that it should not be visible to those who visited him. 'Why,' he asked, 'do you cover the cup?' The other replied, 'To stop it being exposed to the gaze of visitors.' 'Clear off, boy,' he exclaimed, 'do not hide from men what is manifest to the God of the universe. Wishing to live for him alone, I have paid no thought to my reputation with men; for what benefit is it, if the latter think more of my asceticism but God thinks less? For they are not the givers of reward for labors, but God is the bestower.' Who would not be overwhelmed with admiration both at these words and at the mind, so superior to human reputation, that bred them?

12. I learnt of something similar that occurred on some other occasion. It was evening, late evening, and the time for nourishment. So taking the potsherd lying to hand, he ate the soaked lentils—for this was his food. There came someone from the town, entrusted with some military exaction. James, seeing him at a distance, did not put his lentils aside, but continued swallowing the food as usual. And thinking him to be a demonic illusion, he assailed him with words, to drive him off as an enemy; and to show he was not afraid, he continued during this to put lentils in his mouth. The man being assailed with abuse besought him, and declared he was a man, and that he had arrived at this time because obliged by an oath to leave the city towards evening. 'Be of good courage,' said the other, 'and do not be afraid, but pray and then depart. Be my table-companion, and share this food with me.' While saying this, he filled his hand and gave a portion of the lentils. In this way he has expelled from his mind the passion of vainglory together with the others.

13. But of his endurance it is superfluous to speak, since sight is the witness. Often after snow has fallen for three days and as many nights, he has been so buried, when lying prone in prayer to God, that not even a tiny piece of the rags that cover him can be seen. Often his neighbors have to use forks and shovels and in this way remove the snow covering him, in order to drag out and revive his supine body.

14. As a result of these labors he has culled the gifts of divine grace, and these are shared by all who desire it. Through his blessing many fevers have been quenched—and still are—, many agues have abated or departed completely, many demons have been forced to flee; and water blessed by his hand becomes a preventive medicine. Who is ignorant of the resuscitation of a dead child that occurred through his prayer? In the suburbs of the city lived the child's parents, who had begotten many children and escorted them all prematurely to the grave. So when this last child was born, the father hastened to the man of God, begging to obtain a long life for it, and promising to dedicate it to God, should it live. After living for four years, it came to the end of its life. The father was absent; but the moment he returned, he saw the child being already carried out. Snatching it from the bier, he said, 'It is fitting that I fulfil my promise and give the child, even though dead, to the man of God'. So he took it as he had

promised, and laid it before those holy feet, saying what he had already said to his household. The man of God, placing the child before him and kneeling down, lay prostrate as he entreated the Master of life and death. In the late afternoon the child made utterance and called its father. This inspired man, perceiving thereby that the Master had accepted the petition and bestowed life, got up, and after worshipping the One who does the will of those who fear him and hearkens to their requests, completed his prayer and restored the child to its begetter. I myself saw the child and heard the father narrating the miracle; and I have transmitted to many this story worthy of the Apostles,[b] knowing that it will be a cause of great benefit to those who hear it.

15. I myself have often enjoyed his help. I shall recall one or two instances, knowing that it would be the height of ingratitude to consign to silence, and not to make known, his varied good services. The abominable Marcion had sown many thorns of impiety in the territory of the city of Cyrrhus; trying to pull these out by the root, I shook every sail and applied persistently every device.[9] But those who received these attentions from me 'instead of loving me (in the words of the prophet) calumniated me, and returned against me evil for good, and hatred for my love'.[c] They tried to make war invisibly by using magic spells and having recourse to the cooperation of evil demons. Once by night there came a wicked demon, who exclaimed in Syriac, 'Why, Theodoret, do you make war on Marcion? Why on earth have you joined battle with him? What harm has he ever done to you? End the war, stop your hostility, or you will learn by experience how good it is to stay quiet. Know well that I would long ago have pierced you through, if I had not seen the choir of the martyrs with James protecting you.'

16. I heard this, and said to one of my friends sleeping nearby, 'Can you hear, my friend, what is being said?' 'I heard it all,' he replied, 'and though I wanted to get up and peer and find out who was speaking, I kept quiet for your sake, supposing you to be asleep.' So getting up we both peered about, and saw no one moving and heard no one speaking; the others who lived with us had also heard these words. I

[b]Cf. Ac 9:36 ff, 20:9 ff.   [c]Ps 109:5.

realized that by 'the choir of martyrs' was meant the flask of oil of the martyrs, with a blessing gathered from very many martyrs, which was hung up by my bed; and under my head lay an old cloak of the great James, which for me had been stronger than any defences of steel.[10]

17. When I was about to attack the chief village of these same men, and many things got in the way to hinder my setting out, I sent to my Isaiah,[d] begging to enjoy divine reinforcement. 'Have confidence,' he said, 'for all those hindrances have been swept away like spiders' webs; God taught me this by night, not sketching a shadowy dream but displaying a vision. For I saw (he continued), as I was beginning the hymnody, in that part where those places are situated, a fiery serpent crawling from the west to the east and carried through mid-air. After completing three more prayers, I saw it curled up and displaying a circular shape, touching its tail with its head. After finishing eight more prayers, I saw it cut in two and dissolved into smoke.'

18. This is what he foresaw, and we witnessed how the issue agreed with the prediction. For in the morning, under the command of the serpent, originator of evil, those who were formerly of the company of Marcion, but now belong to the host of the Apostles, set out from the west, brandishing naked swords against us. About the third hour of the day they formed up in close order, taking thought only for their own protection, just as the serpent covered his head with his tail. At the eighth hour they dispersed, giving us room to enter the village. And we immediately found a serpent made out of bronze material which they worshipped – for having openly declared war against the Creator and Maker of the universe, they were eager to serve the accursed serpent as being his enemy.[11] Such are the good services which I have myself received from this, to me venerable, person.

19. Since my account has entered on the narration of divine revelations, I shall narrate what I heard from this tongue incapable of deceit. He told this story not out of vanity – for his godly soul is far removed from this passion –, but because a certain need compelled him to tell what he wished to hide. I was asking him to beg the God of the universe to make the crop clear of weeds and free it altogether

[d] Cf. 2 Kgs 19.

from the seeds of heresy, for I was utterly tormented by the error of the abominable Marcion's having so strong a hold. To my earnest entreaty he replied, 'You need neither myself nor some other intercessor with God, for you have the famous John, the mouthpiece of the Word, the forerunner of the Master, who constantly transmits this petition on your behalf'. When I declared that I had faith in the prayers of this saint as in those of the other holy apostles and prophets whose relics had lately been brought to us, he said, 'Have confidence, since you have John the Baptist'.

20. But not even so could I bear to keep silent. I pressed my inquiries all the more in my desire to learn why he made mention of this one in particular. 'I wanted,' he replied, 'to embrace his beloved relics.' When I said I would not bring them unless he promised to tell me what he had seen, he gave the promise, and I on the next day brought what he longed for; and ordering everyone to keep at a distance, he recounted to me alone the following. 'At the time,' he said, 'that you welcomed with Davidic choral singing the arrival from Phoenicia and Palestine of these city-guardians,[12] a thought occurred to me whether these were in reality the relics of the famous John and not of some other martyr of the same name. Now one day later I got up at night for the hymnody, and saw someone clad in white who said, "Brother James, tell me why you did not come to meet us on our arrival". When I asked who they were, he replied, "Those who came yesterday from Phoenicia and Palestine. While everyone welcomed us enthusiastically—the shepherd and the people, townsfolk and countrymen—, you alone did not take part in this veneration". He was alluding to the doubts I felt. At this (James continued) I replied, "Even in the absence of you and the others, I venerate you and worship the God of all things". Again on the next day, at the same time, he himself appeared: "Brother James," he said, "look at the one standing there, whose raiment is like the snow in color, and before whom is placed a furnace of fire." I moved my eyes in that direction and surmised it was John the Baptist, for he wore his cloak, and was stretching out his hand as if baptizing. "It is the one," he said, "whom you have guessed it to be."

21. 'And on another occasion (he continued), when you departed by night to their principal village, in order to punish them as seditious,

and bade me address still more earnest prayer to God, I persevered without sleep entreating the Master. Then I heard a voice saying, "Fear not, James. The great John the Baptist all night entreats the God of the universe; for there would have been great slaughter, had not the insolence of the devil been extinguished by his intercession."' After recounting this to me, he charged me to keep the knowledge to myself and not make others share it; but I, for the sake of the benefit, have not only recounted the story to many, but also entrust it to writing.

22. He said that he had also beheld the patriarch Joseph, with his hoary head and beard, emitting in old age the radiance of youth, and at the summit of virtue naming himself the last of the saints. 'While I,' he continued 'declared him to be the first of those who shared a tomb with him, he called himself the last.'

23. He also recounted to me the attacks of all kinds made on him by the evil demons.[13] 'At my very entry,' he said, 'into this way of life, I used to see someone naked, with the appearance of an Egyptian, shooting fire from his eyes. I, on seeing him, would be filled with fear, have recourse to prayer and could not bear to take food, for it was at this time that he used to appear.[14] When seven, eight, ten days had passed and I remained without food, finally, despising the evil onslaught, I sat down and took food. But he could not bear my elevation of mind, and threatened to strike me with a rod. But I (he continued) said, "If you have been given permission by the Master of the universe, then strike, and I shall receive the blow with pleasure, as being struck by Him; but if you have not been given permission, you will not strike, however infinite your frenzy." On hearing this, he on this occasion fled away.

24. 'His frenzy, however, continued in secret. Water was brought to me from below twice a week. Meeting the carrier and imitating my appearance, he would take the water and, after telling him to depart, pour it away. This he did not merely twice but three times, and the affliction of thirst made war upon me. In my torment, I asked the usual carrier, "Why on earth for fifteen days have you not brought water?" He replied that he had brought it three times already, indeed four times, and that I had received it from him. "And where," I asked, "did I receive this water from you when you brought it?" When he indicated the place, I said: "Even if on innumerable occasions you see me there, do not hand over the jar until you come to this place."

James [of Cyrrhestica]

25. 'After I had in this way frustrated his plot, I was tested again by another one. Crying out at night, he said: "I shall fill you with such a stench, and spread so evil a reputation, that no one from anywhere will look at you." To this (he continued) I made reply: "I shall concede thanks to you, for against your will you will be doing your enemy a kindness, by making him luxuriate all the more in remembering God; for enjoying greater leisure, I shall keep up as my uninterrupted task contemplation of the divine beauty." After a few days had passed, (he continued) when at midday I was performing the customary liturgy, I saw two women coming down from the mountain. When in vexation at this unusual occurrence I tried to throw stones at them, I recalled the threat of the avenging spirit and guessed this to be the evil reputation. So I shouted that even if they sat on my shoulders I would not throw stones at them or chase them away, but have recourse to prayer alone. When I said this, they vanished, and the visual illusion ended as I spoke.

26. 'After this again (he continued) I was praying by night, when the noise of a carriage reached me, as also the cry of a driver and of horses whinneying. The novelty of the thing bewildered me, for I reflected that no governor was staying in the city at that time, that the road was not for carriages, and that the time of day was not suitable for carriages. As I was having these thoughts, there was heard a tumult of a great company approaching and the cries of the rod-bearers in front, hissing to clear the crowd out of the way and make the road ready for the governor. When they seemed to me to be extremely close (he continued), I said, "Who are you? Where have you come from? For what purpose have you come at this time? How long will you keep up your jesting, you wretch, and presume upon the divine forbearance?" This I said as, facing east, I addressed petition to God. The other gave me a push, but had not the strength to knock me down—for divine grace resisted—, and immediately the whole apparition vanished.'

27. He related too how, at the time when those wicked brigands coming from Isauria burnt and plundered most of the east,[15] he was terrified at the thought, not of being killed—he was not so in love with the body—but of enslavement and captivity and witnessing impiety and lawlessness. The devil, perceiving this fear—for he often

heard him express it to his friends —, imitated by night the wailing of women. 'I thought I could hear,' he continued, 'the enemy arriving and setting fire to the villages. I at once parted the hair on my head, drawing some on the left and some on the right down my shoulders to my chest, and made my neck ready to be severed by the sword, so that receiving the blow immediately, I might be spared the sight I deprecated. When day came and some people arrived, after spending the whole night like this, all the time expecting an assault, I asked what they had heard of the Isaurians. They replied that during these days they had heard nothing of them. That (he concluded) was how I discovered that this too was a diabolical illusion.

28. 'On another occasion,' he said, 'in the likeness of a youth in full vigor, resplendent in bloom and adorned with blond hair, he came up to me both grinning and flirting. But I (he continued), was armed with indignation and drove him off with abuse. But he persevered with his wanton look and with a grin and speech that reeked of pleasure. At this point I intensified my anger: "How do you have the strength," I said, "to traverse the whole world and lay such snares for all men?" He replied that he was not on his own, but that a mass of demons was scattered through the whole world, to play tricks and be at work simultaneously; for by their playful appearance they are at work to destroy the whole human race. "But as for you," I said, "go away: you are being ordered by Christ, who by means of swine sent a whole legion into the abyss."[e] As soon as he heard this, he fled, not able either to endure the power of the Master's name or to look at the radiance of the philosophers of His household.'

29. I know many more stories than these, but I do not wish to record them, lest their quantity become for the more weak an excuse for disbelief. To those who see the man of God no story of this kind appears incredible, because the virtue they see confirms the stories. But since this composed narrative will pass down to posterity and most people trust their ears less than their eyes, let us adjust the narration to the weakness of the hearers.

30. Others built him a great tomb a few stades away in the neighboring village, while I prepared a grave for him in the shrine of the

---

[e] Cf. Mk 5:9-13

triumphant Apostles.[16] But on learning of this, the man of God besought me many times to bury his body on the mountain itself; I replied as often that it is not fitting for one who is indifferent to the present life to take thought for his burial. But when I saw that this was close to his heart, I agreed and consented, and made arrangements for the coffin to be carved and brought up; and when I saw that the stone was being damaged by the frost, I ordered a small hut to be made for the coffin. When, following his orders, we had completed the construction and put on the roof, he said: 'I will not allow this tomb to be called that of James. I want it to be a shrine of the triumphant martyrs, and myself like some immigrant to be placed in another tomb, honored to dwell with them.' This he not only declared but accomplished. Collecting from all sources many prophets, many apostles, and as many martyrs as possible, he placed them in a single coffin, in his wish to dwell with the assembly of the saints, and his desire to share with them both the resurrection and the privilege of the vision of God.

31. This is sufficient to prove his modesty of spirit. Although he had amassed such wealth of virtue, while living in extreme poverty, he desired to dwell with the company of the rich. Of what kind are the labors of this, to me venerable, person, how great his contests, how much grace from God he has enjoyed, what victories he has won and with what crowns he has been adorned, these stories are sufficient to teach.

32. Since some people accuse him of peevishness of character and are annoyed at his love of solitude and tranquillity, it is after saying a few words on this that I shall bring the account to an end. As I have said already, he lies exposed to everyone's gaze, being neither fenced round with an enclosure nor sheltered by some hut or tent; each of his visitors, because hindered by no barrier, goes to him at once and wants to make conversation. Other lovers of this philosophy have enclosures and doors and the enjoyment of tranquillity; the recluse opens when wishing to, delays as long as he wants, and has his fill of divine contemplation as long as he wishes. But here there is none of this; and this is the essential reason why he gets annoyed with those who are a nuisance at the very time of prayer. If at his bidding they go away at once, he again concentrates on prayer; but if they continue

to be a nuisance and do not obey when ordered once or even twice, then he is annoyed and sends them away with a rebuke.[17]

33. I myself have had a discussion with him on this matter. I told him that some people were upset at being driven away without even a blessing. 'It would be proper,' I said, 'for those who come for this and make a journey of many days to depart not in vexation but full of joy, to feast the ignorant with stories of your philosophy.' He replied, 'I did not come to the mountain for another's sake but for my own. Bearing the wounds of so many sins, I need much treatment, and because of this I beseech our Master to give me the antidotes to wickedness. How, then, would it not be absurd and utterly senseless to break the sequence of petition and make conversation with men in between? If I happened to be the domestic of a human being like myself, and at the time for serving the master failed to bring the food or drink at the right time but instead made conversation with one of my fellow-servants, what great blows would I not justly receive? And if I went to the governor and, while relating an injustice I had suffered from someone, broke off my discourse in the middle and made some other remarks to one of those present, do you not think that the judge would be annoyed, withdraw his assistance, and have me whipped and driven from the bar? How could it be right for a domestic to behave appropriately towards a master, and a plaintiff towards a judge, but for me, as I approach God, the eternal Master, the Judge most just and King of all things, not to make my approach like these, but during my prayers to turn to my fellow-servants and hold a long conversation with them?'

34. This is what I heard and have transmitted to those who had taken offence; and he seems to me have spoken well and fairly. In addition to what he said, it is characteristic of lovers to overlook everyone else and cleave to the one they cherish and love, to dream of him by night and think of him by day. It is, I think, for this reason that he is annoyed when, in the middle of the contemplation he longs for, he is prevented from being immersed in the beauty he loves.

35. We have composed this in the form of a narrative not of a panegyric, paying close attention to brevity, in order not by length to exhaust our readers. If he outlives this narration for a time, he will doubtless add innumerable other achievements to his earlier ones,

and others will record them. As for us, great is the longing to depart from here. May the Umpire of the athletes of piety grant this man an end worthy of his labors, and make the rest of his course consonant with the earlier part, so that he may reach the finishing-post as victor; and may He through the prayers of this man support our weakness, so that strengthened we may retrieve our many defeats and depart from this life with victory.

NOTES

1. James was the most famous ascetic of the region of Cyrrhus. At first a companion of Maron (§3, and XXII.2), then briefly a recluse (§4), he had been an open-air hermit since 402 (XXII.7). It emerges from this chapter that he had close relations with Theodoret, who stresses the spiritual assistance James gave him in his campaign against the Marcionites (§§15-18, 21). Likewise in 446/7 James added his moral support to Theodoret's pleas to high court officials (*epp.* 42, 44) for a remission of taxes to be granted to Cyrrhus, 'a city which he [James] makes illustrious by living near and protecting with his prayers' (*ep.* 42). Theodoret does not care to mention that in 434 James had been one of the ascetics, the others being Symeon Stylites and Baradatus, who, at the request of the imperial court, pressed a reluctant and aggrieved Theodoret to be reconciled with John of Antioch and accept the end of hostilities with Cyril of Alexandria (Festugière, *Antioche*, 420-1). It is remarkable that in 457 it was the same three ascetics – James, Symeon, and Baradatus – who were singled out by the emperor Leo I to be consulted over the controversial Chalcedonian Definition of 451 (E. Schwartz, *ACO* II, 5, p. 23). Theodoret's very full account of James in the *Rel. Hist.* was clearly justified by much more than local loyalty.
2. See I.11-12 above.
3. On Maron's institution of the open-air life in Cyrrhestica, see XVI, with note 1. See VI.3 for a story about Symeon the Elder being told to Maron in James's presence.
4. This mountain has been identified with Sheih Khoros, four miles west of Cyrrhus.
5. 'Fourteen years ago' implies a date of 426 (see Introduction, II, for the date of the *Rel. Hist.*).
6. Similar is the way soldiers from Antioch secured Symeon Stylites's body and carried it to the city, despite the resistance, not only of the local inhabitants, but also of a band of armed Ishmaelites, who also wished to obtain it (see Antony, *Life of Symeon* 29-31, in Festugière, *Antioche*, 374-5).
7. This is the shrine containing relics of John the Baptist and others, the translation of which is mentioned below, at §§19-20. For fourth and fifth century relics of John the Baptist, see Smith and Cheetham, *Dictionary of Christian Antiquities*, I: 883.
8. On Acacius, bishop of Beroea, see II, note 9.
9. The teaching of Marcion (*fl.* 150) seems to have taken special root in rural Syria, where in the third century Marcionites are likely to have outnumbered Catholics. Their continuing strength in the region of Cyrrhus is indicated by John Chrysostom, writing *c.* 400 as bishop of Constantinople to the bishop of Cyrrhus about the presence of Marcionism in his diocese, 'urging him to expel the disease and offering assistance from the imperial laws' (Theodoret, *Eccl. Hist.* V.31). In *ep.* 81 (of AD 448) and 113 (of 449) Theodoret claims to have converted eight villages of Marcionites, a total of over one thousand souls, and to have extirpated the heresy from his diocese.
10. Cp. IX.15 for a prophylactic object provided by a holy man (Peter's belt).
11. So far from being pagan, Marcionite churches were very similar in appearance and liturgy to Catholic ones (Cyril of Jerusalem, *Catechetical Lectures* XVIII.26). The Marcionites did not so much introduce innovations as exaggerate certain tendencies in Syrian Christianity. They pushed anti-Judaism to the point of rejecting the Old Testament and the more Judaistic parts of the New, and pushed encratism (or continence) to the point of using water not wine in the eucharist and insisting that all the baptized were committed to lifelong sexual abstinence.

12. See Theodoret, *epp.* 66–68 and XXXVI for the great festival with which he consecrated a new church as a shrine of the prophets and apostles, probably before 430. For saints as patrons of cities, see *Cure of Hellenic Maladies* VIII.10: 'While the noble souls of the victors traverse heaven . . . , their bodies are not buried in a single tomb for each one: but cities and villages, among which they are distributed, call them saviours of souls and doctors of bodies, and honor them as city-guardians and protectors; employing them as ambassadors to the Master of the universe, it is through them that they receive the divine gifts.'

13. The following chapters are unparalleled in the *Rel. Hist.* in their treatment of the interior life as a struggle against demonic visitations (though see note XXVIII.2 for this struggle in the context of evangelization). The obvious parallel is Athanasius's *Life of Antony*, esp. 6–13, 23–43. P. Brown, *The Making of Late Antiquity*, 89, comments perceptively, 'One may suspect that hallucination and extreme emotional states were deliberately courted so as to be overcome, and not entered into unwillingly and then naïvely ascribed to the demonic'.

14. This implies that James felt a scruple at being seen eating (like St Antony, *Life* 45). Contrast his later behavior in §12; the scruple had been overcome. For the devil 'with the appearance of an Egyptian', cp. *Martyrdom of Perpetua and Felicity* 10, where Perpetua dreams of the devil in the form of an 'Egyptian of foul aspect'. The idea derives from allegorizing the Egyptians of the Exodus.

15. This Isaurian raid probably dates to 404; see Introduction, note 4.

16. For rival tombs constructed before a holy man's death, cp. III.18.

17. For a holy man refusing his blessing in irritation at being disturbed, cp. *Life of Antony* 48.

XXII-III

THALASSIUS, LIMNAEUS, JOHN

TILLIMA IS A VILLAGE in our region, which formerly received the seeds of the impiety of Marcion, but now enjoys cultivation by the Gospel.[1] South of it is a ridge neither too rough nor too flat; here an ascetic dwelling was built by the wonderful Thalassius, a man adorned with many other good qualities, but surpassing the men of his time in simplicity of character, gentleness, and modesty of spirit. I say this, not relying on hearsay alone, but having had experience; for I visited the man and often enjoyed his sweet company.

2. In his choir was enrolled Limnaeus,[2] now celebrated by all. At a very young age he entered this wrestling-school and received a fine education in this consummate philosophy. At first, knowing the treachery of the tongue, he imposed on it a rule of silence while still an adolescent, and continued for as long as possible saying nothing to anyone. When he had received sufficiently the teaching of the godly old man and made himself an impress of his virtue, he came to the great Maron, whom we recalled above—he came at the same time as the godly James.[3] After reaping much benefit from there again,

and keenly embracing the open-air life, he repaired to another hilltop, lying above a village called Targalla.

3. Here he has continued till today, without a cell or tent or hut, but fenced round by a bare wall built of stones and not joined with clay. It has a small door always sealed with mud, which he never opens to other visitors, but allows me alone to open when I visit him. For this reason, very many gather from all over when they hear of my arrival, desiring to share my entry. To those who visit him at other times he speaks through a small window and gives his blessing, by this means bestowing health on very many; by using the name of our Saviour he ends diseases, drives out demons, and imitates the miracle-working of the Apostles.

4. Not only to those who come to him does he pour out healing, but he has often applied it to his own body also. Some time ago he was assailed by the disease of the gripes. The agonizing pain this causes is known precisely both by those who have experienced it and by those who have been witnesses of it: they roll about like lunatics, turning over on this side and on that, at the same time stretching out and then bending back their legs. At various times they sit, stand, and walk, endeavoring to find some means of repose; and for this reason they sit by baths and often go into them, to enjoy some relief. But why should I describe at length what is known and manifest to all? Struggling with this disease and afflicted with pains of this kind and magnitude, he benefited from no medical help, could not endure a bed, and got no relief from medicines or food; but seated on a plank lying on the ground, he received treatment by prayer and the sign of the cross, and lulled his pains by the spell of the divine name.

5. On another occasion, when walking at night, he stepped with his heal on a sleeping viper, which caught the flat of his foot and inserted its teeth. Trying to protect his foot, he stooped down and moved his hand to it, which merely transferred to his hand the mouth of the beast. When he then used his left hand to help the other one, he attracted the anger of the beast against it as well. When it had satisfied its rage – it had inflicted on him more than ten bites – , it departed and went to its hole, while he was afflicted with bitter pains all over. But not even on this occasion did he accept medical skill, but applied to his wounds the remedies only of faith – the sign of the cross, prayer, and invocation of God.

6. I am therefore of the opinion that the God of the universe allowed the beast to rage against his sacred body in order to reveal undisguised the endurance of this godly soul. We see this same dispensation of His in the case of noble Job. He allowed him to be submerged by many and varied waves, through a wish to display to all the wisdom of the pilot. How else would we know the courage of the one and the endurance of the other, if the adversary of piety had not been given room to shoot all kinds of arrows against them? Therefore this is sufficient to teach the endurance of the man.

7. Let us from a different indication show his humanity: he gathered together many who were deprived of their sight and had been compelled to beg. Building dwellings on both sides, east and west, he invited them to live there and sing hymns to God, telling those who visited him to supply the food they needed. He himself, immured in the middle, exhorts both groups to hymnody. It is possible to hear them hymning the Master continually; and he continues to show such humanity towards his fellow-men. The length of time of open-air contests has been the same both in his case and in that of the great James: they have already completed their thirty-eighth year.

XXIII.[4] 1. John too has keenly embraced this mode of life, a man conspicuous, in addition to other virtues, for gentleness and kindness. Repairing to a jagged ridge, prone to storms and northward-facing, he has now spent twenty-five years there,[5] exposed to the contrasting assaults of the atmosphere. All the other things—not to proceed through them individually—, food and clothing and loads of iron, are much the same as with the ascetics described above. He is so raised above all human things that he reaps no comfort from them. Clear proof of this I shall provide at once. When some well-meaning person planted an almond-tree right by his bed, which then with time became a tree, providing him with shade and feasting his eyes, he ordered it to be cut down, to stop him enjoying any relief therefrom.

2. This life has also been embraced by Moses, who contends on a high hill-top surmounting the village of Rama, by Antiochus, an elderly man who has built an enclosure on a quite uninhabited mountain, and by Antoninus, who in an aged body contends just as youths do. They have the same dress, food, standing posture, prayer, labors all night and all day; neither length of time nor old age nor physical

weakness overcome their endurance, but they preserve in themselves love of labor in full bloom. God, the Umpire of virtue, has very many other contestants in our mountains and plains; it would not be easy merely to number them, let alone record the life of each one. So having offered sufficient benefit from them for those who wish to profit, I shall turn to a different class of narration, while asking to receive the blessing of these men as well.

NOTES

1. Tillima has not been identified. On Theodoret's conversion of Marcionite villages, see XXI.15-18, 21, with note 9.
2. Limnaeus was an ascetic of the region of Cyrrhus, who received his formation in a monastery and then became a disciple of the great Maron (XVI). Then in 402 (XXII.7) he adopted the solitary life, imitating Maron in living in the open air within an unroofed enclosure, near the unidentified village of Targalla. Theodoret knew him personally (§3).
3. For James's period with Maron, see XXI.3.
4. In the manuscripts and editions this is treated as a new chapter. But, as P. Devos has lately pointed out, in *Analecta Bollandiana* 97 (1979) 319-336, comparison with the rest of the *Rel. Hist.* shows that XXII lacks a proper close and XXIII a proper beginning. It is clear that Theodoret intended them to form a single chapter. The content is adequately unified: Limnaeus is the principal subject, with Thalassius briefly treated as his first teacher (XXII.1), and the ascetics of XXIII appended as embracing the same open-air life. Likewise chapters XXIV and XXV have been wrongly separated.
5. So John had been an open-air ascetic, also in the region of Cyrrhus, since 415.

XXIV-V
ZEBINAS, POLYCHRONIUS, ASCLEPIUS

ZEBINAS[1] IS PRAISED even today by those who have had the privilege of seeing him. He is said, on reaching extreme old age, to have practised the same labors till his death, without being compelled by the great burden of old age to change any of those of his youth. He surpassed, they said, all the men of his time in assiduity at prayer; spending all day and night at it, he not only did not experience satiety, but he made his longing all the more fervent. He would say but a few words to those who came to see him, for he could not bear to draw his thought down from heaven; and as soon as he was free of them, he would again address supplication as if he had been separated for not even a short time from the God of the universe. When old age did not allow him to bear without pain continuous standing, he used a stick as a support for it, and leant on this when hymning the Master and when praying.

2. Adorned with hospitality in addition to other good qualities, he told many of those who came to see him to stay till evening; but they, in dread of his all-night standing, would allege lack of leisure,

and so release themselves from these labors. He was also exceedingly admired by the great Maron, who would tell all who visited him to hasten and reap the old man's blessing, naming him father and teacher and calling him the model of every virtue. He even asked to share his grave: but this was disallowed by those who seized his sacred body and carried it off to the place mentioned above.[2] The inspired Zebinas died before him and received the customary rites in the village near him – it is called Cittica. They built a great shrine for his coffin, for he pours forth every kind of healing for those who draw near with faith. He now shares the same roof with martyrs who contended in Persia and are honored by us with annual festivals.[3]

3. His teaching was enjoyed by the great Polychronius;[4] and the most godly James said that this man gave him his first hair-tunic. But I who never saw him – for he reached the end of life before my arrival – see in this famous Polychronius the philosophy of the divine Zebinas; for wax does not receive the impress of signet-rings as much as Polychronius bears the distinctive marks of Zebinas. I have clear knowledge of this from comparing what is done by the former to the stories about the latter; for it is to the same degree that he burns with longing for God and is above all things earthly. Though tied to the body, he has a soul with wings, and flies through the lower and the upper air, rises higher than the heavens and perceives continuously the vision of God. He can never bear to draw his thought down from there, but even when talking with visitors traverses what lies above.

4. I learnt of his all-night vigil in standing posture from the following. Seeing him struggling at the same time with both old age and weakness and not being looked after, I persuaded him by repeated entreaty to take two companions and enjoy solace from them. When he asked for two men conspicuous in virtue who lived alone by themselves in another retreat, I persuaded these wonderful men to choose before everything else looking after the man of God. After being with him for a short time, they tried to escape, for they could not endure standing all night. When I begged the man of God to adjust the labor to the weakness of the body, he replied, 'Not only do I not compel them to share the standing with me continuously, but I also often tell them to lie down'. But they said, 'How could we lie down, who are

men healthy and of middle age, when one grown old in labors remains standing and despises the weakness of the body?' So it was that I learnt of the nocturnal labors of this, to me venerable, person.

5. These men have with time acquired such virtue that they pursue the same philosophy as this great man. Moses—for this is his name—has continued to the present time taking every care of his father and master and receiving an accurate impress of the virtue that flashes forth from this godly soul. Damian—this is the name of the other—repaired to a village lying not far away—its name is Niara.[5] He found a small hut by the threshing-floor, and there he lives, pursuing the same way of life, with the result that those with an accurate knowledge of both this man and the other think on seeing him that they are beholding the soul of the great Polychronius in another body; for there is the same simplicity, mildness, modesty, gentleness of speech, sweetness in company, alertness of soul, and apprehension of God, and the same standing, labor, vigil, food, and poverty in accordance with the divine law—for apart from a little basket containing soaked lentils the cell contains nothing. Such benefit did he derive from the company of the great Polychronius.

6. But I, leaving the disciple, shall return to the teacher, for it is from the spring that the stream pours forth its waters. Polychronius, having with the other passions expelled ambition from his soul and trod down the tyranny of vainglory, was always keen to hide his labors. Iron he could not bear to wear, fearing to derive some harm therefrom, from the soul becoming inflamed with pride. But telling someone to bring him a very heavy root of oak, as if needing it for some other purpose, he would at night place in on his shoulders and pray with this burden, as also during the day when he enjoyed leisure; if someone arrived and knocked on the door, he would hide it away in some place. Someone who saw it told me; and wishing to discover how great was the weight, I found I could scarcely lift it up with both hands. On seeing me, he told me to put it down; but I on the contrary begged to take it away, in order to remove the cause of his labor. But when I saw he was distressed, I yielded to his desire for victory.

7. As a result of these labors, God-given grace blossoms forth in him, and many miracles are worked by his prayers. When that terrible drought consumed men and drove them to prayer,[6] a great number of

priests came to see him. Among them was one from the region of Antioch, appointed to shepherd many villages. He begged the more senior of those present to persuade this man to extend his hand over a flask, but they replied that he would not consent. When prayer followed, and this, to me inspired, person was praying, the man stood behind him and held out the flask in his hands: it gushed forth, so that two or three of those present held out their hands and drew them back filled with oil.

8. Nevertheless, although emitting such rays of grace, being laden with every kind of achievement and gathering each day the wealth of philosophy, he is so modest in spirit that he embraces both feet of each of those who come to see him, while putting his forehead to the ground, whether he is a soldier, an artisan, or a peasant. I shall relate something that can demonstrate both his simplicity and his modesty. A worthy man, who had been assigned to the governorship of the province[7] and repaired to Cyrrhus, wished to enjoy with me the sight of these great athletes. Having gone round the others, we came also to see this one whose virtue we are now relating. When I had said that the visitor with me was a governor and also an upholder of justice and lover of the pious, the inspired man extended both hands to take hold of both his feet: 'I wish,' he said, 'to address a request to you.' When the other, extremely put out, begged him to get up and promised to do whatever he might bid – for he supposed him to be appealing on behalf of one of his subjects–, the inspired man said, 'Therefore, since you have promised, and confirmed your promise with an oath, offer prayers to God earnestly on my behalf'. The other, striking his forehead, begged to be released from his oath, as unworthy to offer supplication to the Master even on his own behalf. What words would suffice as worthy eulogy of a man who preserves such modesty of spirit at such a summit of philosophy?

9. His love of labor has not been confuted by the afflictions of every kind that have fallen upon him; but although beset with varied disease, he perseveres in the same labors. It was with difficulty, and after repeated recourse to many arguments, that we built this small cell, contriving a little warmth for his utterly frozen body. Many men have repeatedly offered him money in their lifetime, or bequeathed it to him when dead, but he has never accepted anything from anybody,

but charges them to be the almoners of their offerings. The great James sent him a goat's hair cloak which someone had brought him, but even this he sent back,[8] considering it too effective a covering and too well made—for he always uses clothes that are extremely simple and cheap. To such an extent does he count poverty more desirable than every kingdom that he does not always have essential nourishment. This I know, having often come to ask for his blessing and found nothing else but two solitary dried figs. The man's honeyed ways are thrice desired by those who see them and extremely lovely to those who hear of them. I know that no man, even of those specially fond of mocking, has ever cast a reproach upon him; instead, all praise and extol him, and when they visit him are reluctant to depart.

XXV.[9]1. Of this company is also the wonderful Asclepius, who is ten stades distant[10] but who has keenly embraced the same way of life. He has the same food, dress, modesty of character, hospitality, brotherly love, kindness, and gentleness, intercourse with God, consummate poverty, abundance of virtue, wealth of philosophy, and all the other things we related concerning that sacred person. He is said, at the time he was numbered with the brethren who inhabit the village, to have embraced the ascetic and disciplined life, and to have derived no harm from mixing with the multitude. Therefore, for having been preeminent in each life, both the social and the eremitical,[11] he will with good reason receive the honor of a double crowning.

2. Many others also have emulated his virtue; not only ours but also the neighboring cities and villages are full of this philosophy. One of these is the most divine James, a recluse in a cell at a village called Nimouza, who, though near the very end of life—for he is more than ninety years old—, is a solitary recluse, giving replies, without being seen, through a small hole dug slantwise, and neither using fire nor employing lamplight. Twice has he dug through his door and bid me come in, thereby honoring me and showing the affection he has for me. Those who are now alive do not need my account, for they can, if they wish, become the eyewitnesses of the philosophy of these men. As for those to come, who do not share in seeing them, these particulars are sufficient for their benefit, since they show the distinctive character of their philosophy. So concluding at this point my account of these men, and asking in return for the gift of their blessing, I shall proceed to another narrative.

NOTES

1. Zebinas was a hermit near Cittica (unidentified) in the region of Cyrrhus. He clearly died before Theodoret's arrival at Cyrrhus (423), as is confirmed by Maron's outliving him (§2).
2. For Maron see XVI, with §4 on his burial.
3. The date of these martyrs is unknown, but for Persian persecution of Christians in Theodoret's own time see his *Eccl. Hist.* V.39(38).
4. Polychronius, as a disciple of Zebinas and still alive, would have been an ascetic at the time of writing for at least twenty years. Note that he enjoyed a special reputation not only at Cyrrhus but also in the region of Antioch (XXIV.7).
5. There is still even now a village called Niara, twelve miles south-east of Cyrrhus.
6. The date of this exceptional drought is unknown; it is presumably the same as the one mentioned at XXVI.19.
7. The province of Euphratensis, extending down the west bank of the Euphrates.
8. Cp. Aphrahat rejecting the gift of a fine tunic (VIII.4).
9. In the manuscripts and editions this is treated as a new chapter. But as P. Devos has pointed out (see XXII-III, note 4), this is simply a repetition of the error he detected in the division of XXII-III. XXIV and XXV form a single chapter in precisely the same way that XXII and XXIII do, especially since 'his virtue' of XXV.2 (line 1) refers not to Asclepius (the subject of 'ch. XXV') but to the Polychronius of XXIV. As in XXII-III, the structure is centered on a single ascetic, here Polychronius, who is preceded by his master, Zebinas (XXIV.1-2), and followed by a rapid mention of ascetics of the same variety; while in XXII-III the common feature was the open-air life, in XXIV-V it is perpetual standing.
10. Ten stades is one mile.
11. Canivet's Greek text gives not 'eremitical' but 'anachoretic'; but 'eremitical' is the reading of the vast majority of manuscripts, and is in fact adopted in Canivet's own translation.

XXVI
SYMEON
(Stylites)

THE FAMOUS SYMEON[1], the great wonder of the world, is known of by all the subjects of the Roman empire and has also been heard of by the Persians, the Medes, the Ethiopians; and the rapid spread of his fame as far as the nomadic Scythians has taught his love of labor and his philosophy. I myself, though having all men, so to speak, as witnesses of his contests that beggar description, am afraid that the narrative may seem to posterity to be a myth totally devoid of truth. For the facts surpass human nature, and men are wont to use nature to measure what is said; if anything is said that lies beyond the limits of nature, the account is judged to be false by those uninitiated into divine things. But since earth and sea are full of pious souls educated in divine things and instructed in the grace of the all-holy Spirit, who will not disbelieve what is said but have complete faith in it, I shall make my narration with eagerness and confidence. I shall begin from the point at which he received his call from on high.

2. There is a village lying on the border between our region and Cilicia; they call it Sisa.[2] Originating from this village, he was taught by his parents first to shepherd animals, so that in this respect too he

might be comparable to those great men the patriarch Jacob,[a] the chaste Joseph,[b] the lawgiver Moses,[c] the king and prophet David,[d] the prophet Micah and the inspired men of their kind.[3] Once when there was much snow and the sheep were compelled to stay indoors, he took advantage of the respite to go with his parents to the house of God. I heard his sacred tongue recount the following: he told how he heard the Gospel utterance which declares blessed those who weep and mourn, calls wretched those who laugh, terms enviable those who possess a pure soul, and all the other blessings conjoined with them. He then asked one of those present what one should do to obtain each of these. He suggested the solitary life and pointed to that consummate philosophy.[4]

3. Therefore, having received the seeds of the divine word and stored them well in the deep furrows of his soul, he hastened—he said—to a nearby shrine of the holy martyrs. In it he bent his knees and forehead to the ground, and besought the One who wishes to save all men to lead him to the perfect path of piety. After he had spent a long time in this way, a sweet sleep came upon him, and he had the following dream: 'I seemed,' he said, 'to be digging foundations, and then hear someone standing by say that I had to make the trench deeper. After adding to its depth as he told me, I again tried to take a rest; but once more he ordered me to dig and not relax my efforts. After charging me a third and a fourth time to do this, he finally said the depth was sufficient, and told me to build effortlessly from now on, since the effort had abated and the building would be effortless.' This prediction is confirmed by the event, for the facts surpass nature.

4. Getting up from there, he repaired to the dwelling of some neighboring ascetics. After spending two years with them and falling in love with more perfect virtue, he repaired to that village of Teleda which we mentioned above, where the great and godly men Ammianus and Eusebius had pitched their ascetic wrestling-school. The inspired Symeon, however, did not enter this one, but another which had sprung from it; Eusebônas and Abibion, having enjoyed sufficiently the teaching of the great Eusebius, had built this retreat of philosophy.[5] Having shared throughout life the same convictions and

[a] Cf. Gen 30:29-43.   [b] Cf. Gen 37:2.   [c] Cf. Ex 3:1.   [d] Cf. 1 Sam 16:11.

the same habits, and displayed, as it were, one soul in two bodies, they made many love this life as they did. When they departed from life with glory, the wonderful Heliodorus succeeded to the office of superior over the community. He lived for sixty-five years,[6] and spent sixty-two years immured within; for it was after three years of rearing by his parents that he entered this flock, without ever beholding the occurrences of life.[7] He claimed not even to know the shape of pigs or cocks or the other animals of this kind. I too had often the benefit of seeing him; I admired his simplicity of character and was especially amazed at his purity of soul.

5. After coming to him, this all-round contestant in piety spent ten years contending. He had eighty fellow contestants, and outshot all of them; while the others took food every other day, he would last the whole week without nourishment. His superiors bore this ill and constantly quarreled with it, calling the thing lack of discipline; but they did not persuade him by their words, nor could they curb his zeal. I heard the very man who is now superior of this flock recount[8] how on one occasion Symeon took a cord made from palms—it was extremely rough even to touch with the hands—, and girded it round his waist, not wearing it on the outside but making it touch the skin itself. He tied it so tightly as to lacerate in a circle the whole part it went round. When he had continued in this manner for more than ten days and the now severe wound was letting fall drops of blood, someone who saw him asked what was the cause of the blood. When he replied that he had nothing wrong with him, his fellow contestant forcibly inserted his hand, discovered the cause and disclosed it to the superior. Immediately reproaching and exhorting, and inveighing against the cruelty of the thing, he undid the belt, with difficulty, but not even so could he persuade him to give the wound any treatment. Seeing him do other things of the kind as well, they ordered him to depart from this wrestling-school, lest he should be a cause of harm to those with a weaker bodily constitution who might try to emulate what was beyond their powers.

6. He therefore departed, and made his way to the more deserted parts of the mountain. Finding a cistern that was waterless and not too deep, he lowered himself into it, and offered hymnody to God. When five days had passed, the superiors of the wrestling-school had

a change of heart, and sent out two men, charging them to look for him and bring him back. So after walking round the mountain, they asked some men tending animals there if they had seen someone of such a complexion and dress. When the shepherds pointed out the cistern, they at once called out several times, and bringing a rope, drew him out with great labor—for ascent is not as easy as descent.

7. After staying with them for a short time, he came to the village of Telanissus, which lies under the hill-top where he now stands;[9] finding a tiny cottage in it, he spent three years as a recluse. In his eagerness to be always increasing his wealth of virtue, he longed to fast forty days without food, like the men of God Moses[e] and Elijah.[f] He urged the wonderful Bassus, who at the time used to make visitations of many villages, as supervisor of the village priests,[10] to leave nothing inside and seal the door with mud. When the other pointed out the difficulty of the thing and urged him not to think suicide a virtue, since it is the first and greatest of crimes, he replied: 'But you then, father, leave me ten rolls and a jar of water; and if I see my body needs nourishment, I shall partake of them.' It was done as he bade. The provisions were left, and the door was sealed with mud. At the end of the forty days, Bassus, this wonderful person and man of God, came and removed the mud; on going in through the door he found the complete number of rolls, he found the jar full of water,[11] but Symeon stretched out without breath, unable either to speak or to move. Asking for a sponge to wet and rinse his mouth, he brought him the symbols of the divine mysteries; and so strengthened by these, he raised himself and took a little food—lettuce, chicory and suchlike plants, which he chewed in small pieces and so passed into the stomach.

8. Overwhelmed with admiration, the great Bassus repaired to his own flock, to recount this great miracle; for he had more than two hundred disciples, whom he ordered to possess neither mounts nor mules, nor to accept offerings of money, nor to go outside the gate whether to buy something necessary or see some friend, but to live indoors and receive the food sent by divine grace. This rule his disciples have preserved to this day. They have not, as they become more numerous, transgressed the injunctions that were given them.

[e]Cf. Ex 24:18.   [f]Cf. 1 Kgs 19:8.

9. But I shall return to the great Symeon. From that time till today—twenty-eight years have passed—he spends the forty days without food.[12] Time and practice have allayed most of the effort. For it was his custom during the first days to chant hymns to God standing, then, when because of the fasting his body no longer had the strength to bear the standing, thereafter to perform the divine liturgy seated, and during the final days actually to lie down—for as his strength was gradually exhausted and extinguished he was compellled to lie half-dead. But when he took his stand on the pillar, he was not willing to come down, but contrived his standing posture differently: it was by attaching a beam to the pillar and then tying himself to the beam with cords that he lasted the forty days. Subsequently, enjoying henceforward still more grace from above, he has not needed even this support, but stands throughout the forty days, not taking food but strengthened by zeal and divine grace.

10. After spending three years, as I said, in this cottage, he repaired to that celebrated hill-top, where he ordered a circular enclosure to be made. After procuring an iron chain of twenty cubits, nailing one end to a great rock and fixing the other to his right foot, so that not even if he wished could he go outside these limits, he lived all the time inside, thinking of heaven and compelling himself to contemplate what lies above the heavens—for the iron chain did not hinder the flight of his thought. But when the wonderful Meletius, who had at that time been appointed to supervise the territory of the city of Antioch[13] and was a wise man of brilliant intelligence and gifted with shrewdness, told him that the iron was superfluous, since the will was sufficient to impose on the body the bonds of reasoning, he yielded and accepted the advice with compliance: And bidding a smith be called, he told him to sever the chain. When a piece of leather, which had been tied to his leg to prevent the iron injuring his body, had to be torn apart (for it had been sown together), people saw, they said, more than twenty large bugs lurking in it; and the wonderful Meletius said he had seen this. I myself have mentioned it in order to show from this example as well the endurance of the man: for though he could easily have squeezed the leather with his hand and killed them all, he steadfastly put up with their painful bites, welcoming in small things training for greater contests.

11. As his fame circulated everywhere, everyone hastened to him, not only the people of the neighborhood but also people many days' journey distant, some bringing the paralysed in body, others requesting health for the sick, others asking to become fathers; and they begged to receive from him what they could not receive from nature. On receiving it and obtaining their requests, they returned with joy; and by proclaiming the benefits they had gained, they sent out many times more, asking for the same things. So with everyone arriving from every side and every road resembling a river, one can behold a sea of men standing together in that place, receiving rivers from every side. Not only do the inhabitants of our part of the world flock together, but also Ishmaelites, Persians, Armenians subject to them, Iberians, Homerites, and men even more distant than these; and there came many inhabitants of the extreme west, Spaniards, Britons, and the Gauls who live between them.[14] Of Italy it is superfluous to speak. It is said that the man became so celebrated in the great city of Rome that at the entrance of all the workshops men have set up small representations of him, to provide thereby some protection and safety for themselves.

12. Since the visitors were beyond counting and they all tried to touch him and reap some blessing from his garments of skins, while he at first thought the excess of honor absurd and later could not abide the wearisomeness of it, he devised the standing on a pillar,[15] ordering the cutting of a pillar first of six cubits, then of twelve, afterwards of twenty-two and now of thirty-six — for he yearns to fly up to heaven and to be separated from this life on earth. I myself do not think that this standing has occurred without the dispensation of God, and because of this I ask fault-finders to curb their tongue and not to let it be carried away at random, but to consider how often the Master has contrived such things for the benefit of the more easygoing. He ordered Isaiah to walk naked and barefoot,[g] Jeremiah to put a loincloth on his waist and by this means address prophecy to the unbelieving,[h] and on another occasion to put a wooden collar on his neck[i] and later an iron one,[j] Hosea to take a harlot to wife[k] and again to love a woman immoral and adulterous,[l] Ezekiel to lie on his

[g]Cf. Is 20:2.   [h]Cf. Jer 13:1.   [i]Cf. Jer 27:2.   [j]Cf. Jer 28:13.   [k]Cf. Hos 1:2.
[l]Cf. Hos 3:1.

right side for forty days and on his left for one hundred and fifty,[m] and again to dig through a wall and slip out in flight, making himself a representation of captivity,[n] and on another occasion to sharpen a sword to a point, shave his head with it, divide the hair into four and assign some for this purpose and some for that[o] — not to list everything. The Ruler of the universe ordered each of these things to be done in order to attract, by the singularity of the spectacle, those who would not heed words and could not bear hearing prophecy, and make them listen to the oracles. For who would not have been astounded at seeing a man of God walking naked? Who would not have wanted to learn the cause of the occurrence? Who would not have asked how the prophet could bear to live with a harlot? Therefore, just as the God of the universe ordered each of these actions out of consideration for the benefit of those inured to ease, so too he has ordained this new and singular sight in order by its strangeness to draw all men to look, and to make the proffered exhortation persuasive to those who come — for the novelty of the sight is a trustworthy pledge of the teaching, and the man who comes to look departs instructed in divine things. Just as those who have obtained kingship over men alter periodically the images on their coins, at one time striking representations of lions, at another of stars and angels, and at another try to make the gold piece more valuable by the strangeness of the type, so the universal Sovereign of all things, by attaching to piety like coin-types these new and various modes of life, stirs to eulogy the tongues not only of those nurtured in the faith but also of those afflicted by lack of faith.[16]

13. Words do not testify that these things have this character, but the facts themselves proclaim it; for the Ishmaelites, who were enslaved in their many tens of thousands to the darkness of impiety, have been illuminated by his standing on the pillar.[17] For this dazzling lamp, as if placed on a lampstand, has sent out rays in all directions, like the sun. It is possible, as I have said, to see Iberians and Armenians and Persians arriving to receive the benefit of divine baptism. The Ishmaelites, arriving in companies, two or three hundred at the same time, sometimes even a thousand, disown with shouts their ancestral

[m]Cf. Ezk 4:4-6.   [n]Cf. Ezk 12:4-5.   [o]Cf. Ezk 5:1-4.

imposture;[18] and smashing in front of this great luminary the idols they had venerated and renouncing the orgies of Aphrodite[19] – it was this demon whose worship they had adopted originally –, they receive the benefit of the divine mysteries, accepting laws from this sacred tongue and bidding farewell to their ancestral customs, as they disown the eating of wild asses and camels.[20]

14. I myself was an eyewitness of this, and I have heard them disowning their ancestral impiety and assenting to the teaching of the Gospel. And I once underwent great danger: he told them to come up and receive from me the priestly blessing, saying they would reap the greatest profit therefrom. But they rushed up in a somewhat barbarous manner, and some pulled at me from in front, some from behind, others from the sides, while those further back trod on the others and stretched out their hands, and some pulled at my beard and others grabbed at my clothing. I would have been suffocated by their too ardent approach, if he had not used a shout to disperse them. Such is the benefit that the pillar mocked by lovers of mockery has poured forth; such is the ray of divine knowledge which it has made descend into the minds of barbarians.

15. I know another case of such behavior by these men. One tribe begged the man of God to utter a prayer and blessing for their chieftain; but another tribe that was present objected to this, saying that the blessing ought to be uttered not for him but for their own leader, since the former was extremely unjust while the latter was a stranger to injustice. A long dispute and barbarian quarrel ensued, and finally they went for each other. I myself exhorted them with many words to stay calm, since the man of God had power sufficient to give a blessing to both the one and the other; but these said that that man should not get it, while those tried to deprive the other of it. By threatening them from above and calling them dogs, he with difficulty extinguished the dispute. I have told this out of a wish to display the faith in their understanding; for they would not have raged against each other, if they did not believe the blessing of the inspired man to possess the greatest power.

16. On another occasion I witnessed the occurrence of a celebrated miracle. Someone came in – he too was a tribal chieftain of Saracens – and begged the godly person to assist a man who on the road had

become paralysed in the limbs of his body; he said he had undergone the attack at Callinicum—it is a very great fort. When he had been brought right to the center, Symeon bade him disown the impiety of his ancestors. When he gladly consented and performed the order, he asked him if he believed in the Father and the only-begotten Son and the Holy Spirit. When the other professed his faith, he said: 'Since you believe in these names, stand up!' When he stood up, he ordered him to carry the tribal chieftain on his shoulders right to his tent, and he was of great bodily size. He at once picked him up and went on his way, while those present stirred their tongues to sing hymns to God.

17. He gave this order in imitation of the Master, who told the paralytic to carry his bed.[p] But let no one call the imitation usurpation, for His is the utterance, 'He who believes in me will himself do the works that I do, and greater than these will he do'.[q] Of this promise we have seen the fulfilment; for while the Lord's shadow nowhere performed a miracle, the shadow of the great Peter canceled death, drove out diseases, and put demons to flight.[r] But it is the Master who through His servants performed these miracles too; and now likewise it is by the use of His name that the godly Symeon performs his innumerable miracles.[21]

[18.[22] It happened that another miracle occurred in no way inferior to the preceding. A not undistinguished Ishmaelite, who was one of those who had found faith in the saving name of Christ the Master, made prayer to God with Symeon as the witness, and a promise as well: the promise was to abstain thereafter till death from all animal food.[23] At some time he broke this promise, I know not how, by daring to kill a bird and eat it. But since God chose to bring him to amendment by means of a reproof and to honor His servant who had been the witness of the broken promise, the flesh of the bird was changed in nature to stone, with the result that not even if he wanted to was he now able to eat—for how was it possible,[24] since the body which he had got hold of for eating had been petrified? Astounded by this extraordinary sight, the barbarian repaired to the holy man with great speed, bringing to light his secret sin, proclaiming his transgression to all, asking from God forgiveness for his offence and calling the saint to his aid, that through his all-powerful prayers he might free

[p]Cf. Mt 9:6.   [q]Jn 14:12.   [r]Cf. Ac 5:15.

him from the bonds of sin. Many have been eyewitnesses of this miracle by touching the part of the bird by the breast, which is composed of bone and stone.]

19. I have been, not only an eyewitness of his miracles, but also a hearer of his predictions of the future. The drought that occurred,[25] the great crop-failure of that year and the simultaneous famine and plague that followed, he foretold two years beforehand, saying that he had seen a rod threatening mankind and indicating the scourging it would cause. On another occasion he revealed beforehand an attack of what is called the grasshopper, and that it would not cause serious harm, for the mercy of God would follow hard on the punishment. When thirty days had passed a countless swarm so swooped down as to intercept the rays of the sun and create shade; and this we all saw distinctly. But it harmed only the fodder of the irrational animals, while causing no injury to the food of human beings. Also to me, when under attack from someone, he disclosed the death of my enemy fifteen days in advance, and from experience I learnt the truth of his prediction. [He also saw on one occasion two rods descend from the sky and fall on the land both east and west. The godly man explained it as a rising of the Persian and Scythian nations against the Roman empire; he declared the vision to those present, and with many tears and unceasing prayers stopped the blows with which the world was threatened. Certainly the Persian nation, when already armed and prepared for attack on the Romans, was through the opposition of divine power driven back from the proposed assault and fully engaged in domestic troubles within.][26]

20. Although I know very many other occurrences of this kind, I shall omit them, to avoid length in the account—and the preceding are sufficient to show the spiritual perception of his mind. His reputation is also great with the king of the Persians. As the envoys who came to see Symeon related, he wished to inquire carefully about the man's way of life and the nature of his miracles; and his spouse is said to have asked for oil honored by his blessing and to have received it as a very great gift. All the king's courtiers, struck by his reputation, and despite hearing from the Magians many calumnies against him,[27] wished to inquire precisely, and on being informed called him a man of God. The rest of the crowd, going up to the muleteers, servants

and soldiers, offered them money, begging to receive a share in the blessing attached to the oil.

21. The queen of the Ishmaelites, being sterile and longing for children, first sent some of her highest officials to beg that she become a mother, and then when she obtained her request and gave birth as she had wished, took the prince she had borne and hastened to the godly old man.[28] Since women are not allowed access, she sent the baby to him together with a request to receive blessing from him. 'Yours,' she said, 'is this sheaf; for I brought, with tears, the seed of prayer, but it was you who made the seed a sheaf, drawing down through prayer the rain of divine grace.'[s] But how long shall I strive to measure the depth of the Atlantic Ocean? For just as the latter cannot be measured by men, so the daily deeds of this man transcend narration.

22. More than all this I myself admire his endurance. Night and day he is standing within view of all; for having removed the doors and demolished a sizeable part of the enclosing wall,[29] he is exposed to all as a new and extraordinary spectacle—now standing for a long time, and now bending down repeatedly and offering worship to God.[30] Many of those standing by count the number of these acts of worship. Once one of those with me counted one thousand two hundred and forty-four of them, before slackening and giving up count. In bending down he always makes his forehead touch his toes—for his stomach's receiving food once a week, and little of it, enables his back to bend easily.

23. As a result of his standing, it is said that a malignant ulcer has developed in his left foot, and that a great deal of puss oozes from it continually. Nevertheless, none of these afflictions has overcome his philosophy, but he bears them all nobly, both the voluntary and the involuntary, overcoming both the former and the latter by his zeal. He was once obliged to show this wound to someone; I shall recount the cause. Someone arrived from Rabaena,[31] a worthy man, honored with being a deacon of Christ. On reaching the hill-top, he said, 'Tell me, by the truth that has converted the human race to itself, are you a man or a bodiless being?' When those present showed annoyance at the question, Symeon told them all to keep silence, and said to him, 'Why on earth have you posed this question?' He replied, 'I hear everyone

---

[s]Cf. Ps 126:5.

repeating that you neither eat nor lie down, both of which are proper to men—for no one with a human nature could live without food and sleep.' At this Symeon ordered a ladder to be placed against the pillar, and told him to ascend and first examine his hands, and then to place his hand inside his cloak of skins and look at not only his feet but also his severe ulcer. After seeing and marveling at the excess of the wound and learning from him that he does take food, he came down from there, and coming to me recounted everything.[32]

24. During the public festivals he displays another form of endurance: after the setting of the sun until it comes again to the eastern horizon, stretching out his hands to heaven he stands all night, neither beguiled by sleep nor overcome by exertion.[33]

25. Despite such labors and the mass of his achievements and the quantity of his miracles, he is as modest in spirit as if he were the last of all men in worth. In addition to his modest spirit, he is extremely approachable, sweet and charming, and makes answer to everyone who addresses him, whether he be artisan, beggar, or peasant. And he has received from the munificent Master the gift also of teaching. Making exhortation two times each day, he floods the ears of his hearers, as he speaks most gracefully and offers the lessons of the divine Spirit, bidding them look up to heaven and take flight, depart from the earth, imagine the expected kingdom, fear the threat of hell, despise earthly things, and await what is to come.

26. He can be seen judging and delivering verdicts that are right and just. These and similar activities he performs after the ninth hour—for the whole night and the day till the ninth hour he spends praying. But after the ninth hour he first offers divine instruction to those present, and then, after receiving each man's request and working some cures, he resolves the strife of those in dispute.[34] At sunset he begins his converse from then on with God.

27. Although engaged in these activities and performing them all, he does not neglect care of the holy churches—now fighting pagan impiety, now defeating the insolence of the Jews, at other times scattering the bands of the heretics, sometimes sending instructions on these matters to the emperor, sometimes rousing the governors to divine zeal, at others time charging the very shepherds of the churches to take still greater care of their flocks.[35]

28. I have proceeded through all this trying from a drop to indicate the rain, and using my forefinger to give readers of the account a taste of the sweetness of the honey. The facts celebrated by all are many times more numerous than these, but I did not promise to record everything, but to show by a few instances the character of the life of each one. Others, doubtless, will record far more than these; and if he lives on, he will perhaps add greater miracles. I myself desire and beg God that, helped by his own prayers, he may persevere in these good labors, since he is a universal decoration and ornament of piety, and that my own life may be brought into harmony and rightly directed in accordance with the Gospel way of life.

/ After a further span of life with many miracles and labors – having alone of men of any time remained unconquered by the flames of the sun, the frosts of winter, the fierce blasts of the winds and the weakness of human nature – since he had henceforth to be with Christ and receive the crowns of his immeasurable contests, he proved by his death, to those who disbelieved it, that he is a man. And he remained even after death unshakable, for while his soul repaired to heaven, his body even so could not bear to fall, but remained upright in the place of his contests, like an unbeaten athlete who strives with no part of his limbs to touch the ground. Thus, even after death does victory remain united to the contestants according to Christ. Certainly cures of diseases of every kind, miracles, and acts of divine power are accomplished even now, just as when he was alive, not only at the tomb of the holy relics but also by the memorial of his heroism and long contending – I mean the great and celebrated pillar of this righteous and much-lauded Symeon –, by whose holy intercession we pray both that we ourselves may be preserved and made firm in the true faith, and that every city and country upon which the name of our Lord Jesus Christ is invoked may enjoy protection, untried by every kind of damage and injury from both the sky and their enemies. To Him be glory for ever and ever.][36]

NOTES

1. This chapter provides what is easily our most reliable account of the most renowned of late antique holy men. The other two sources of note are a Greek *Life* by one Antony, allegedly an immediate disciple of Symeon, and a Syriac *Life* written a few years after the saint's death (though with some later additions). Antony offers a full and reliable account of the saint's death and obsequies, but his account of his life is slight and unreliable. The *Syriac Life* is much longer than the others, and represents the traditions of the monastery of Telanissus that sprang up rapidly round Symeon's pillar. It adds many vivid details, including a full repertoire of miracle stories essential for determining the scope of the saint's apostolate; but it is marred by numerous legendary accretions. A comparison between these two accounts and that of Theodoret, written twenty years before the saint's death, shows the latter to be sober and reliable. Theodoret uses the following sources: (1) personal acquaintance with Symeon (§2, 14-19, 22), (2) accounts by other eyewitnesses (§4, 23), (3) monastic tradition independent of that of Telanissus (§5, 8), (4) the monastic tradition of Telanissus itself, which must account for some unexpected parallels between Theodoret, and the *Syriac Life* (see n. 15, 16, 21 below). The early date of Theodoret's account and this wide range of sources, gives it a unique value, even if it lacks the freshness and empathy that mark Theodoret's account of the hermits with whom he enjoyed a much more intimate relationship.

The most important items in the learned literature on Symeon are H. Lietzmann, *Das Leben des heiligen Symeon Stylites*, Texte und Untersuchungen XXXII – which includes the text of Antony's *Life* and a translation of the Syriac one – and Festugière, *Antioche*. These works agree on the following chronology, based on the plethora of slightly divergent data in the sources: birth of the saint, in a village on the border of Syria and Cilicia, between 385 and 390; entry into a monastery at Teleda in 403; departure in 412 to Telanissus, where Symeon settled in an enclosure on a hill above the village and by 423 adopted as his mode of life perpetual standing on a pillar (whence his name 'Stylites', from *stylos*, a pillar); death in 459. Only the last of these dates is entirely certain; but the others are at least approximately correct.

2. Sisa was on the Syrian side of the boundary, in the territory of the city of Nicopolis.

3. Symeon's having been a shepherd is doubtless a typological accretion: his social status is better indicated by the 'very wealthy' aunt mentioned in the *Syriac Life* 11.

4. Symeon's conversion bears a suspicious similarity to that of Antony of Egypt; see his *Life* 2-3.

5. Tchalenko, *Villages Antiques*, I: 134-5, conjecturally identifies this monastery with that of Burj es-Sab', lying on the slope of Mt Barakat, immediately above the village of Teleda; its tower (dating to 572) is still to be seen. The *Syriac Life* 11 tells us that Symeon chose this monastery because he had a cousin there.

6. The tense of 'lived' is curiously ambiguous: it could mean either that Heliodorus was sixty-five when he became superior (Canivet's translation), or that he was sixty-five when Symeon entered the monastery (Festugière, *Antioche*, 349), or that he was sixty-five at the time Theodoret was writing (P. Peeters in *Analecta Bollandiana* 61, p.39), or that he lived a total of sixty-five years (Canivet, *Le monachisme syrien*, 169). The last seems the most natural rendering, even though it involves a clash with the *Syriac Life* 22, which gives seventy-nine years as Heliodorus's lifespan.

7. Contrast Daniel the Stylite (b. 409) being refused admission to a monastery at the age of five, and being with difficulty admitted at the age of twelve (*Life* 3-4).

173

8. Theodoret first visited Teleda in the early 410s (IV.10), and so probably heard of the episode narrated here soon after its occurrence.

9. Telanissus, the modern Deir Sim'an, lies in a valley of the limestone plateau in the east of the territory of Antioch. The date of Symeon's arrival here is given as 410 at *Syriac Life* 24; the figure of forty-seven years for the subsequent period till his death (459), given at *Syriac Life* 116 and supported by other sources, implies a date of 412.

10. Bassus originated from Edessa (*Syriac Life* 26). He was clearly a *periodeutes*, an itinerant priest entrusted with the supervision of churches in a rural area. An inscription at Telanissus commemorates a later *periodeutes*, John (*Dictionnaire d'Archéologie et de Liturgie*, XIV: 378).

11. Cp. *Sayings of the Fathers* (Syriac version) I.68 for an Egyptian monk 'who made a vow not to drink any water during the fast of forty days', and kept it.

12. See Introduction, XIV with note 5 for this chronological crux, on which depends the dating of the composition of the *Rel. Hist.*

13. In other words Meletius was a *chorepiscopus*, with the same responsibilities as a *periodeutes*, but episcopal rank. See Jones, *The Later Roman Empire*, 879.

14. Evidence of Symeon's reputation in Gaul is contained in several sixth-century texts: *Life of Genovefa* 27 (Gallic traders visiting Symeon); Gregory of Tours, *History of the Franks* VIII.15, X.24, and *The Glory of the Confessors* 26. This last passage tells of Symeon's inflexible refusal to see any woman, even his mother, and of the immediate death of a woman who tried to infringe this rule; the story, described as taken from 'the book of his life', is a variant of the story told in Antony, *Life of Symeon* 14.

15. This passage is puzzling in that Symeon's world-wide fame, described in the preceding section, was presumably the result rather than the cause of his mounting the pillar. It cannot be a coincidence that at this point the *Syriac Life* also discourses on Symeon's fame 'in every region' (§52).

16. For contemporary doubts about Symeon's histrionic asceticism, see Theodore Lector, *Eccl. Hist.* II.41: 'The monks of Egypt, learning that the holy Symeon was standing on a pillar, criticized the strangeness of the thing . . . , and sent him a certificate of excommunication. But when they learnt of the man's life and crown, they re-entered into communion with him.' Cp. *Life of Daniel the Stylite* 7: Mesopotamian monks, visiting Telanissus c. 430, accused Symeon of vainglory, but were won over when they actually spoke to him. The defence of Symeon advanced by Theodoret here – the need for a striking sign to wake the world from slumber – is identical to that in the *Syriac Life* 117, and adduces the same biblical precedents. We are doubtless in the presence of a standard defence circulated by the monks of Telanissus.

17. Canivet (in note *ad loc.*) judges the rest of this paragraph to be an interpolation on the inadequate ground that it interrupts the narrative.

18. See IV.12 for a monk at Teleda – Abba – of Ishmaelite origin. The Ishmaelites were Arab tribesmen of the Syrian desert, many of them in alliance with Rome; they were also known as Saracens. Doubtless those here are the Tanukhaye of the region of Chalcis. Many Saracens of Phoenicia and Arabia (Transjordan) were already converted in the fourth century, but the conversion of those in northern Syria occurred in the fifty century, mainly through the work of holy men such as Symeon. See J. Trimingham, *Christianity among the Arabs in Pre-Islamic Times*, esp. ch. 3.

19. 'Aphrodite' may be the great Syrian goddess Atargatis, who was sometimes identified with Venus (Plutarch, *Life of Crassus* 17.6), or perhaps the specifically Ishmaelite goddess Allat, as suggested by R. MacMullen, *Christianizing the Roman Empire*, 2–3.

20. This renouncing of camel meat shows that Syrian Christians respected the prohibition in Deut 14:7.

21. Partly the same argument, with the same citation of Jn 14:12 and Acts 5:15, occurs in the *Syriac Life* 99.

22. This paragraph, absent from the best manuscripts, is to be rejected as an interpolation.
23. Vegetarianism was a common form of asceticism: see III, note 9.
24. Canivet's Greek text has two additional words: 'How was it possible *to be able to eat*, since . . .?' These words are a clumsy repetition from the previous sentence and are found only in a few manuscripts: they are clearly to be excluded as a gloss.
25. This is probably the same drought as that of XXIV.7.
26. Lacking in most manuscripts, the bracketed section is an interpolation. The two scourges are the Persians and the Huns. The Persians invaded the empire in 440–41, until forced to withdraw by an invasion in their rear by the Ephthalites of Central Asia; the Huns began making serious inroads in 441, when they overran the Balkans. This dates the prophecy to 441, one year after the probable date of the composition of the *Rel. Hist.*
27. For the Magians as the chief stimulators of the Persian persecution of Christians, see Theodoret, *Eccl. Hist.* V.39(38).
28. Cp. the conversion *c.*360 of the Saracen chieftain Zocomus by a holy man who by prayer to God obtained a son for him (Sozomen, *Eccl. Hist.* VI.38).
29. According to the *Life* by Antony 12, there was a double wall, of which the inner had a gate; when the gate was shut – as throughout each Lent (*Syriac Life* 88) – Symeon could only be seen from within the enclosure.
30. See the *Syriac Life* 88, 'Three of the vertebrae of his back became dislocated through his incessant praying, during which he would bend down and then straighten up before his Lord'.
31. Rabaena was a large village in north-west Euphratensis, near modern Marash.
32. Cp. Daniel the Stylite replying to an enquirer, 'Believe me, brother, I both eat and drink sufficiently for my needs; for I am not a spirit nor disembodied, but I too am a man and am clothed with flesh' (*Life of Daniel* 62). On the episode here see P. Brown, 'The Rise and Function of the Holy Man', 130–1.
33. Symeon committed himself to perpetual standing by tying his feet to the pillar, *Syriac Life* 83: 'His feet were bound and fettered as if in the stocks, so that he could move neither of them either to the right or to the left, till the bones and sinews of his feet became visible as a result of the pain and his belly was lacerated by standing.' See *Syriac Life* 116 for Symeon's dispensing with sleep altogether.
34. For Symeon's work as judge and mediator, see *Syriac Life* 57: 'How many victims of oppression were through his word freed from their oppressors, how many statements of liability were torn up as a result of his efforts! . . . How many slaves were manumitted, and the certificates of their slavery torn up before the saint! How many orphans and widows were brought and nourished near our Lord (i.e. by the Church) through the insistence of the blessed one! . . . He edified the priests of God through his great assiduity; through his assiduity were the laws and ordinances of the Church confirmed.'
35. On several occasions the imperial court requested Symeon's intervention in the great doctrinal disputes of the time. In 432 Theodosius II got Symeon to press John of Antioch to be reconciled to Cyril of Alexandria; in 434 Titus, *comes domesticorum*, got Symeon to press Theodoret himself on the same issue. Theodoret yielded, though he was deeply distressed by the pressure brought to bear on him (Festugière, *Antioche*, 418–23). Again after the Council of Chalcedon (451) he advised the dowager empress Eudocia at Jerusalem in favor of Chalcedon and reconciliation with bishop Juvenal of Jerusalem; and in 457 he responded to the emperor Leo's circular letter, again in favor of Chalcedon (W. Frend, *The Rise of the Monophysite Movement*, 148, 153). Monophysite sources tell of Theodoret personally visiting Symeon after the Council of Chalcedon to press for his support of its Definition.

36. This feeble homiletic close is an interpolation, found only in one family of manuscripts, the same family that includes the interpolations at §§18 & 19. Symeon died in 459, almost twenty years after the composition of the *Rel. Hist.* The tomb of Symeon was at Antioch, whither his body was translated immediately after his death.

XXVII
BARADATUS

THE AVENGING SPIRIT common to men has devised many ways of evil in his zeal to consign the whole human race to total destruction, and the nurslings of piety have devised many and differing ladders for the ascent into heaven. Some, contesting in companies – myriad are such communities, defeating enumeration – enjoy unageing crowns and attain the desired ascent; others, embracing the solitary life, practising conversation with God alone and receiving no human consolation, enjoy in this way proclamation as victors. Some living in tents and others in cells chant hymns to God; others embrace the life in holes and caves. Many, of whom I have recalled some, have not been induced to have a cave or hole or hut or cell, but giving their bodies to the naked air endure contrasts of temperature, sometimes frozen by unrelieved frost, sometimes burnt by the fire of the sun's rays. Of these again the life is various: some stand all the time, others divide the day between sitting and standing; some, immured in enclosures, shun the company of the many; others, with no such covering, are exposed to all who wish to see them.

2. I am obliged at the present juncture to proceed through each of these, for I wish to record the life of the wonderful Baradatus;[1] for he too has devised new tests of endurance. First, immuring himself for a long time in a cell, he enjoyed divine consolation alone. From there repairing to the ridge situated above, and constructing out of wood a small chest that did not even match his body, in this he dwelt, obliged to stoop the whole time — for its length was not equal in size to the height of his body. It was not even fitted together with planks, but had openings like a lattice, and was similar to windows that have rather broad openings for the light; because of this he was neither safe from the assault of the rains nor free from the flames of the sun, but endured both of them like the other open-air ascetics, whom he surpassed only in the labor of reclusion.

3. Having spent a long time in this way, he later came out, yielding to the instances of the inspired Theodotus, who had been appointed to the episcopal see of Antioch.[2] However, he stands all the time, stretching out his hands and hymning the God of the universe, and covering his entire body with a tunic of skins — only round the nose and mouth has he left a small opening for breath, in order to receive and inhale the common air, since otherwise human nature cannot live. He endures all this labor, even though with a body not robust but much afflicted by numerous ailments; but his bubbling zeal, inflamed by divine love, compels to labor one who cannot labor.

4. Adorned in mind with understanding, he is excellent at composing questions and answers; he sometimes syllogizes better and more powerfully than those well versed in the labyrinths of Aristotle.[3] Although he is at the very summit of virtue, he does not allow his spirit to soar above, but orders it to crawl below at the skirts of the mountain, for he knows what harm is incurred by an understanding swollen with vanity. Such, in summary, is this man's philosophy. May it be that it so increases as to reach the finishing-post of the race, for the glory of these victors is the common joy of the pious. For me may it be that, supported by the prayers of these men, I do not get far from this mountain, but ascend it gradually and luxuriate in gazing upon them.

NOTES

1. Baradatus was a hermit in the region of Antioch who lived at first in a cell, and then inside a chest till dissuaded by bishop Theodotus of Antioch (§3). He subsequently practised perpetual standing. See XXI, note 1 for the imperial court singling him out in both 434 and 457 as one of the preeminent ascetics of the East.
2. Theodotus was bishop of Antioch in the 420s; he is the recipient of Theodoret, *epp.* XXXII, XLV.
3. Cp. Theodoret, *Cure of Hellenic Maladies* V.72: those who know the Persians 'report that they are extremely skilful at syllogisms and are capable of refuting the complex arguments of others . . . , not because they have read the labyrinths of Chrysippus and Aristotle . . . , but they have had nature alone as their teacher'.

XXVIII
THALELAEUS

NOR SHALL I BE SILENT about the story of Thalelaeus;[1] for the spectacle is full of wonder, and not only have I heard the accounts of others but have myself been an eyewitness of the extraordinary spectacle. At twenty stades from Gabala—it is a small and charming city—he repaired to a hill on which there was a precinct dedicated to demons and honored with many sacrifices by the impious of old. Here he pitched a small hut. They always served those miscreants, they said, in an attempt to appease by service their great cruelty, for they caused harm to many passing by or of the neighborhood, not only men but also asses and mules, oxen and sheep, not making war on irrational animals but by means of them plotting against men. On this occasion, when they saw him arrive, they tried to frighten him, but were unable to do so, since faith fenced him round and grace fought on his behalf. Therefore, filled with rage and frenzy, they proceeded against the trees planted there—there happened to be many flourishing fig and olive trees on this hill. They say that more than five hundred of these were suddenly uprooted; I heard this recounted by the neighboring peasants, who were formerly engulfed by the darkness of impiety but received through his teaching and miracle-working the light of the knowledge of God.

2. Since even by doing this the wicked demons had failed to frighten the athlete of philosophy, they again applied other devices. By wailing and displaying torches at night, they tried to terrify him and instil confusion in his thought. But when he laughed at all their assaults, they afterwards left him and fled away.

3. Making two wheels of two cubits in diameter, he joined both wheels together with planks not fitted to each other but separated apart. Then seating himself inside and fixing these separated planks firmly with bolts and nails, he hung the wheel up in the air. Fixing three other tall wooden stakes in the ground and connecting their upper ends with other pieces of wood, he fastened the double wheel in the midst of them and raised it up, the inside of the wheel having a height of two cubits and a breadth of a cubit. Sitting or rather suspended in this, he has spent ten years up till now. Since he has a very big body, not even sitting can he straighten his neck, but he always sits bent double, with his forehead tightly pressed against his knees.

4. On coming to see him, I found him reaping the benefit of the divine Gospels, gathering benefit therefrom with extreme concentration. I questioned him, out of desire to learn the reason for this novel mode of life. He replied to me in Greek, for he happens to be Cilician in race: 'Burdened,' he said, 'with many sins and believing in the penalties that are threatened, I have devised this form of life, contriving moderate punishments for the body, in order to reduce the mass of those awaited.[2] For the latter are more grievous not only in quantity but also in quality; for they are involuntary, and what happens against our will is particularly disagreeable, while what is voluntary, even if wearisome, is less painful—for my labor is self-chosen and not compulsory. So if (he concluded) by these slight afflictions I lessen those awaited, great is the profit I shall derive therefrom.' Hearing this, I was overwhelmed with admiration for his shrewdness, because he not only contended beyond the course laid down and devised other contests of his own will, but also knew the reason for them and taught it to others.

5. The local inhabitants have declared that many miracles occur through his prayer, with not only men but also camels, asses, and

mules enjoying healing. In consequence, all this people, formerly in the grip of impiety, have disowned their ancestral imposture and accepted the splendor of divine light. With their assistance he has demolished the precinct of demons and erected a great shrine to the triumphant martyrs, opposing to those falsely called gods the godly dead.[3] May it be that by their intercession this man too may with the same victory reach the goal of the contests, and that we, aided by both them and him, may become fervent lovers of the contests of philosophy.

NOTES

1. Thalelaeus was a hermit on a hill twenty stades (two miles) outside Gabala, a city on the Mediterranean coast sixty miles south of Antioch. He lived at first in a cell, and then, from 430 (§3), in the strange contraption of a suspended cylinder, which may be compared to Baradatus's chest (XXVII.2). He converted the peasants of the district to Christianity (§1,5). Theodoret once visited him (§4).
2. For a holy man's emphasis on his own sinfulness, cp. XXI.33.
3. For the less attractive side of the monastic campaign against the traditional paganism of the countryside, see the account of the demolition of temples against the wishes of the natives in Libanius, *Oration* XXX (Loeb *Selected Works* II: 100ff.) 8-9 (AD 386).

XXIX
Marana and Cyra

AFTER RECORDING THE WAY of life of the heroic men, I think it useful to treat also of women who have contended no less if not more; for they are worthy of still greater praise, when, despite having a weaker nature, they display the same zeal as the men and free their sex from its ancestral disgrace.[1]

2. At this point I shall treat of Marana and Cyra,[2] who have defeated all the others in the contests of endurance. Their fatherland was Beroea, their stock the glory of their fatherland, and their upbringing appropriate for their stock. But despising all these, they acquired a small place in front of the town, and entering within it, walled up the door with clay and stones. For their maidservants who were eager to share this life with them they built a small dwelling outside this enclosure, and in this they told them to live. Through a small window they keep a watch on what they are doing, and repeatedly rouse them to prayer and inflame them with divine love. They themselves, with neither house nor hut, embrace the open-air life.

3. In place of a door a small window has been constructed for them, through which they take in the food they need and talk with

the women who come to see them. For this intercourse the season of Pentecost has been laid down; during the rest of the time they embrace the quiet life. And it is Marana alone who talks to visitors; no one has ever heard the other one speak.

4. They wear iron, and carry such a weight that Cyra, with her weaker body, is bent down to the ground and is quite unable to straighten her body. They wear mantles so big as to trail along behind and literally cover their feet and in front to fall down right to the belt, literally hiding at the same time face, neck, chest, and hands.

5. I have often been inside the door in order to see them; for out of respect for the episcopal office they have bidden me dig through the door. And so I have seen that weight of iron which even a well-built man could not carry. After long entreaty I succeeded in getting it off them for the nonce,[3] but after our departure they again put it on their limbs—round the neck the collar, round the waist the belt, and on hands and feet the chains assigned to them.

6. In this mode of life they have completed not merely five or ten or fifteen years, but forty-two; and despite having contended for so long a time, they love their exertion as if they had only just entered on the contests. For contemplating the beauty of the Bridegroom, they bear the labor of the course with ease and facility, and press on to reach the goal of the contests, where they see the Beloved standing and pointing to the crown of victory. Because of this, in suffering the assaults of rain and snow and sun they feel neither pain nor distress but from apparent afflictions reap joy of heart.

7. Emulating the fast of the inspired Moses,[a] they have three times spent the same length of time without food, for it was at the end of forty days that they took a little nourishment. Three times also have they emulated the abstinence from eating of the godly Daniel, completing three weeks and only then supplying nourishment to the body. On one occasion, out of a desire to behold the sacred places of the saving sufferings of Christ, they hastened to Aelia,[4] enjoying no nutriment on the way. It was after reaching that city and accomplishing their worship that they took nourishment, and then returning back completed the journey without food—and

[a] Cf. Ex 24:18.

there are not less than twenty stages. Conceiving a desire to behold as well the shrine of the triumphant Thecla in Isauria,[5] in order from all sources to kindle the firebrand of their love for God, they journeyed both there and back without food – to such a degree has divine yearning driven them to frenzy, so much has divine love for the Bridegroom driven them mad. Since by such a way of life they have adorned the female sex, becoming as models for other women, they will be crowned by the Master with the wreaths of victory. I myself, having displayed the benefit therefrom and culled their blessing, shall pass on to another account.

NOTES

1. See XXX.5 with n.3 for the equality in asceticism of men and women.
2. Marana and Cyra were two noblewomen of Beroea, who founded a small convent on the outskirts of the city. This they directed, while themselves living in a separate, unroofed enclosure (cp. XVIII.1 and XXII.7 for this combination of reclusion with the open-air life). They had been living this life since 398 (§6).
3. For a bishop exercising a moderating influence in cases of excessive mortification, cp. XXI.6–7, XXIV.4, XXVII.3.
4. Theodoret himself had made a pilgrimage to Jerusalem (*Cure of Hellenic Maladies* XI.71), as had Peter the Galatian (IX.2). See E. Hunt, *Holy Land Pilgrimage in the Later Roman Empire*.
5. The first mention of pilgrimage to the shrine of St Thecla in Isauria occurs in Gregory Nazianzen and Egeria in the 380s. The most distinguished Syrian pilgrim was Theodore of Mopsuestia († 428), who visited the shrine to ask for the gift of interpreting the Scriptures. See Canivet, *Le monachisme syrien*, 278, n.102.

XXX
DOMNINA

EMULATING THE LIFE of the inspired Maron, whom we recalled above, the wonderful Domnina[1] set up a small hut in the garden of her mother's house; her hut is made of millet stalks. Passing the whole day there, she wets with incessant tears not only her cheeks but also her garments of hair, for such is the clothing with which she covers her body. Going at cockcrow to the divine shrine nearby, she offers hymnody to the Master of the universe, together with the rest, both men and women. This she does not only at the beginning of the day but also at its close, thinking the place consecrated to God to be more venerable than every other spot and teaching others so. Judging it, for this reason, worthy of every attention, she has persuaded her mother and brothers to spend their fortune on it.

2. As food she has lentils soaked in water; and she endures all this labor with a body reduced to a skeleton and half-dead—for her skin is very thin, and covers her thin bones as if with a film, while her fat and flesh have been worn away by labors. Though exposed to all who wish to see her, both men and women, she neither sees a face

nor shows her face to another, but is literally covered up by her cloak and bent down onto her knees, while she speaks extremely softly and indistinctly, always making her remarks with tears. She has often taken my hand, and after placing it on her eyes, released it so soaked that my very hand dripped tears. What discourse could give due praise to a woman who with such wealth of philosophy weeps and wails and sighs like those living in extreme poverty? For it is fervent love for God that begets these tears, firing the mind to divine contemplation, stinging it with pricks and urging it on to migrate from here.

3. Though spending in this way both the day and the night, nor does she neglect the other forms of virtue, but ministers, as far as she can, to the heroic contestants, both those we have mentioned and those we have omitted. She also ministers to those who come to see her, bidding them stay with the shepherd of the village and sending them all they need herself, for the property of her mother and brothers is available for her to spend, since it reaps a blessing through her. To myself too when I arrived at this place—it is to the south of our region—she sent rolls, fruit, and soaked lentils.

4. But how long can I expatiate in my eagerness to relate all her virtue, when I ought to bring into the open the life of the other women who have imitated both her and those we recalled above? For there are many others, of whom some have embraced the solitary life and others have preferred life with many companions—in such a way that communities of two hundred and fifty, or more, or less, share the same life, putting up with the same food, choosing to sleep on rush-mats alone, assigning their hands to card wool, and conscreating their tongues with hymns.[2]

5. Myriad and defeating enumeration are the philosophic retreats of this kind not only in our region but throughout the East; full of them are Palestine, Egypt, Asia, Pontus, and all Europe. From the time when Christ the Master honored virginity by being born of a virgin, nature has sprouted meadows of virginity and offered these fragrant and unfading flowers to the Creator, not separating virtue into male and female nor dividing philosophy into two categories. For the difference is one of bodies not of souls: 'in Christ Jesus,' according to the divine Apostle, 'there is neither male nor female'.[a] And a single

[a] Gal 3:28.

faith has been given to men and women: 'there is one Lord, one faith, one baptism, one God and Father of all, who is above all and through all and in us all'.[b] And it is one kingdom of heaven which the Umpire has set before the victors, fixing this common prize for the contests.[3]

6. As I have said, numerous are the pious wrestling-schools of men and women not only among us but also in all Syria, Palestine, Cilicia, and Mesopotamia. In Egypt, it is said, some retreats have five thousand men each,[4] who work and in-between sing hymns to the Master, not only providing themselves with the necessary food out of their labor, but also supplying guests who come and are needy.

7. But to recount everything is impossible not only for me but for all writers. Even if it were possible, I consider it superfluous and an ambition without gain; for those who wish to cull some profit, what has been said is sufficient to provide what they desire. We have recalled different lives, and added accounts of women to those of men, for this reason: that men old and young, and women too, may have models of philosophy, and that each person, as he receives the impress of his favorite life, may have as a rule and regulator of his own life the one presented in our account. Just as painters look at their model when imitating eyes, nose, mouth, cheeks, ears, forehead, the very hairs of the head and beard, and in addition the sitting and standing postures, and the very expression of the eyes, whether genial or forbidding, so it is fitting that each of the readers of this work choose to imitate a particular life and order their own life in accordance with the one they choose. Just as joiners straighten their planks with a measuring-cord and remove what is excessive to the point where, applying the rule, they see the plank is equal, so too one who wishes to emulate a particular life must apply it to himself in place of a rule, and cut off the excesses of vice, while supplying what is lacking in virtue. It is for this reason that we have undertaken the labor of composition, offering to those who wish it a means of benefit. I ask my future readers, as they luxuriate effortlessly in the labors of others, to repay my labors with prayer.

8. I also beg those whose life I have written down not to leave me tarrying at a distance from their spiritual choir, but to draw me up,

---

[b]Eph 4:5–6.

who am lying below, lead me up to the summit of virtue and join me to their own choir, so that I may not only praise the wealth of others, but also myself have some cause to give praise — by deed, word, and thought glorifying the Saviour of the universe, with whom to the Father be the glory together with the Holy Spirit, now and always and for ever and ever. Amen.

NOTES

1. Domnina was a female ascetic in the southern part of the region of Cyrrhus (§3). She lived in a cell in a garden owned by her relatives, who fed her and funded her alms. She had especially close links with the local church: she attended morning and evening prayer each day, and the parish priest put up her many visitors (§3). In all, she belonged to the tradition of pious virgins, living at home, who first feature in Syrian writing in the early third-century Pseudo-Clementine *Epistles on Virginity*. Her fierce austerities betray, however, the influence of the eremiticism of the fourth and fifth centuries.

2. For convents of women, see too IX.12 and XXIX.2. For manual labor, see X.2–3, with n.3.

3. On the moral and spiritual equality of men and women, cp. *Cure of Hellenic Maladies* v.57: God 'applies the same laws to men and women, since the difference lies in the shape of the body and not in the soul. The woman like the man is rational . . . , and knows like him what to shun and what to pursue; sometimes she discovers what will be of benefit better than the man does. . . . Moreover, the prizes of virtue are offered to women as to men, since the contests of virtue are shared.'

4. Cp. Cassian, *Institutes* IV.1 (*c*.420), which describes Pachomius's foundation at Tabennisi as the largest monastery in Egypt, containing 'more than five thousand brethren under the rule of a single abbot'.

EPILOGUE: ON DIVINE LOVE

HOW GREAT AND HOW MANY[1] are the athletes of virtue and with which crowns they are decked, is clearly demonstrated by the accounts we have written of them. Even if they do not contain all their contests, yet even a few suffice to show the character of the whole life.[2] It is not by wearing away all the gold that is applied to it but by being rubbed against a little of it that a stone shows it to be good coin or bad. Likewise in the case of an archer, one could learn accurately from the discharge of only a few arrows whether he uses the bow well, hitting the target, or if he shoots outside, being unpractised in the skill. It is possible in the same way too to test the other men of skill, not to mention them individually: athletes, runners, actors of tragedy, pilots, shipwrights, doctors, peasants, and, in a word, all the others who put their hand to some skill; for slight experiment is sufficient to prove the skill of those with knowledge and convict the ignorance of those who adopt the mere name. Therefore, as I said, the recording of even a few of the achievements of each one is sufficient to teach their whole purpose in life. It is our present task to examine, inquire, and discover exactly from what impulse they embraced this way of life, and by what thoughts they attained the very summit of philosophy; for that it was not through confidence in the strength of the body that they became enamored of what is beyond human nature, transcended the limits imposed on it, and jumped beyond the bounds fixed for contestants in piety, experience is a clear teacher.

2. No one who has not shared in this philosophy has ever displayed their endurance. Even if shepherds are exposed to snow, it is not all the time, for they use caves or return home, and cover their feet with shoes and protect the other parts of the body with warm clothing; and they enjoy nourishment two or three times a day, perhaps even four. Moreover, eating meat and drinking wine warm their bodies better than any hearth. For when such nourishment suffers conversion and, sifted as by some strainer and reaching the liver, undergoes change into blood, it passes into the heart through the hollow vein; now warmed, from there, through the dispersed veins acting like conduits, it permeates all the parts of the body. Wherever it arrives, it does not merely moisten but also warms like fire, and heats the body better than soft clothes. For it is not, as some suppose, tunics, coats, and cloaks that supply heat to the body, or they would warm wood and stones on which they were laid; but no one has ever witnessed wood or stone becoming warmer under clothes. Therefore these do not supply warmth to the body either. Instead, they preserve the warmth of the body; they ward off the attack of the cold air, and by absorbing the vapors that exude from the body are warmed by them and lie more warmly on the body. Experience is the witness: often when we lie on a cold bed, we make warm the mattress, which was cold shortly before, by the contact of the body. Therefore nourishment warms the body more than any clothing. Those who take it to the point of repletion have a sufficient protection against the attack of the freezing cold, for they fortify the body by it, and make it withstand such a time of year. But those who enjoy neither food nor drink each day and, when they do, do not wait for repletion but curb their appetite at its height, and do not partake of what can warm the body but either eat grass like irrational animals or use only soaked pulses—how could they draw heat from such nourishment? What quantity, or quality, of bloodstream could result therefrom?

3. Therefore the habits of others in no way resemble theirs. Neither do the two have the same clothing, for theirs is very rough and quite incapable of warming, nor is their nourishment similar, but diametrically opposite. For shepherds and others like them, every time of day is a time for nourishment; for they define the time by their appetite, and even if hunger assails them in the morning, they take nourishment straightaway. In addition, they take whatever is on offer; for eating this and not that is not laid down, but they enjoy without scruple everything they want. But in the other case, there are days and times, kinds of nourishment and limits of quantity, and taking one's fill is excluded. Therefore let none of our critics by adducing farm-laborers, shepherds, and sailors attempt to belittle the contests of these great athletes.[3] For the farm-laborer, while toiling by day, is looked after at home by night, his wife providing him every service; the shepherd likewise shares in all the things we mentioned above. The sailor feels the rays of the sun on his body, but applies to his body treatment by means of water; for he swims as much as he wishes, and applies the cold of the water as an antidote to the burning heat of the rays. But these enjoy no service from anyone; for they do not live with wives, who devise every kind of comfort for their husbands. Nor, when the sun's rays assail hotly, do they apply relief by means of water; neither in winter-time do they oppose nourishment to the freezing cold, nor do they apply to the labors of the day rest by night like some medicine. Indeed, their fatigues by night are greater and more numerous than those by day: for in the night they undertake struggle against sleep and do not permit this sweet defeat; but they overcome this most pleasant tyranny, and continue all night chanting hymns to the Master. Therefore no one uninvolved in their philosophy has displayed their endurance.

4. If no other men have been able to hold out against such labors, it is clearly desire for God that has made them surpass the limits of nature. Kindled by the firebrand from on high, they bear gladly the attack of the freezing cold, and it is by dew from there that they mitigate the burning heat of the sun's rays. It is this desire that nourishes, waters, and clothes them, gives wings and teaches to fly, makes them transcend the heavens, reveals the Beloved in so far as it is possible, and through imagination inflames yearning for contemplation, stirs

up longing for it, and kindles the flame more fiercely. Just as those enamored of bodies fuel their longing by the sight of the objects of their passion and make that madness more grievous, so those who have received the goad of divine love, by imagining that divine and pure beauty, make sharper the pricks of love, and the more they yearn to enjoy, the more they draw their fill. While surfeit follows on the pleasure of bodies, divine desire does not admit the laws of satiety.

5. Such was Moses the great lawgiver, who often, in so far as man can attain to it, was counted worthy of divine contemplation and often heard the blessed voice, who was in the darkness for forty days together and received the divine legislation, who not only did not experience satiety but attained a desire still more fervent and intense. For as if he had felt a kind of torpor under the intoxication of that desire, or been utterly maddened with longing, he did not acknowledge his own nature, but yearned to see what it is not lawful to see. As if he had forgotten who was the Master and was thinking only of his longing, he said to the God of the universe, 'Behold, thou sayest to me, "You have found favor before me and I know you before all". Therefore, if I have found favor in your sight, reveal yourself to me: may I see you clearly.'[a] Such was the intoxication he had received from divine love, and the intoxication did not quench his thirst but made it more intense; the supply of drink intensified his desire, and eating increased his appetite. Just as fire, the more it is fed, displays greater activity—for it is increased, not dulled, by the addition of fuel—, so too love of God is kindled by contemplating the things of God, and derives therefrom an activity more intense and fervent. The more a man devotes himself to the things of God, the more does he kindle the fire of love. This has been taught not only by the great Moses but also by the holy spouse of whom the inspired Paul says, 'I have yoked you to one husband to present a pure virgin' to God.[b] It is she who in the Song of Songs exclaims to the Bridegroom, 'Show me your face, and make me hear your voice, for your voice is sweet and your face is comely.'[c] Though she conceived her love as a result of the words spoken about him, she is not satisfied by words, but yearns also to hear his voice. Given wings by the accounts of his

[a] Ex 33:12–13 (LXX).   [b] 2 Co 11:2.   [c] Sg 2:14.

comeliness, she desires the vision itself, expressing her longing by the praises she utters. 'Show me your face,' she says, 'and make me hear your voice, for your voice is sweet and your face is comely.'

6. He who arranged the marriage and presented the bride—I mean the inspired Paul—was also enamored of this beauty, and uttered this expression of desire: 'Who will separate us from the love of God? Tribulation, or distress, or persecution, or hunger, or nakedness, or peril, or sword? As it is written, For your sake we are being put to death all the day long; we have been reckoned as sheep for slaughter.' He then indicates the cause of endurance: 'in all these things,' he says, 'we more than conquer, through God who has loved us'.[d] Let us examine who we are and what benefits we have enjoyed, and that it was not we who loved first, but being loved we gave love in return;[e] while hating we were loved, and 'while enemies we were reconciled.'[f] We did not ourselves beg to obtain reconciliation, but received the Only-begotten as intercessor; those who had wronged were consoled by him they had wronged. In addition to this, let us reflect upon him who was crucified for us, the saving passion, the repose of death, the hope of resurrection that has been given to us.

7. When we examine these and the like, we overcome the melancholy things that fall to our lot; and by applying the memory of benefits to the temporary hardships of the body, we bear gladly the attack of things distressing. When we weigh up against longing for the Master all the sorrows of life, we find them light indeed. Even if we assemble together all that is pleasurable and seems delightful, divine yearning, when put in the balance, shows them to be more feeble than a shadow and more perishable than spring blossoms. This he expresses clearly both by what we have cited and by what we are about to cite: 'I am convinced,' he says, 'that neither death, nor life, nor angels, nor principalities, nor powers, neither things present nor things to come, neither height nor depth, nor any other creation will be able to separate us from the love of God in Christ Jesus our Lord.'[g] For when, in placing at the head only what is melancholy, he has listed tribulation, distress, persecution, hunger, nakedness, peril, and sword (that is, violent death), he then with good reason adds to things painful

---

[d]Rom 8:35–37.   [e]Cf. 1 Jn 4:10, 19.   [f]Rom 5:10.   [g]Rom 8:38–39.

things delightful – to death life, things of the mind to things of sense, to things seen the unseen powers, to the present and passing the future and abiding, and in addition to these the depth of hell and the height of the kingdom. Listing all these, he finds them all, both the unpleasant and the delightful, inferior to longing, and deprivation of love more bitter than punishment in hell, and shows that, if it were possible, we would choose the threatened punishment together with divine love rather than the promised kingdom of heaven without it. Then, intoxicated with yearning, he seeks what is not at hand and strives to compare this to divine longing: 'neither height nor depth,' he says, 'nor any other creation will be able to separate us from the love of God in Christ Jesus our Lord.'

8. Not only, he says, do I prefer longing for the Saviour and Creator to all things seen and unseen together, but even if any other creation should appear greater and finer than this one, it will not persuade me to give love in exchange.[4] Even if someone offers what is delightful, but without love, I will not accept it; even if he imposes what is melancholy, on account of love, it will appear to me lovely and utterly desirable; hunger on account of love is more delightful to me than every luxury, persecution more pleasant than peace, nakedness more agreeable than a purple robe and cloth of gold, peril more sweet than every security, violent death more to be chosen than every sort of life. For the cause of suffering becomes for me a consolation, and for the sake of one both lover and beloved I accept these showers. For, 'Him who knew not sin He made to be sin for our sake, so that we might become the righteousness of God in him';[h] he who was rich became poor for our sake, so that we by his poverty might become rich.[i] And, 'He redeemed us from the curse of the law by becoming a curse for our sake'.[j] And, 'He humbled himself, by becoming obedient unto death, death on a cross'.[k] And, 'While we were yet sinners, Christ died for us.'[l] Reflecting on these and similar sayings, I would not accept the kingdom of heaven without the love relating to them; I would not flee retribution in hell, if it was reasonable for one who has this love to undergo punishment.[5] He teaches this plainly in another place: 'For the love of Christ constrains us,

[h] 2 Co 5:21.   [i] Cf. 2 Co 8:9.   [j] Gal 3:13.   [k] Phil 2:8.   [l] Rom 5:8.

since we made this judgment, that one has died for all, so that the living might no longer live for themselves, but for him who for their sake died and rose again.'[m] So those who do not live for themselves but for him who for their sake died and rose again, gladly endure doing and suffering all things for his sake.

9. Sufferings great and grievous in nature he compares to longing, and calls them slight and easy to bear: 'For our light momentary tribulation,' he says, 'is working for us an eternal weight of glory utterly beyond all measure'—then he teaches how to compare them—'because we look not to things seen but to things unseen, for the things seen are temporary, but the things unseen are eternal.'[n] It is fitting, he says, to compare to things present things to come, to things temporary things eternal, to tribulation glory. For tribulation possesses the immediate, but glory the eternal; it is because of this that the former is light and easy to bear, the latter precious and valuable. This also is why he has added to both 'beyond all measure', to both the slightness of the tribulation and the weight of the glory; the former, he says, are immeasurably slight and light and temporary, and the latter are likewise beyond measure glorious, precious, valuable, and eternal. And elsewhere he exclaims in the same vein, 'I am content with weaknesses, insults, hardships, persecutions, and calamities for the sake of Christ; for when I am weak, then am I strong.'[o]

10. It was wounded by this same yearning that the great Peter did not consent to escape his future denial, despite foreknowledge, but thought it better to follow and deny than to escape and profess.[p] That his following was the product of desire and not presumption, the facts bear witness; for not even after his denial could he bear to forsake the Teacher, but wept bitterly, as the story teaches,[q] and lamented his defeat and weakness, and remained stalwart, held by the bonds of longing. Moreover, on receiving the good news of the Resurrection, he was the first to repair to the tomb.[r] Again, when fishing in Galilee, and learning that it was the Lord standing on the shore and addressing them, he could not bear the boat's slowness in cleaving the surface of the sea, but yearned to become winged and get to the bench through

[m] 2 Co 5:14–15. [n] 2 Co 4:17–18. [o] 2 Co 12:10. [p] Cf. Mt 26:34, 58.
[q] Cf. Mt 26:75. [r] Cf. Jn 20:6.

Epilogue: on Divine Love

the air as quickly as possible. Since his nature lacked wings, he used instead of the air the waters and instead of wings his arms.[s] By swimming he reached the one he loved, and received as prize for the race greater honor than the others; for when He bade them sit down and distributed the food they had found, He at once began a conversation with him, asking indeed and inquiring how great was his longing, and revealing to the others the desire of the great Peter. 'Simon Peter,' he said, 'do you love me more than these?' The other invoked him as witness to his love: 'Lord,' he said, 'you know that I love you'[t] – for you penetrate into the souls of men and perceive clearly the movements of their thought, and nothing human escapes you; 'for you know all things, both things final and the things of old'.[u] At this the Master added, 'Shepherd my sheep'.[v] For I, he meant, have no needs, but I consider care of my sheep the greatest service, and I accept for myself attention paid to them. Therefore it is fitting that you give your fellow servants a share of the solicitude you enjoy, that you feed them as you are fed, shepherd them as you are shepherded, and that you repay through them the gratitude you owe me.

11. This question the Master asked a further two times; two times did the great Peter reply, and two times did he receive ordination by the Shepherd. But when the inquiry was made a third time, the blessed Peter did not reply with the same confidence and fearlessness; instead, he was filled with fear and felt perturbation in his soul, agonized over his decision and was alarmed, suspecting that the Master foresaw a further denial and was laughing at his words of love.[w] For his mind ran back to his earlier words, and reminded him that already on an earlier occasion he had repeatedly promised not to forsake the Teacher till death, only to hear that before the cock crew he would deny him three times; he had found, not his own promise accomplished, but the prophecy of the Master confirmed. The memory of this frightened him, and did not let him give the fitting answer with confidence; instead, he felt sharp and bitter pricks. Nevertheless, he yielded to the Master in knowledge, not resisting as before, nor saying, 'Even if I have to die with you, I will never forsake you'.[x] But professing that

[s]Cf. Jn 21:7.   [t]Jn 21:15.   [u]Ps 139:4f (LXX).   [v]Jn 21:16.   [w]Cf. Jn 21:17.
[x]Mt 26:35.

the Master himself shared his awareness of his love, and conceding that accurate knowledge of all things belongs only to the Creator of all things, he said, 'Lord, you know all things, you recognize all things, you know that I love you you.ʸ That I love you, you know and bear witness. Whether I shall persevere in my love, you yourself know clearly. I will ask no questions about the future, nor will I argue about things I do not know. I have learnt from experience not to contradict the Master. You, fount of truth, you, abyss of knowledge, I have been taught to abide by the limits you set.'

12. On perceiving his alarm, and knowing his love exactly, the Master by foretelling his end destroyed his fear, gave witness to his love, confirmed Peter's profession, and applied the remedy of profession to the wound of denial.ᶻ I think that he made this threefold interrogation for this reason: to apply to the wounds remedies of the same sequence, and to lay bare to those of the disciples present the fire of his love. The prophecy of his end both comforted Peter and taught the others that his denial resulted from the divine plan, not from his own intention. Our Saviour and Lord himself hinted at this when he said to him, 'Simon, Simon, Satan has been granted leave to sift you like wheat, and I have made intercession for you, that your faith may not fail; but when you have turned again, strengthen your brethren.'ᵃᵃ Just as I, he means, support you when tottering, so be yourself a support to your brethren when they are shaken, and give them a share of the assistance you enjoy; do not give a push to those who are slipping, but raise them up when in danger. It was for this reason that I allow you to stumble, but do not let you fall—to contrive by means of you to keep standing those who totter.⁶

13. So it was that this great 'pillar'ᵇᵇ supported a tottering world, and did not let it fall completely, but set it upright and made it firm. Ordered to shepherd the sheep of God, he put up with being maltreated on their behalf, and rejoiced at being tortured. On leaving the wicked sanhedrin with his companion, he exulted 'at being counted worthy to be dishonored for the name' of the Lord.ᶜᶜ On being thrown into prison, he was happy and jubilant.ᵈᵈ And when, under

---

ʸCf. Jn 21:17.   ᶻCf. Jn 21:18–19.   ᵃᵃLk 22:31–32.   ᵇᵇCf. Gal 2:9.
ᶜᶜAc 5:41.   ᵈᵈCf. Ac 12:4.

Nero, he was condemned to death on a cross for the sake of the crucified one, he asked the executioners not to be nailed to the gallows like the Master, but to be impaled in the reverse way to him — out of fear, doubtless, lest the identity of the suffering win him from the ignorant equality in honor; it was for this reason that he begged for his hands to be nailed below and his feet above.[7] He had learnt to chose the lowest place not only in honor but also in dishonor. And if it had been possible to undergo this death ten or fifty times, he would have accepted it with every joy, being inflamed with yearning for God. This the godly Paul also exclaimed, saying on one occasion, 'I die every day, by my pride in you, which I have in Christ Jesus',[ee] and on another, 'I have been crucified with Christ; it is no longer I who live, but Christ who lives in me'.[ff]

14. Therefore he who has conceived divine love despises all earthly things together and tramples on all the pleasures of the body. He looks down upon wealth and glory and honor from men; he thinks that the royal purple is no different from spiders' webs; he likens the stones that are precious to pebbles on the bank. He does not consider health of body enviable, nor does he call disease a misfortune, nor does he term poverty bad luck, nor does he use wealth and luxury to define happiness. But they are of the fine opinion that each of these is always to be compared to river streams that flow past trees planted on the banks and stop by none of them; for beauty, poverty and wealth, health and disease, honor and dishonor, and the other things that brush past the nature of men, are likewise observed not to remain always with the same people, but to change their possessors, and pass continually from some to others. Many fall from plenty into extreme poverty, while many ascend from being poor into the list of the rich; and disease and health travel through all bodies, so to speak, both of the hungry and of those lapped in luxury.

15. Virtue, or philosophy,[8] is an abiding good. It overcomes the hands of the robber, the tongue of the slanderer, and the showers of darts and spears of the enemy; it does not become the victim of fever, nor the plaything of a storm, nor the casualty of shipwreck. Time does not remove its power, but increases its power. The substance of

[ee] 1 Co 15:31.   [ff] Gal 2:20.

it is love for God. It is impossible for one who does not become fervently enamored of God to succeed in philosophy. But rather, this thing is itself called 'philosophy' (friendship with wisdom), since God is, and is called, Wisdom. Concerning the God of the universe the blessed Paul says, 'To the incorruptible, invisible, unique, wise God'.[gg] Concerning the Only-begotten he says, 'Christ, the power of God and the wisdom of God'.[hh] And again, He has been given 'to us as wisdom from God, righteousness and sanctification and redemption'.[ii] Therefore the true 'philosopher' [friend of wisdom] could appropriately be called the 'friend of God'. The 'friend of God' despises everything else and looks at the Beloved alone. He puts serving him before all the rest together; he says, performs, and thinks only those things that please and serve the One he loves, and abominates everything that he forbids.

16. It was this love that Adam belittled when he became hardhearted towards his benefactor, and so reaped thorns, labors, and hardships as the reward for his ingratitude. It was this love that Abel maintained firm towards the bestower of good things, when, despising the pleasure of the belly, he preferred the service of God,[jj] and so was decorated with imperishable wreaths, and traverses every generation, harvesting fame through memory. It was this love that Enoch conceived, true and authentic, when he sowed well and reaped better, and so as the reward for serving God carried off translation[kk] and at the same time eternal life and, through every age, a renowned and celebrated memory. What should one say of the friendship with God of Noah, which even the huge crop of the lawless could not disprove? But when all turned aside and chose the opposite course, he alone traveled on the straight path, putting the Creator before all things together; on account of this, he alone with his children attained being saved, a seed was left to nature, and a spark was preserved for the race.[kl] So too Melchizedek the great high-priest, who abhorred the senselessness of those who chose to revere idols, dedicated his own priesthood to the Creator of the universe; on account of this, he carried off that great reward of becoming the type and shadow of the

---

[gg] 1 Tim 1:17.   [hh] 1 Co 1:24.   [ii] 1 Co 1:30.   [jj] Cf. Gen 4:4.   [kk] Cf. Gen 5:24.
[kl] Cf. Gen 6:5ff.

one who was truly without father or mother or genealogy, having neither beginning of days nor end of life.[ll]

17. My account, however, proceeding on its way, has reached the one who was actually styled the 'friend' of God,[mm] and who observed and taught exactly the rules of friendship. Who of those with any education in the things of God does not know how Abraham the great patriarch obeyed the call of God, how he left his fathers' house and preferred the foreign land to his fatherland?[nn] When once he became enamored of the one who had called him, he decided to put everything else second to this friendship. Despite falling many times into many hardships, he did not desert his beloved on the ground of his not accomplishing his promises; but though oppressed by thirst and prevented from drinking water from wells he had dug, he neither was angry with the one who had called him, nor avenged himself on those who were wronging him.[oo] He underwent the attack of hunger also,[pp] yet did not quench the firebrand of love. He was deprived of his wife, who was resplendent with beauty, decked with self-control, and made his life agreeable in every way.[qq] Yet he did not lose together with his wife his love for God; but with the aid of God, who was testing his patience in allowing him to undergo the attacks of injustice, he persevered in the same love. He became an old man without becoming a father; yet he kept the same disposition towards the one who had promised to make him a father but hitherto had not done so. When at a late date he obtained the promise[rr] and triumphed over the nature of Sarah, surpassed the limitations of old age and was made the father of Isaac,[ss] it was for only a short time that he enjoyed pleasure therefrom. He was ordered to offer the child, now an adolescent, in sacrifice to the One who had given him, to return the gift to the Bestower, to become the priest of the fruit of the promise, to present for sacrifice the great source of the nations, to make his hands red with the blood of his only son.[tt] Nevertheless, although the sacrifice involved all this and much more again than this, the patriarch did not resist, nor invoke the rights of nature, nor adduce the promises,

---

[ll]Cf. Heb 7:3. [mm]Cf. Is 41:8. [nn]Cf. Gen 12:1-4. [oo]Cf. Gen 21:25-30.
[pp]Cf. Gen 12:10. [qq]Cf. Gen 20:2. [rr]Cf. Heb 6:15. [ss]Cf. Gen 21:2.
[tt]Cf. Gen 22:2.

nor mention the care of his old age and burial; but casting aside every human consideration, opposing yearning to yearning and setting law against law—the divine against that of nature—, he hastened to the work of sacrifice, and would without any doubt have inflicted the blow, had not the Munificent One, accepting his zeal, swiftly prevented the killing. Yet, I do not know if any account would suffice to describe this love: if he did not even spare his only son when the Beloved ordered this, whom would he not have despised on his account?

18. The great Isaac himself also conceived the same love for the Master—as did his son, the patriarch Jacob. The divine Scriptures celebrate the love for God of both of them; and the very God of the universe himself in no way separates the branches from the root, but calls himself 'the God of Abraham and of Isaac and of Jacob'.[uu] Of these men the pious fruit was Joseph, who was like an old man among the young and vigorous among the old men. His friendship with God neither envy could destroy,[vv] nor slavery quench,[ww] nor the wheedling of a mistress remove,[xx] nor threats and terror extinguish; neither could calumny, prison and length of time overthrow it,[yy] nor power, authority, luxury and wealth drive it from his mind.[zz] But he remained the same, looking at the Beloved and fulfilling his laws. It was this love that Moses conceived, when, despising life in a palace, he 'chose rather to share ill-treatment with the people of God than to have a temporary enjoyment of sin'.[α] But why should I lengthen and extend the discourse beyond due measure? It was because they practised and were adorned with divine love that the whole company of prophets achieved the most perfect virtue and left behind a fame of everlasting remembrance. Moreover, the choir of the Apostles and the throngs of martyrs, on receiving this fire, looked down on all things visible, and preferred innumerable forms of death to every kind of agreeable life. Enamored of the divine beauty, reflecting on God's love for us, and pondering on his innumerable benefits, they thought it disgraceful not to yearn for that ineffable beauty or to be ungrateful towards their Benefactor. On account of this, they kept till death their covenant with him.

[uu] Ex 3:16. [vv] Cf. Gen 37:4. [ww] Cf. Gen 37:28. [xx] Cf. Gen 39:7.
[yy] Cf. Gen 39:20. [zz] Cf. Gen 41:39-45. [α] Heb 11:25.

19. It was enamored of this beauty that the new athletes of virtue also, whose life we have recorded in brief, have leapt into those great conflicts that surpass human nature. This they were taught clearly by the divine Scriptures. For they chant with the great David, 'Lord my God, how exceeding great you are! You have clothed yourself with confession and magnificence, casting on light like a garment, stretching out the sky like a curtain'—and the remaining verses that teach his wisdom and power.[β] And again, 'The lord reigns, he has clothed himself with majesty; the Lord has clothed and girded himself with power';[γ] for, 'He has established the world, which shall not be shaken';[δ] here likewise his wisdom and beauty are proclaimed, and also his power. In another place, 'You are comely in beauty beyond the sons of men';[ε] here he has also praised the human beauty of God the Word. He also hymns his wisdom: 'Grace,' he says, 'has been poured upon your lips.'[ε] He also points to his power: 'Gird your sword upon your thigh, mighty one, in thy comeliness and beauty; exert yourself, prosper and reign, on behalf of truth and gentleness and justice'.[ζ] For these are his—wealth, and beauty, and power. Isaiah too exclaims, 'Who is this who comes from Edom, the red of his garments from Bozrah, himself comely in his apparel, force with strength?'[η] For even human apparel did not hide the divine beauty; but even though clothed in this, he emits sparks from his beauty, to compel and entice the beholders to feel desire. It is this too that the holy bride says, who addresses him in the Song of Songs: 'Your name is myrrh outpoured; therefore the young girls have loved you, drawn thee and hastened after you, for the aroma of your myrrh'.[θ] For the souls of the young, when they partake of thy fragrance, hasten in their yearning to reach thee; held by the aroma as if by a chain, they cannot bear to break the bond, for it is sweet and they wear it willingly.[9] With this agree also the words of the inspired Paul, 'We are the fragrance of Christ in those who are being saved and in those who are perishing, to one an aroma of death to death, to the other an aroma of life to life'.[ι]

[β] Ps 104:1ff.   [γ] Ps 93:1.   [δ] Ps 96:10.   [ε] Ps 45:2.   [ε] Ibid.   [ζ] Ps 44:3-4.
[η] Is 63:1.   [θ] Sg 1:3-4 (LXX).   [ι] 2 Co 2:15-16.

20. Being taught, therefore, by divine Scripture that he is beautiful, has indescribable wealth, is the fount of wisdom, is able to do whatever he wishes, possesses immeasurable love for men, pours forth rivers of kindness, and in everything wishes solely to benefit men – and being taught by the God-bearing men about the myriad and uncountable varieties of his beneficence –, they have been wounded by the sweet darts of love, and, as limbs of the bride, exclaim with her, 'We are wounded with love'.^{κ} The great John exclaims. 'Behold the lamb of God, who takes away the sin of the world'.^{λ} The prophet Isaiah foretold what was to come as if it had already taken place, when he said: 'He was wounded for our transgressions and bruised for our sins; the chastisement for our peace was upon him; by his scar we were healed' – and the remaining verses which proceed through the sufferings of salvation.^{μ} There is also the proclamation of Paul, exclaiming, 'He who did not spare his own Son, but gave him up for us all, how will he not also give us all things together with him?'^{ν} And again, 'We are ambassadors for Christ, as if God is making his appeal through us. We beseech you on behalf of Christ, be reconciled to God; for him who knew not sin he made to be sin for our sake, so that we might become the righteousness of God in him.'^{ξ}

21. Finding these and all similar statements in those who became the servants of the Word of God, they receive from all sources the goads of divine love; despising all things, they contemplate the Beloved, and prior to the incorruption for which they hope they have rendered the body spiritual. Let us too conceive this longing; let us become bewitched by the beauty of the Bridegroom, eager for the promised goods, paying heed to the multitude of benefits, fearing the punishment for ingratitude, and so in our love be maintainers of his laws. For this is the definition of friendship: liking and hating the same things. This is why He said to Abraham, 'I shall bless those who bless you, and those who curse you shall I curse'.^{ο} And David to Him, 'Greatly honored by me have been thy friends, O God'.^{π} And again, 'Have I not hated, Lord, those who hate thee, and wasted away

^{κ}Cf. Sg 5:8. ^{λ}Jn 1:29. ^{μ}Is 53:5 ff. ^{ν}Rom 8:32. ^{ξ}2 Co 5:20–21.
^{ο}Gen 12:3. ^{π}Ps 139:17 (LXX).

Epilogue: on Divine Love

because of thine enemies? With perfect hatred have I hated them; they have become for me enemies.'ᴾ And elsewhere, 'I have hated the lawbreakers, and loved thy law.'ˢ And in another place, 'How I have loved thy law, O Lord; the whole day it is my meditation'.ᵀ 10 Therefore the clear proof of love for God is the keeping of his divine laws. 'He who loves me will keep my commandments,' said Christ the Master,ᵁ with whom to the Father be the glory with the Holy Spirit, now and always and for ever and ever. Amen.

ᴾ Ps 139:21. ˢ Ps 119:13. ᵀ Ps 119:97. ᵁ Cf. Jn 14:23.

NOTES

1. The treatise *On Divine Love* is attached by most of the early manuscripts to the *Rel. Hist.* (Canivet, *Le monachisme syrien*, 88), to which indeed it refers back (§1, 19). However, the final pages of the *Rel. Hist.* (XXX.5-8) have already provided an emphatic conclusion to the whole work; moreover, the defense of open-air hermits against their critics in §2-3 of the treatise reads as a reply to those who had criticized the *Rel. Hist.* itself. It is reasonable to conclude that *On Divine Love* did not form part of the original edition of the *Rel. Hist.*, as written in around 440, but was composed by Theodoret as the epilogue to a second, otherwise unchanged, edition of the work. There is no indication in the text itself of the date of composition. The seventeenth-century scholar J. Garnier argued (PG 84: 252-3) for a date of 449/50 on two grounds: first, the emphasis on suffering for Christ (§6-9) points to the period when Theodoret was in monastic exile, having been deprived of his see by the Council of Ephesus of 449; secondly, the treatment of St Peter's task of strengthening his brethren (§12-13) is reminiscent of Theodoret's appeal to Pope Leo in 449 (*ep.* 113), even if in the latter Theodoret does not cite the same texts. These feeble arguments, rightly dismissed by Tillemont, (*Mémoires*, XV: 329) and Glubokovsky (*Blazhennyi Theodorit*, 428-9), receive some reinforcement from Canivet (*Le monachisme syrien*, 91-94), who adds further parallels between *On Divine Love* and letters written by Theodoret between 447 and 451. Of these one is so close as to suggest direct dependence: *ep.* 21 (448/9) develops Rom 8:35-39 to precisely the same effect, and with the same vocabulary, as *On Divine Love* §§6-8. However, the same treatment and application of this text occurs also in Theodoret's *Commentary on the Pauline Epistles* (PG 82: 145), which probably dates to the 430s (F. Young, *From Nicaea to Chalcedon*, 284). It remains true that if parallels, close or loose, linked *On Divine Love* to letters of 447-51 rather than those earlier or later, this would support Garnier's dating. The comparison cannot be made, however, since we possess very few letters of Theodoret's dating to between 438 and 446 or after 451. One must conclude that an attempt to tie down the date of *On Divine Love* is futile.

By 'divine love' Theodoret means 'love for God', and the theme of the treatise is that it is an ardent love of God that motivates the ascetics, just as it had the great saints of the Old and New Testament. In the *Rel. Hist.* this theme is never developed, but is often touched on briefly: Prol. 5, II.2, III.2, IV.3-4, V.7, VI.8, IX.2, XV.6, XVIII.2,4, XXI.34, XXIV.3, XXVII.3, XXIX.7, XXX.2. Of the various words Theodoret uses to refer to this love, I have, in this treatise, consistently translated *agape* by 'love', *eros* by 'desire', *pothos* by 'yearning', *philtron* by 'longing', *philia* by 'friendship'; but there is here no difference in meaning between them.

2. For this commonplace, cp. Prol.8 and XXX.7 .

3. The criticism that open-air hermits showed no greater endurance than shepherds or farm-laborers was not a standard item in the disparagement of monks (for which see John Chrysostom, *Against the Detractors of the Monastic Life*; PG 47: 319-392), but a reaction to the emphasis on their endurance in the *Rel. Hist.* itself (see Introduction, xxxii).

4. The 'love of God' from which nothing created can separate us is, in Rom 8:39, God's love for us. The interpretation that the verse refers to our love for God, and that the meaning is that the true lover of God loves Him for His sake alone without thought of reward in this life or the life to come, occurs also in Theodoret's Antiochene predecessors John Chrysostom (*Homilies on the Epistle to the Romans* XV.5) and Theodore of Mopsuestia (PG 66: 832C).

Epilogue: on Divine Love

5. The theme that the lover of Christ values this love even above his own salvation also comes in John Chrysostom's treatment of the passage (see preceding note). Cp. also Clement of Alexandria, *Stromateis* IV.22.136; 'If someone, let us imagine, could offer the gnostic a choice between the knowledge of God and eternal salvation, and if these two things, which are in fact utterly identical, were separate, then he would, without any hesitation, choose the knowledge of God, judging preferable for its own sake that character which transcends faith and through love attains to knowledge.'

6. To Theodoret's interpretation of Jn 21 at §§10–12, cp. John Chrysostom, *Homilies on John* 87 and 88, which share in common (1) adducing in the same context Rom 8:35ff. and 2 Co 4:17f., (2) Peter's 'yearning' in swimming to Jesus, (3) Peter's alarm at being asked the third time, 'Do you love me?', and the contrast between his modest answer this time and his earlier refusal to believe he would deny Christ. Still more extensive, however, are the parallels with Theodore of Mopsuestia's *Commentary on John* (which are set out in Canivet, *Le monachisme syrien*, 100–1). These include (1) feeding Christ's flock being the way to serve Christ, who needs nothing for himself, (2) Peter's threefold confession atoning for his threefold denial, (3) Peter's alarm at being asked a third time, 'Do you love me?', fearing that Christ was hinting at a further denial, (4) Christ prophesying Peter's martyrdom to reassure him. Since in addition there are numerous close verbal parallels, it is clear that Theodoret is writing with Theodore's commentary in front of him.

7. This legend of Peter being martyred head downwards, which was already traditional material when incorporated in the second century *Acts of Peter*, is also adduced, to the same effect, in Theodore of Mopsuestia's *Commentary on John*.

8. For Christian asceticism as 'Philosophy', see Prol., note 4.

9. Theodoret in his *Commentary on the Song of Songs* (PG 81: 28–213) adopts the traditional typological exegesis, refusing to follow Theodore of Mopsuestia, who rejected it. F. Young, *From Nicaea to Chalcedon*, 284–7, is concerned to bring out Theodoret's exegetical independence, despite such counter-examples as those listed in notes 4–6 above.

10. The theme that virtue consists in sharing God's loves and hates occurs also in an earlier work of Theodoret's *The Cure of Hellenic Maladies* XII.12, with an almost identical repertoire of biblical citations.

LIST OF WORKS CITED

I. PRIMARY SOURCES

Abbreviations

ACW   Ancient Christian Writers (Westminster, Maryland).
ANF   The Ante-Nicene Fathers (Eerdmans, Michigan).
CS   Cistercian Studies (Kalamazoo, Michigan).
CSCO   Corpus Scriptorum Christianorum Orientalium (Paris; Louvain)
GCS   Die Griechischen Christlichen Schriftsteller der ersten Jahrhunderte (Berlin).
LCL   Loeb Classical Library (Harvard University Press).
MGH   Monumenta Germaniae Historica (Berlin; Hanover; Stuttgart).
NPNF   Nicene and Post-Nicene Fathers of the Christian Church (rpt. Eerdmans, Grand Rapids, Michigan).
PG   Migne, Patrologia Graeca (Paris).
PL   Migne, Patrologia Latina (Paris).
SC   Sources Chrétiennes (Paris).
SH   Subsidia Hagiographica (Brussels).
TU   Texte and Untersuchungen zur Geschichte der altchristlichen Literatur (Leipzig; Berlin).

Acta Conciliorum Oecumenicorum, ed. E. Schwartz. Berlin 1914–71.
Acts of Judas Thomas, trans. in M.R. James, *The Apocryphal New Testament* (Oxford 1924) 365–438.
Acts of Peter, trans. in M.R. James, *The Apocryphal New Testament*, 300–36.
Ad Diognetum, The Apostolic Fathers, LCL, Vol. 2 (1913) 348–79.
Ammianus Marcellinus, *Res Gestae*, LCL (3 vols., 1935–9).
Antony, *Life of Symeon*, TU XXXII (1908) Heft 4, 20–78.
Aphrahat, *Demonstrations*, Patrologia Syriaca I & II. Paris 1894, 1907.
Athanasius, *Life of Antony*, PG 26: 835–976; trans. ACW 10 (1950).
Basil, *Longer Rules*, PG 31: 889–1052.
Cassian, *Conferences* & *Institutes*, SC 42, 54, 64, 109 (1955–65); trans. NPNF, 2nd Series, XI (1894) 201–545.
Chronicle of Edessa, CSCO, Scriptores Syri III, vol. 4 (1903).
Clement of Alexandria, *Opera*, ed. Stählin & Früchtel, 3 vols. (GCS, 1960–72); trans. ANF II (1885) 171–604.
Clement, Pseudo-, *Epistles on Virginity*, PG 1, 379–452; trans. ANF VIII (1886), 55–66.
Cyprian, *Opera*, Corpus Scriptorum Ecclesiasticorum Latinorum, III (Vienna 1868–71); trans. ANF V (1886) 275–595.

208

List of Works Cited 209

Cyril of Jerusalem, *Catechetical Lectures*, PG 33; 331-1180; trans. NPNF, 2nd Series, VII (1894) 1-157.
Egeria, *Travels*, SC 296 (1982); trans. J. Wilkinson, London 1971.
Ephraem, *Carmina Nisibena*, CSCO 218-219, 240-241 (1961-3).
_____ *Hymni et Sermones*, ed. T. Lamy, 4 vols. Mechlin 1882-1902.
_____ *Hymns on Fasting*, CSCO 246-247 (1964).
Ephraem, Pseudo-, *Hymns on Julian Saba*, CSCO 322-323 (1972).
Eunapius, *Lives of the Philosophers*, with Philostratus, *Lives of the Sophists*, LCL (1921).
Eusebius, *Ecclesiastical History*, LCL (2 vols., 1926-32).
_____ *Life of Constantine*, in *Werke*, Band 1, GCS 7 (1902), 3-148; trans. NPNF, 2nd Series, I (1890) 481-540.
Gregory of Tours, *Opera*, MGH, Scriptores Rerum Merovingicarum I (1885).
Hermas, *The Shepherd*, The Apostolic Fathers, LCL, Vol. 2 (1913) 1-305.
History of the Monks in Egypt, SH 34 (1961); trans. B. Ward and N. Russell, CS 34 (1980).
Homily on Easter (of 387), SC 48 (1957).
Jerome, *Letters (ep.)*, PL 22: 325-1224; trans. NPNF, 2nd Series, VI (1893) 1-295.
John Chrysostom, *Against the Detractors of the Monastic Life*, PG 47: 319-92.
_____ *Homilies on John*, PG 59: 23-482; trans. NPNF, 1st Series, XIV (1889) 1-334.
_____ *Homilies on Romans*, PG 60; 391-682; trans. NPNF, 1st Series, XI (1889) 329-564.
_____ *Homilies on the Statues*, PG 49: 15-222; trans. NPNF, 1st Series, IX (1889) 331-489.
_____ *Huit Catéchèses Baptismales*, SC 50 (1957).
_____ *Letters (ep.)*, PG 52: 549-760.
_____ *On the Priesthood*, PG 48: 623-92; trans. NPNF, 1st Series, IX (1889) 33-83.
John Moschus, *The Spiritual Meadow*, PG 87: 2851-3112.
Libanius, *Opera*, ed. Foerster, 12 vols., Leipzig 1903-22; partial trans. in *Selected Works*, LCL (3 vols., 1969-).
Life of Alexander the Acoemete, Patrologia Orientalis VI (Paris 1911) 645-705.
Life of Daniel the Stylite, SH 14 (1923), 1-94; trans. in Dawes & Baynes, *Three Byzantine Saints* (Oxford 1948) 7-71.
Life of Genovefa, MGH, Scriptores Rerum Merovingicarum III (1896) 204-38.
Life of Pachomius (First Greek), SH 19 (1932); trans. CS 45 (1980), 297-407.
Life of Shenouti (Bohairic), CSCO 129 (1951); trans. CS 73 (1983).
Life of Symeon Stylites (Syriac), German trans., TU XXXII (1908) Heft 4, 80-180.
Marcellinus, *Chronicon*, MGH, Auctores Antuiquissimi, XI (1894) 37-108.
Martyrdom of Perpetua and Felicity, in H. Musurillo, ed., *The Acts of the Christian Martyrs* (Oxford 1972) 106-31.
Martyrdom of Polycarp, in Musurillo, *The Acts of the Christian Martyrs*, 2-21.
Palladius, *Dialogue on the Life of John Chrysostom*, PG 47: 5-82.
_____ *Lausiac History*, ed. C. Butler, Cambridge 1904; trans. ACW 34 (1965).
Plato, *Dialogues*, LCL.
Plutarch, *Life of Crassus*, in Plutarch's *Lives*, LCL, III (1916) 314-423.

Porphyry, *Life of Pythagoras* & *To Marcella*, ed. des Places (Paris 1982).
Procopius, *History of the Wars*, LCL (5 Vols. 1914-28).
Rabbula, *Monastic Canons*, in A. Vööbus, ed., *Syriac and Arabic Documents regarding Legislation relative to Syrian Asceticism* (Stockholm 1960) 24-86.
Sayings of the Father: Alphabetical Collection, PG 65: 71-440; trans. Benedicta Ward, *The Sayings of the Desert Fathers*, CS 59 (1975).
─────── *Syriac Version*, trans. A Wallis Budge, *The Paradise of the Holy Fathers* (London 1907) vol. 2.
Sozomen, *Ecclesiastical History*, GCS 50 (1960); trans. NPNF, 2nd Series, II: 236-427.
Sulpicius Severus, *Life of Martin*, SC 133 (1967); trans. NPNF, 2nd Series, XI (1894) 3-17.
Theodore of Mopsuestia, *Commentary on John*, CSCO, Scriptores Syri IV, vol. 3 (1940).
─────── *Commentary on Romans*, PG 66: 787-876.
Theodoret, *Commentary on Psalm 50*, PG 80: 1237-54.
─────── *Commentary on Romans*, PG 82: 35-226.
─────── *Commentary on the Song of Songs*, PG 81: 28-213.
─────── *Cure of Hellenic Maladies*, SC 57, 2 vols. (1958).
─────── *Ecclesiastical History*, GCS 44 (1954); trans. NPNF, 2nd Series, III (1892) 33-159. (Where the chapter numeration of these two editions varies, I have placed that of the NPNF edition in brackets.)
─────── *Epitome of Heretical Myths*, PG 83, 335-556.
─────── *Letters* (ep.). SC 40, 98, 111 (1955-65).
─────── *Religious History*, edd. P. Canivet and A. Leroy-Molinghen. SC 234, 257 (1977-79).
Zosimus, *Historia Nova*, ed. L. Mendelssohn. Leipzig 1887.

LIST OF WORKS CITED

II. SECONDARY SOURCES

Bartelink, G.J.M., 'Quelques observations sur παρρησια dans la littérature paléochrétienne', *Graecitas et Latinitas Christianorum Primaeva*, Suppl. III. Nijmegen, 1970.
Beck, E., 'Asketentum und Mönchtum bei Ephräm', *Il Monachesimo Orientale*, OCA 153 (1958) 341-362.
Brock, S., 'Early Syrian Asceticism', *Numen* 20 (1973) 1-19.
Brown, P.R.L., *Augustine of Hippo*. University of California Press, 1967.
Brown, P.R.L., *The Cult of the Saints*. University of Chicago Press, 1981.
Brown, P.R.L., *The Making of Late Antiquity*, Harvard University Press, 1978.
Brown, P.R.L., 'The Rise and Function of the Holy Man in Late Antiquity', *Society and the Holy in Late Antiquity*. London: Faber, 1982: 103-152.
Brown, P.R.L., 'Sorcery, Demons and the Rise of Christianity', *Religion and Society in the Age of St Augustine*. London: Faber, 1972: 119-146.
Bury, J.B., *History of the Later Roman Empire*, 2 vols. London, 1923.
Butler, H.C., *Early Churches in Syria*. Princeton, 1929.
Canivet, P., *Le monachisme syrien selon Théodoret de Cyr*. Paris, 1977.
Dawes, E. and Baynes, N.H., ed., *Three Byzantine Saints*. Oxford, 1948-Crestwood N.Y.: St Vladimirs, 1977.
Delehaye, H., *Les Saints Stylites*, Subsidia Hagiographica 14. Brussels, 1923.
Devos, P., 'La structure de l'Histoire Philothée de Théodoret de Cyr: Le nombre de chapitres'. *Analecta Bollandiana* 97 (1979) 319-336.
Dictionnaire d'Archéologie Chrétienne et de Liturgie. Paris, 1907-1953.
Festugière, A.J., *Antioche païenne et chrétienne: Libanius, Chrysostome et les moines de Syrie*. Paris, 1959.
Frend, W.H.C., *The Rise of Christianity*. London: Darton Longman & Todd; Philadelphia: Fortress Press, 1984.
Frend, W.H.C., *The Rise of the Monophysite Movement*. Cambridge University Press, 1972.
Garnier, J., *Auctarium Theodoreti*. Paris, 1684, reprinted in PG 84.
Gibbon, E., *The History of the Decline and Fall of the Roman Empire* (ed. J.B. Bury) 7 vols. London, 1896-1900.
Glubokovsky, N., *Blazhennyi Theodorit*, 2 vols. Moscow, 1890.
Guillaumont, A., 'Messaliens', *Dictionnaire de Spiritualité* 10 (1980) 1074-1083.
Harnack, A., *The Mission and Expansion of Christianity, The First Three Centuries* 2 vols. London and New York, 1908.

Hausherr, I., 'Comment priaient les pères', *Revue d'Ascétique et de Mystique* 32 (1956) 33–58, 284–297.
Holum, K.G., *Theodosian Empresses*. University of California Press, 1982.
Hunt, E.G., *Holy Land Pilgrimage in the Later Roman Empire*. Oxford University Press, 1982.
Jones, A.H.M., *The Later Roman Empire*. Oxford, 1964.
Jouguet, P., *Papyrus de Théadelphie*. Paris, 1911.
Kelly, J.N.D., *Jerome*. London: Duckworth, 1975.
Lampe, G.W.H., *A Patristic Greek Lexicon*. Oxford University Press, 1961.
Lassus, J., *Sanctuaires chrétiens de Syrie*. Paris, 1947.
Leroy-Molinghen, A., 'A propos de la Vie de Syméon Stylite', *Byzantion* 34 (1964) 375–384.
Liebeschuetz, J.H.W.G., *Antioch: City and Imperial Administration in the Later Roman Empire*. Oxford University Press, 1972.
Lietzmann, H., 'Das Leben des heiligen Symeon Stylites', *Texte und Untersuchungen* 32 (1908) Part 4.
Lupus, C., *Opera Omnia*, VII. Venice, 1726.
MacMullen, R., *Christianizing the Roman Empire*. Yale University Press, 1984.
Murray, R., 'The Exhortation to Candidates for Ascetical Vows at Baptism in the Ancient Syrian Church', *New Testament Studies* 21 (1975) 59–80.
Murray, R., 'The Features of the Earliest Christian Asceticism', *Christian Spirituality*, ed. P. Brooks. London: SCM, 1975: 65–77.
Peeters, P., 'La légende de Saint Jacques de Nisibe', *Analecta Bollandiana* 38 (1920) 285–373.
Peeters, P., 'S. Syméon Stylite et ses premiers biographes', *Analecta Bollandiana* 61 (1943) 29–71.
Pena, I. and others, *Les Reclus Syriens*. Milan, 1980.
Petit, P., *Libanius et la vie municipale à Antioche*. Paris, 1955.
Price, R.M., 'Holy Men's Letters of Rebuke', *Studia Patristica* XVI (1985) 56–59.
Prosopography of the Later Roman Empire, 2 vols. Cambridge University Press, 1971–1980.
Quasten, J., *Patrology*, 3 vols. Utrecht, 1950–1960, repr. Christian Classics, 1983.
Roey, A. van, 'Remarques sur le moine Marcien', *Studia Patristica* XII (Berlin, 1975) 160–177.
Rousseau, P., *Ascetics, Authority and the Church in the Age of Jerome and Cassian*. Oxford University Press, 1978.
Schiwietz, S., *Das morgenländische Mönchtum*, Bd III: 'Das Mönchtum in Syrien und Mesopotamien'. Mödling bei Wien, 1938.
Smith, W. and Cheetham, S., *Dictionary of Christian Antiquities*, 2 vols. London, 1876–1880.
Streeter, B.H., *The Four Gospels*. London, 1924.
Tchalenko, G., *Villages antiques de la Syrie du Nord*, 3 vols. Paris, 1953–1958.
Tillemont, L.-S. Le Nain de, *Histoire des Empereurs*, 6 vols. Paris, 1700–1738.

Tillemont, Le Nain de, *Mémoires pour servir à l'Histoire Ecclésiastique des six premiers siècles*, 16 vols. Paris, 1693-1712.
Trimingham, J.S., *Christianity among the Arabs in Pre-Islamic Times*. New York: Longman, 1979.
Vööbus, A., *History of Asceticism in the Syrian Orient*, 2 vols., CSCO 184, 197. Louvain, 1958-1960.
Young, F.M., *From Nicaea to Chalcedon*. London: SCM, 1983.

INDEX OF NAMES

Abba	IV.12.
Abel (O.T.)	I.1, Epil 16
Abibion	XXIV.4
Abraham (O.T.)	I.1, Epil 17-18
Abraham (Antiochene)	VII.4
Abraham (Carrhae)	XVII
Abraham (Chalcidene)	III.17
Acacius	II.9,16,18,22; III.11; IV.7; XXI.10
Acepsimas	XV
Adam (O.T.)	Epil 16
Agapetus	III.4, 5,19
Agrippa	IV.8,9
Alexander (Alexandria)	I.10
Alexander (Antioch)	XII.7
Alypius	III.14,18
Amanus	VI.4,13; IX.10; X.1
Ammianus	IV.2-6; XXVI.4
Ananias (N.T.)	I.9
Anthemius	VIII.4
Antioch	II.15-20; III.22; VI.6; VIII.2,5-10; IX.3,9,16; X.1,6,8; XI.1; XII.2; XIII.7,11,19; XIV.4; XXIV.7; XXVII.3
Antiochus	XXIII.2
Antoninus	XXIII.2
Apamea	III.4-5
Aphrahat	II.16; VIII; X.8
Aphrodite	XXVI.13
Aphthonius	V.6,8
Apollinarianism	III.16
Arianism	II.15-16,21; III.16
Aristotle	XXVII.4
Arius	I.10
Armenians	XXVI.11,13
Asclepius	XXV.1
Asia	XXX.5
Asikha	XVIII.1
Asterius (Cyrrhus)	II.21-22
Asterius (Gindarus)	II.7-10,16
Astrion	XIII.13

Index of Names

Avitus	III.12
Balaam (O.T.)	II.22
Baradatus	XXVII
Basil (Caesarea)	XII.1
Basil (Seleucobelus)	III.20
Bassus	XXVI.7-8
Beroea	II.9; III.9; XXI.10; XXIX.2
Britons	XXVI.11
Callinicum	XXVI.16
Capersana	XIX.1
Carrhae	XVII.5
Chalcis	III.18
Cilicia	X.1, XXX.6
Cittica	XXIV.2
Constantine the Great	I.10
Cyra	XXIX
Cyril	XIV.1
Cyrrhus (city)	II.21-22; III.1,14,18; XXI.9-14
Cyrrhus (region)	XIV; XVI.3; XVII.2; XXI; XXII.1; XXIII.2; XXIV.8; XXV.2; XXX.3
Damian	XXIV.5
Daniel	IX.4
David (O.T.)	XXVI.2
David	IV.9-12
Diodore	II.16; VIII.6-7
Dionysius	II.21
Domnina	XXX
Edessa	VIII.1
Egypt	XXX.6
Elijah (O.T.)	Pr 10; I.13; III.1; XVII.6; XXVI.7
Elisha (O.T.)	Pr 10; I.5; XIII.17
Emesa	XVII.3
Enoch (O.T.)	I.1; XXXI.16
Ethiopians	XXVI.1
Euchites	III.16
Euphrates	V.1; XVII.10; Epil 16
Eusebius (Asikha)	XVIII
Eusebius (Chalcidene)	III.4-12,18-19
Eusebius (Chalcis)	III.11
Eusebius (Teleda)	IV.2-9; XXVI.4

216   A History of the Monks of Syria

Eusebonas	XXVI.4
Eutychius	XIV.1
Ezekiel (O.T.)	IV.4; XXVI.12
Flavian	II.16; III.11; VIII.6-7; XIII.4
Gabala	XXVIII.1
Galatia	IX.1
Gauls	XXVI.11
Gindarus	II.9
Gregory	V.9
Heliodorus	XXVI.4
Heliopolis	IX.9
Helladius	X.9
Homerites	XXVI.11
Hosea	XXVI.12
Iberians	XXVI.11,13
Imma	VII.1-2
Isaac (O.T.)	Epil 17-18
Isaiah (O.T.)	XXVI.12
Isauria	XXIX.7
Isaurians	X.5; XII.6; XXI.27
Ishmaelites	VI.4, XXVI.13,18,21
Isidore	III.11
Jacob (O.T.)	XXVI.2; Epil 18
James (Cyrrhestica)	VI.3; XXI; XXII.2; XXIV.3,9
James (Nimouza)	XXV.2
James (Nisibis)	I; XXI.2
James (Teleda)	II.6; IV.8
Jeremiah (O.T.)	XXVI.12
Jerusalem (Aelia)	(IX.2), XXIX.7
Jews	VI.2-3; XXVI.27
Job (O.T.)	XXII.6
John the Baptist	II.11; XXI.19-21
John	XXIII.1
Joseph (O.T.)	XXI.22; XXVI.2; Epil 18
Joshua (O.T.)	Pr 10
Jovian	VIII.5
Julian (Antioch)	X.8
Julian the Apostate	II.14, VIII.5
Julian Saba	II; IV.8

Index of Names

Koryphe	IV.2
Lebanon	XVII.2
Letoius	XIV.4
Limnaeus	XXII
Lupicinus	XIII.15
Macedonius Gouba	XIII
Maesymas	XIV
Malchus	XIV.1
Marana	XXIX
Marato	X.9
Marcianus	III
Marcionites	XXI.15–21; XXII.1
Marianus	IV.3
Maris	XX
Maron	VI.3; XVI: XXI.3; XXII.2; XXIV.2; XXX.1
Marosas	IV.12
Melchizedek (O.T.)	I.1, Epil 16
Meletius (Antioch)	II.15
Meletius (chorepiscopus)	XXVI.10
Mesopotamia	XXX.6
Moses (O.T.)	Pr 10; I.1; II.8,13; XXVI.2,7; Epil 4
Moses (Antiochene)	XIV.1
Moses (Cyrrhestica)	XXIV.5
Moses (Rama)	XXIII.2
Niara	XXIV.5
Nicaea	I.10
Nicerte	III.4
Nimouza	XXV.2
Nisibis	I.2,7,11,12,14
Noah (O.T.)	I.1; Epil 16
Olympius	IV.10
Omeros	XX.1
Osrhoene	II.1
Ovodianus	XIII.13
Palestine	IX.2, XXX.6
Palladius	VII
Paratomus	VII.4
Paul (N.T.)	Pr 4; II.18; Epil 5–9

218   A History of the Monks of Syria

Pergamius	IX.5
Persia, Persians	I.4,6,11–12; VIII.1,4; XXIV.2; XXVI.13,19–20
Peter (N.T.)	I.9; II.11,16; IV.4; XXVI.17; Epil 10–13
Peter the Egyptian	XIV.1
Peter the Galatian	IX
Phinehas (O.T.)	I.10
Polychronius (Cyrrhestica)	XXIV.3–9
Polychronius (Cyrrhus)	XXI.11
Pontus	XII.1; XXX.5
Publius	V
Rabaena	XXVI.23
Rama	XXIII.2
Rhosus	X.1; XI.1
Romanus	XI
Rome	XXVI.11
Romulus	X.9
Sabellianism	III.16
Sabinus	III.21–22
Salamanes	XIX
Sapor II	I.11–12
Saracens	XXVI.16
Scythians	VIII.5; XXVI.1,19
Seleucia	XIII.15
Seleucobelus	III.20
Severus	XIV.1
Sinai	II.13; VI.7,12
Sisa	XXVI.2
Sodom	VI.7
Spaniards	XXVI.11
Symeon the Elder	VI
Symeon (Nicerte)	III.4
Symeon Stylites	XXVI
Targalla	XXII.2
Tarsus	X.9
Telanissus	XXVI.7
Teleda	IV.2; XXVI.4
Thalassius	XXII.1–2
Thalelaeus	XXVIII
Thecla, St	XXIX.7

Index of Names

Theodoret	IV.9–12; V.10; VIII.15; IX.4,15; XII.4; XIII.1,18; XVIII.2; XX.2–4; XXI.5–34; XXII.1,3; XXIV.4–9; XXV.2; XXVI.2,14–16,19,22–23; XXVIII.4; XXIX.5; XXX.2–3
Theodoret's mother	VI.14; VIII.15; IX.4–9,14–15; XIII.3,16–17
Theodosius I	XIII.7
Theodosius II	XVII.9–10; XXVI.27
Theodosius	X; XI.1
Theodotus (Antioch)	XXVII.3
Theodotus (Hierapolis)	III.10
Theodotus (Zeugma)	V.6–7
Theotecnus (I)	V.6–7
Theotecnus (II)	V.7,9
Thrace	VIII.5
Tillima	XXII.1
Valens	II.15; VIII.5,8–12
Zebinas	XXIV.1–3
Zeno	XII
Zenobiana	III.18
Zeugma	V.1

INDEX OF SUBJECTS

Angels	XII.6; XIII.14
Ascetic practices:	
chains	III.19; IV.6,12; X.2; XI.3; XXI.8; XXIII.1; XXIV.6,10; XXIX.4-5
enclosure	II.2; IV.3-4; VII.1; VIII.1; IX.3; XV.1; XVIII.2-3; XIX.1; XX.1; XXI.4; XXII.3; XXV.2; XXVI.7; XXVII.1-2; XXIX.2
fasting	Pr 5; III.12-13; XXVI.7-9; XXIX.7; Epil 2; see *Diet*
living in caves, holes, tombs	I.2; II.2,4; III.19; VI.1,7-9; IX.3; XII.2; XIII.2; XXVI.6; XXVII.1
open-air life	I.2; IV.12; XVI.1; XVIII.1; XXI.3,5,13,32; XXII.2; XXIII.1-2; XXVI.10,12; XXVII.1-2; XXIX.2,6
sleeping on the ground	Pr 5; I.7; X.2
standing ceaselessly	IV.12; XVII.2; XXIII.2; XXIV.1,4,5; XXVI.9,12,22-24; XXVII.1,3
vigils	Pr 6-7; XVII.2,6; XXIII.2; XXIV.1,4,22; XXVI.24,26; Epil 3
Asceticism, themes of:	
angelic life	Pr 2; III.15; IV.9; XXI.3; XXVI.23
likeness to Christ	I.6,8; III.8; XI.2; XVII.3; XXVI.17
similarity to the Apostles	I.3,9,13; II.4,11,19; V.5; VI.4; VIII.2; IX.14,15; XXI.14; XXII.3
similarity to the Prophets	I.5,13; II.8.11; III.1; IV.3,4; VI.4,11,12; XI.2; XXVI.2,12; XXIX.7
spiritual combat	Pr 4-6; XXI.1,3
Bishops visiting monks	III.11 ; XII.7; XV.4; XVIII.2; XIX.2; XX.3,4; XXI.5-8,17; XXII.3; XXIV.4-9; XXV.2; XXVI.4,14; XXVII.3; XXVIII.4; XXIX.5; XXX.2-3
Charisms:	
authority over animals	VI.2,10
familiar access to God (*parrhēsia*)	I.3,14; III.9; VII.3; VIII.15; IX.7; XVIII.4

Index of Subjects

foreknowledge	I.3; II.14; XIII.15,17; XV.4; XXI.17; XXVI.19
gift of tears	III.17; V.7; XXX.1-2
visions	XXI.20-22
Civil officials:	
agens in rebus	XII.2
ambassador	VIII.4
Comes Orientis	II.20; IX.5; XIII.11
provincial governor	XXIV.8
Clergy:	
chorepiscopoi	XXVI.10
periodeutae	XXVI.7
priests	II.15-16; VIII.6-7; XIV.2; XVII.4; XXIV.7; XXX.3; see *Ordination of monks*
deacons	XX.4; XXVI.23
lectors	XII.4
Convents of women	IX.12; XXIX.2; XXX.4-5
Curials	XIII.13; XIV.4
Demons	Pr 4,6; II.6; III.7; IV.2; XVI.1; XVII.5; XXI.15,23,28; XXVI.13; XXVIII.1-2,5; see *Miracles: exorcism*
Devil, The	III.9; IV.7; VI.13; XXI.18,23-28; XXVII.1
Diet:	
bread	II.2,4,13; III.3,12; V.3; VIII.3; IX.3; XI.1; XII.3; XIII.3; XX.3
plants and vegetables	I.2; II.4; III.12; VI.1; VIII.3; XV.1; XVII.6; XVIII.1; XXI.12; XXIV.5; XXX.2; Epil 2
meal	III.21; V.3; XIII.3
no cooking	I.2; III.21; XVII.6; XXI.11
food each day	III.3; IV.5
less than each day	II.2; III.12; IV.5,12; IX.3; XXVI.5,22; Epil 2
only water to drink	II.2; V.9; IX.3; XI.1; XII.3; XV.2; XXI.24
no water	IV.12; XVII.6; XXVI.7
Dress:	
rags	VI.9; XII.2; XIV.2
single tunic	VIII.4
of skins	XVIII.1; XXVI.12; XXVII.3
Eucharist, monks at	XII. 5; XIII.4; XX.4.

222   A History of the Monks of Syria

Festivals of martyrs   XX.2; XXIV.2

Languages:
  Greek   IV.13, V.5-6; VIII.2; XVII.9; XXVIII.4
  Syriac   IV.13, V.5-6; XIII.2,7; XXI.15

Manual labor   X.2-3; XXX.4,6
Martyrs: see *Festivals* and *Shrines*
Military personnel   III.9; VIII.2; XIII.6,7,15; XXI.9
Miracles:
  cures   II.19,20; IX.5,7; XIII.9,13; XIV.3;
                              XVI.2; XXVI.16
  childbirth involved   IX.14; XI.4; XIII.16,17; XXVI.21
  raising the dead   XXI.14
  of rebuke or punishment   I.4-6,8-13; II.21-22; VIII.9; IX.12;
                              XIV.4; XV.3 ; XXVI.18
  magic overcome   VIII.13, XIII.10-11
  exorcism   III.9,22; IX.4,9,10; XIII.10; XVI.2
  with animals   VIII.11,14; XXVIII.5
  with inanimate nature   II.7-8; VI.5; X.7; XIV.2,4
  miscellaneous   II.17, VII.3
Miracles by material means:
  blessed oil   III.9, VIII.13; cp. XXIV.7 and XXVI.20
  blessed water   VIII.14; XIII.9,13,17; XXI.14
Monasteries (coenobitic):
  Antiochene   II.9, IV.2,5,8-13; VI.13; XXVI.4,8
  Apamene   III.4
  Chalcidene   III.5
  Cilicia   X.3,9
  Cyrrhestica   XVIII.1; XXII.2
  Egypt   XXX.6
  Euphratensis   V.3-10
  Mesopotamia   II.3-5

Ordination of monks:
  priests   III.11; IV.10; XIII.4; XV.4; XVII.4;
                              XIX.2
  bishops   I.9; II.9; III.5; V.8; X.9; XVII.5

Paganism   I.4; IV.2; VI.4; XIV.4; XVI.1;
                                  XVII.2,5; XXVI.13,27; XXVIII.1,5
Pastoral work of monks:
  seeing visitors   III.12,20; V.2; X.4; XI.3; XII.4; XVII.7;
                              XXI.33; XXIV.2,8; XXVI.11,20-26;
                              XXIX.3; XXX.3

Index of Subjects

blessing	VI.14; VIII.15; IX.4; XII.4; XIII.18; XVIII.3; XXI.33; XXII.3; XXIV.2,9; XXVI.15
mediation	XIII.7, XIV.4; XVII.3
evangelization	I.4; VI.4; XVII.2-5; XXVI.13,16; XXVIII.1,5
opposing heresy	II.16-22; III.16-17; VIII.2,7-8; XXI.17; XXVI.27
other work	XIV.2; XXII.4
Pilgrimage:	
Holy Land	IX.2, XXIX.7
Isauria	XXIX.7
Mt Sinai	II.13; VI.7-12
Prayer:	
communal	II.5; IV.5; V.5; X.3; XXII.7
solitary	II.4; IV.5; VI.12; XII.2; XXI.32-34; XXIV.1; XXVI.10; Epil 4
Psalmody	II.2,5; III.2,5; V.2,5; VI.10; X.2; XVII.2; XXI.17,20; XXII.7; XXVI.6,9; XXX.1,4
Relics	XXI.16,19-20, 30
Scripture reading	III.2,5,6; IV.6; V.2; XIII.8
Shrines:	
of martyrs	II.21, X.8, XIII.19; XX.2; XXI.30; XXIV.2; XXVI.3; XXVIII.5; XXIX.7
of monks	VII.4, X.8; XIII.19; XVI.4; XXIV.2; XXVI.28
of Prophets	XXI.10,20,22,30

www.ingramcontent.com/pod-product-compliance
Lightning Source LLC
Chambersburg PA
CBHW031240290426
44109CB00012B/371